THE HOLY SPIRIT
AND MODERN THOUGHT

The Holy Spirit and Modern Thought

An Inquiry into the Historical, Theological, and Psychological Aspects of the Christian Doctrine of the Holy Spirit

LINDSAY DEWAR

FOREWORD BY HENRY P. VAN DUSEN

HARPER & BROTHERS
PUBLISHERS NEW YORK

Matri dilectissimae

SYNOPSIS

v

FOREWORD

BY HENRY P. VAN DUSEN

'It has become almost a convention that those who undertake to write about the Holy Spirit should begin by deploring the neglect of this doctrine in the thought and life of the Church today.'[1]

This assertion from the opening pages of one of the most noteworthy current treatments of the Holy Spirit records a truism among students of the subject—the relative silence of recent theology on the Holy Spirit.

However, this is not a new discovery of a merely contemporary lacuna. At the beginning of this century, the volume on the Holy Spirit in the *Studies in Theology* series noted in its Preface:

'It is a frequent and well-founded complaint that the doctrine of the Holy Spirit has been strangely neglected by theologians. Our theological text-books, as a rule, pass over the subject with a few conventional pages.'[2]

And, near the middle of the last century, Frederick Denison Maurice, pointing to the same neglect, ventured a forecast which still awaits fulfilment:

'I cannot but think that the reformation in our day, which I expect to be more deep and searching than that of the sixteenth century, will turn upon the Spirit's presence and life, as that did upon the Justification by the Son.'[3]

Modern theology's 'neglect' of the Holy Spirit can claim notable historical antecedents. It is a truism of the history of Christian thought that, long after the Church had clarified its mind with respect to Christ and had embodied its conclusions in creedal affirmations, it had nothing definite to say about the Holy Spirit.[4] And for the very good reason that it had given

---

[1] George S. Hendry: *The Holy Spirit in Christian Theology* (1956), p. 11.
[2] T. Rees: *The Holy Spirit in Thought and Experience* (1914), p. vii.
[3] Quoted in *The Spirit*, edited by B. H. Streeter (1919), p. viii.
[4] Cf. Henry P. Van Dusen, *Spirit, Son and Father* (1958), p. 71 f.

comparatively little attention to the subject.[5] Broadly speaking,
that 'neglect' continued through the centuries and has persisted
to this day. With a few inconsequential exceptions, there has
been hardly a period in the Church's history, hardly a school of
Christian theology, hardly an individual theologian who has
given to the Holy Spirit the attention which its importance as an
aspect of the Godhead, according to the historic creeds 'co-eternal'
and 'co-equal' with the Father and the Son, merited.

ii.

There is evidence that, in our day at long last, a beginning is
being made toward overtaking that age-long 'neglect.' Within
the past half-dozen years, there have appeared a half-dozen books
of some worth on this theme, as many as in the preceding half-
dozen decades. It is not easy to explain this quickened interest
in the Holy Spirit. But it is a heartening fact. For, as Dr Ernest
Scott was never weary of stressing, absence of vital belief in the
Holy Spirit has always paralleled spiritual sterility, and recovery
of the reality of the Spirit is either an evidence of or a prelude
to spiritual renewal grounded in revitalized experience.

'The belief in the Spirit has always sprung out of an experience.
It has been strongest in times of religious awakening, when men
have grown suddenly aware that the truths they had clung to
half mechanically are the great realities. . . . It carries with it, if
the testimony of the past means anything, the promise of a new
and more vital faith.'[6]

iii.

To the lengthening shelf of contemporary treatments of the
Holy Spirit, Canon Dewar's volume is a welcome addition. Its
importance is at least two-fold.

Its first three Parts trace the development of understanding of
the Holy Spirit from the earliest Hebrew thought until the dawn
of modern theology. Here, a vast chronicle is compressed within
all too brief compass. Inevitably, the historian's interests and
convictions influence his choice of material and determine his
emphases. Authorities on particular periods must be expected

[5] Cf. H. B. Swete: *On the Early History of the Doctrine of the Holy Spirit*, p. 5.
[6] E. F. Scott: *The Spirit in the New Testament* (1923), p. vi.

to challenge the selections and the stresses. The review of the Biblical sources is most notable for its firm establishment of one of the author's major theses—the 'natural' as well as the 'supernatural' operations of the Holy Spirit. This lays the groundwork for one of the most original and challenging contentions of the writer's own constructive position. In Part III, sections 1 and 2, Canon Dewar has provided the most comprehensive succinct conspectus of the thought of the early Christian centuries from the Apostolic Fathers through Augustine which is to be found in comparable space. Here he is dealing with material which is at once especially congenial to his own conviction and least familiar to the ordinary reader. The latter are certain to find it of great interest and value. Adherents of the widely neglected tradition which flowed from the 'radical' or 'sectarian' Reformation—Protestants of Baptist, Congregational, Methodist, Disciple, Mennonite, Moravian, Brethren, etc. affinity—may claim that their heritage has received less than adequate attention and may question the choice of George Fox as their representative spokesman. And they may feel that this is the more regrettable both because it is precisely this wing of Protestantism which has been most alive to the significance of the Holy Spirit through the modern period and because it is new expressions of 'radical' or 'sectarian' Protestantism—Adventist, Pentecostal, Holiness, etc.—which constitute the most vital, dynamic and rapidly multiplying groups in contemporary Christianity and are in part responsible for the present increased attention to the Holy Spirit. At the suggestion of the American publisher, Canon Dewar has added a brief Appendix on 'The Doctrine of the Holy Spirit in Radical Protestantism.'

iv.

It is in Part IV, however, that this volume breaks fresh ground and should direct current discussion of the Holy Spirit into relatively unexplored territories. The result can hardly fail to prove immensely stimulating and provocative, and possibly revolutionary.

From his own very considerable acquaintance with modern psychology, the author examines the bearing of Extra-sensory Perception, psychokinesis and psychoanalysis upon our understanding of the Holy Spirit, and vice versa. More particularly, he explores the thesis that the 'unconscious,' both individual and collective, may reveal the working of the Holy Spirit. This suggestion was anticipated just over half a century ago. Probably the most novel and germinal proposition in William James' justly famous *The Varieties of Religious Experience* was advanced in these words:

'Let me propose then, as an hypothesis, that whatever it may be on its *farther* side, the "more" with which in religious experience we feel ourselves connected is on its *hither* side the subconscious continuation of our conscious life.'[7]

James' suggestion was taken up by no less distinguished a theologian than William Sanday, Lady Margaret Professor of Divinity at Oxford. It furnished him a determinative principle for a wholly novel interpretation of the Person of Jesus Christ:

'The proper seat or *locus* of all divine indwelling, or divine action upon the human soul, is the subliminal consciousness. . . .

'The same, or the corresponding, subliminal consciousness is the proper seat or *locus* of the Deity of the incarnate Christ.'[8]

But these bold conjectures were too daring and too unconventional for their day. They have lain almost unnoted, unexamined and unexploited through the intervening decades.[9] Moreover, neither James nor Sanday discussed the *Holy Spirit's* relation to the 'unconscious'; they were concerned respectively with its significance for thought of God and Christ.[10]

Those decades have witnessed immense advances, both theoretical and clinical, in understanding of the human unconscious. Of these, Canon Dewar takes full advantage. The time was ripe for a fresh examination of the implications for Christian theology of varied manifestations of psychic phenomena. It is the special merit of this book that it rightly fastens upon the Holy Spirit as

---

[7] *Ibid.*, p. 512.

[8] William Sanday: *Christologies Ancient and Modern*, 'Presuppositions of a Modern Christology' (1910), p. 159.

[9] Sanday's thesis was subjected to brief and critical examination by the foremost historian of christological theory, H. R. Mackintosh, in a 'Note' in his *The Doctrine of the Person of Jesus Christ* (1912), pp. 487 ff.

[10] In a footnote, James quoted a reference to the Holy Spirit in an article by W. C. Brownell in *Scribner's Magazine*, vol. xxx, p. 112: 'The influence of the Holy Spirit, exquisitely called the Comforter, is a matter of actual experience, as solid a reality as that of electro-magnetism.'

the particular aspect (or 'Person') of the Divine Reality in terms of which these phenomena can be understood and interpreted as congruous with, indeed vital constituents of, a full-orbed Christian Faith.[11]

It is hardly to be hoped for, or expected, that so bold an incursion into such newly discovered and highly controversial territory will win instant or complete assent. But it is of the highest consequence that such exploration should be attempted. For that, we are greatly in Canon Dewar's debt. At the least, his work opens a quite new phase in our comprehension of the Holy Spirit. All subsequent investigation and interpretation must take it into account. But that is a minimal estimate of the possible fruitfulness and influence of this discussion. If the author's hypothesis is pursued with the vigor it deserves, Maurice's prophecy may yet see fulfillment—'a reformation in our day, . . . more deep and searching than that of the sixteenth century, turning upon the Spirit's presence and life, as that did upon the Justification by the Son.'

NEW YORK
APRIL 1960

---

[11] Canon Dewar mentions both James and Sanday, but not in this connection.

PREFACE

This book should be read as a whole. No attempt, for example, should be made to pass judgement on the Biblical section until the last section has been read. It is an endeavour to bring into a single survey evidence from widely separated fields—evidence, as I believe, brought together for the first time.

One of the crucial questions which arise in connexion with the doctrine of the Holy Spirit is that which concerns His personality. The latter has been insufficiently recognised—to state the matter mildly—as is proved by the too common habit of referring to Him as 'it.' We are still hampered by the presuppositions of the unitarian theology which the Church took over from its Hebrew ancestry. As Dr Leonard Hodgson has said: 'Christianity began as a Trinitarian religion with a unitarian theology.'[1] It took the Church three hundred years to avoid a decisive defeat at the hands of unitarianism. But its experience of redemption through Christ stood firm and unitarianism was finally defeated at Nicaea in 325 A.D. Unfortunately the formulae finally adopted by the Church, *mia ousia, treis hupostaseis,* and *una substantia, tres personae,* were susceptible of an interpretation which does not accord fully personal status to the Holy Spirit. This has been seized upon by some modern scholars to support what is, in fact, a binitarian theology. Thus Dr Wheeler Robinson in his book, *The Christian Experience of the Holy Spirit,* has written: 'We cannot possibly make sense of the classical doctrine of the Trinity without deliberately eliminating the full and rich content of the term "person" which fifteen centuries have bequeathed to us. . . . No question is more frequently asked about the doctrine of the Holy Spirit than this—"Are we to believe in His personality?"— yet in most instances it is asked in a way that shows that the questioner is reading a modern connotation into the term. If this is done, the problem of the three "Persons" becomes insoluble.'[2] I disagree emphatically. It is the belief in God as 'One

[1] L. Hodgson: *Doctrine of the Trinity* (Nisbet 1943), p. 103.
[2] *Op. cit.* pp. 254–255.

Person' which makes the problem insoluble. As Archbishop
Temple wrote: 'To attribute to *a* Person at once the eternal
comprehension of the universe and the disappointment of Jesus
Christ over Jerusalem or His cry of desolation on the Cross is to
talk nonsense. It is one God; but it is two Persons—so far as
human terms have any applicability at all.'[3] And if two Persons,
why not three, if the evidence requires?

Here we see the influence of the *damnosa haereditas* of unitarianism. My submission is that the true inference to be drawn
from Christian experience is not that which Dr Wheeler Robinson
draws. It is that we must take the Trinitarianism seriously and
that what is required, as Dr Leonard Hodgson has shown, is not
a surrender of Trinitarianism but a revision of our idea of unity
as applied to God. This is *not* to be taken as mathematical unity.
That is exactly what we do not mean when we profess our belief
in 'one God.' For that would imply that there might conceivably
be two or more Gods. We mean 'one' in the sense of unique.
As Christians we believe in a unique Being whom we call God,
who has revealed Himself in Christian experience as three Persons
in an eternal and indivisible Trinity. 'And in the Trinity none is
afore, or after other: none is greater or less than another.'

In this book I have tried to show that it is only by recognising
the fully personal nature of the Holy Spirit—which, of course,
does not mean personal with the limitations of human personality—that we can rightly understand His operations. Thus, for
instance, the 'gift of the Holy Spirit' must be understood to be
not the bestowal of a *thing* but the action of a person. If that
had always been recognised, many of our theological disputes—
about the grace of baptism, for example—would never have arisen.

Furthermore, I have laid great stress on the work of the Holy
Spirit outside the bounds of Christianity, in the widest sense of
that term. This is an aspect of His work which, as I venture to
think, has been too much neglected by Christian theologians. I
have tried to show the significance of His working in every
human being. This has been borne strongly upon me in the
psychiatric work which I have tried to do for many years. In
this I have been much helped by Dr C. G. Jung's writings, and

[3] W. Temple: *Christus Victor* (Macmillan 1924), p. 277.

I have attempted to show in this book how the doctrine of the Holy Spirit is greatly illuminated if approached from Jung's standpoint. Indeed, I venture to think that, in turn, it throws some light on some of the obscurities in Jung's theories.

It is necessary for the sake of clearness to say something about the way the terms 'Natural' and 'Supernatural' are used in this book. As I understand the matter, the word 'supernatural' involves a conscious reference to the transcendent. That is to say, the supernatural is recognised to be 'above' and 'beyond' Nature. It does not contradict it but it crowns or completes it. It does not, of course, necessarily involve the miraculous. The 'natural,' on the other hand, is of this world only. It is solely concerned with man's life on earth. Nevertheless, man, in order to be man, is not devoid of the guidance of the Holy Spirit, though indeed he need not recognise the fact, and only too frequently fails to do so. What we call the natural 'instincts' and the dictates of the Natural Law (in the traditional as contrasted with the modern sense of the phrase) are, however, manifestations of the working of the Holy Spirit at the natural level. In other words, a man or a woman who was totally devoid of the operations of the Holy Spirit would be less than human. The 'supernatural' operations of the Holy Spirit, on the other hand, are those which are not universal in all normal human beings, but peculiar to this or that person, or to this or that religious tradition. In the Christian tradition they are performed through the medium of the Incarnate Son of God. When the Holy Spirit works in this way He is called in the New Testament 'the Spirit of Christ'—a phrase which is often used in these days, or rather, misused, to signify no more than a Christian frame of mind.

In the historical section of this book I realise that I have laid myself open to criticism in two respects. First, I have attempted to cover a great deal of ground in a small compass. It is arguable that giants like S. Augustine and John Calvin cannot be treated in brief. However, since a full treatment was obviously impossible, and it seemed equally impossible to omit the historical section, I have had to make the attempt, however inadequate it may be. In the second place, I recognise that I may well have failed ot do justice to the Protestant tradition which springs from Luther and Calvin, and, still more, to do justice to the more radical forms of Protestantism. I can only plead that I have done my best, and that, since I was brought up in the Presbyterian tradition, I have at least knowledge of it from the inside. I am especially grateful to Dr Van Dusen, who has a full understanding of the Protestant doctrine of the Spirit, for his kindness in writing a foreword to this edition. It is my sincere hope that, however inadequate my treatment of this aspect of the subject may be, I have written nothing which will wound any Christian conscience.

I would add my thanks to the Rev. T. S. Wetherall, Principal of S. Chad's College, Durham, and to the Rev. R. D. Macrory, formerly Vice-Principal of Bishops' College, Cheshunt, for reading the typescript and giving me help with their criticisms: also to the Rev. Dr T. G. Jalland for reading the patristic section and advising me upon it.

LINDSAY DEWAR

MUCH HADHAM
HERTFORDSHIRE

PART I

THE OLD TESTAMENT PREPARATION

THE OLD TESTAMENT PREPARATION

THE MEANING OF THE WORD 'RUACH'

ANY examination of the Old Testament doctrine of the Spirit must begin with a careful consideration of the Hebrew word *ruach*, which is regularly used there to denote what we call 'spirit.' This word, like the Greek *pneuma*, is derived from a root meaning to breathe, and there is no reason for refusing to accept this clue to its interpretation. But whereas *pneuma* is, as a rule, not applied to anything non-material until it comes under the influence of Biblical writers,[1] from the first *ruach* in the Old Testament signifies not only the wind or breath but also the 'spirit' of God and 'the spirit of life' in a living organism. Thus, for instance, we read in the early narrative in Genesis 7. 22: 'All in whose nostrils was the breath of the *ruach* of life died.' This, of course, includes human beings. And it is quite clear from the early account of the creation of man in Genesis 2. 7, in which we read that God 'breathed into his [man's] nostrils the breath of life,' that *ruach* refers to the 'spirit' of life in man from the first.

There is, however, another word in the Old Testament which is used to denote the essence of man and that is the word *nephesh*, usually translated 'soul.' But this rendering is not accurate. The root meaning of *nephesh* is undoubtedly 'breath,' although there is only one passage in the Old Testament which definitely illustrates this.[2] It stands for something much wider than what we call 'soul,' i.e. for the life or personality generally.

This association between 'breath' and 'life' is widespread among primitive peoples, and, indeed, is easily intelligible. Our own usage recognizes this, for we say 'while there is breath there is life.' But in Hebrew breath was generally indicated by a different word (*neshamah*) and *nephesh* was retained to denote what we should call the more 'spiritual' or vital aspect of an organism, whether animal or human.

We must not, indeed, expect to find any clear-cut or systematic

---

[1] Cf. Kittel's *Wörterbuch z. N.T.*, VI, pp. 355 ff.
[2] Job 41. 21: 'His breath kindleth coals, and a flame goeth forth from his mouth.'

3

use of psychological terms among ancient peoples. Words are used with ill-defined meanings among all primitive peoples, and in no instance is this more so than with psychological terms. Indeed, even in modern speech such terms are freely used in the most confusing and inaccurate manner. Thus, for example, the word 'feeling' is used in at least five different senses. It may denote (1) emotion, as in the phrase 'an angry feeling'; (2) organic sensation, as in 'feeling sick'; (3) intuition, as in the expression 'a feeling that something will happen'; (4) tactile sensation, as in 'a feeling of roughness'; (5) pleasure, and its opposite, as in 'a pleasurable feeling.' If we to-day can be so loose and inaccurate in our use of psychological terms, we should not be surprised if the ancient Hebrews used a word like *ruach* with a variety of meanings.

Returning to this word *ruach*, therefore, we must not expect to be able to pin-point its meaning in the Old Testament. There is bound to be a good deal of ambiguity about it, and each instance of its use should be carefully studied in the light of the context. Nevertheless, it is perhaps possible to trace a general tendency whereby this word which at first only by *implication* denoted the 'internal essence' of man (see the passage in Genesis 2 already mentioned), *nephesh* being the word commonly used in the pre-exilic writings, becomes increasingly used to denote man's essential being. Almost certainly the reason for this is, as Professor Wheeler Robinson has suggested, the influence of another usage of this term, viz. the phrase 'the *ruach* of God.' As the influence of the *ruach* of God upon man was increasingly understood—the result of the teaching of the great Hebrew prophets—this word *ruach* was increasingly used to denote what we call 'the spirit' of man.

THE SPIRIT OF GOD

We must next inquire what is the meaning of the phrase, the Spirit (*ruach*) of God? It is one which meets us on the first page of the Bible. 'And the earth was without form and void, and the Spirit of God moved on the face of the waters' (*Gen.* 1. 2). The word translated 'moved' is rare; it occurs in only one other passage of the Old Testament, where it refers to a vulture hovering over its young.[1] Therefore 'brooded' would be the best rendering here; and, if so, the Spirit (*ruach*) of God in this passage appears to denote the divine, vitalizing energy. Moreover, this would cover a great many of the instances in which the phrase, the Spirit of God, occurs in the Old Testament. This vitalizing energy is not only creative but also sustaining. 'Thou takest away their *ruach* and they die, and return to their dust. Thou sendest forth Thy *ruach* and they are created' (*Ps.* 104. 29, 30).

There is one passage in the Old Testament which is of cardinal importance for the understanding of what is meant by God's Spirit. It is to be found in Isaiah 31. 3: 'Now the Egyptians are men, and not God; and their horses flesh, and not spirit.' Here men and flesh, and God and spirit are clearly parallel. In other words, flesh is the essence of man and spirit is (so to say) the essence of God. Thus we read in the Fourth Gospel: 'God is Spirit' (not 'a spirit'). This is the consistent Hebrew mode of thought. And so what we should call 'inspiration' is the result of the Spirit of God (i.e. the spirit who is God, or God who is spirit) coming upon humanity. Thus, for example, we have the picture of the ideal king in Isaiah 11 who is imaginatively depicted as arising from the truncated dynasty of David. 'The Spirit of God shall rest upon him, the spirit of wisdom and understanding, the spirit of counsel and practical ability, the spirit of the knowledge of and the fear of the Lord,' where there seems to be an ascending scale of three pairs of attributes. The first pair consists of purely intellectual gifts, the second pair denotes the ability to put them into practice, and the third pair consists of religious gifts enabling their possessor to know the Lord.

In three passages of the Old Testament we have the Spirit of God understood as imparting holiness. The best known of these is to be found in Psalm 51. 13: 'Take not Thy holy Spirit from me,' which, in the Hebrew, is 'the Spirit of Thy holiness.' We must, as theologians, beware of reading into this passage Christian conceptions of the Holy Spirit, if we are seeking to understand the Old Testament point of view. The other two passages are to be found in Isaiah 63. 10 and 13: 'But they rebelled, and grieved

[1] Deut. 32. 11.

His Holy Spirit. . . . Where is He that put His Holy Spirit in the midst of them?'

As we survey the various and numerous passages in the Old Testament which contain references to the Spirit of God, it is possible to classify them in two groups: (a) those which speak of the Spirit of God coming suddenly and intermittently upon human beings; and (b) those which speak of the Spirit of God abiding or resting permanently upon individuals. An examination of these two types of relationship existing between the Spirit of God and man will throw a good deal of light upon the conception.

First, then, we have those passages—and they are numerous— in which the Spirit of God comes suddenly upon a person. For example, there is the case of Saul upon whom the Spirit of God came mightily as he met the band of prophets (1 Sam. 10. 10). Again, there is the case of Samson, upon whom the Spirit of God came with such power that he rent the young lion as he would have rent a kid (Judges 14. 6). In passages of this kind, when the coming of the Spirit is sudden it also seems to be intermittent. This is clear (for example) in the case of Samson, who seems to have received frequently a temporary access of the Spirit of God to enable him to perform feats of strength. It must not, however, be overlooked that he could summon this strength to his aid when he willed, provided that he was not disobedient to God. But when he disregarded the vow which had pledged him to be a Nazirite he cut himself off from the source of power. After he had been shaven, we are told, 'The Lord was departed from him' (Judges 16. 20), although he was unaware of the fact until he tried to put forth his strength. From this we may infer that even in those cases in which the Spirit of God seems to come and go, there is a real sense in which 'It' was understood to be present all the time, until 'It' was driven out. Thus we read in the case of Saul, after he had disobeyed his conscience: 'The Spirit of the Lord had departed from Saul, and an evil spirit from the Lord troubled him' (1 Sam. 16. 14). But no attempt is made to elucidate the relationship between the Spirit of God and evil spirits from the Lord.

Turning to the second group of passages, where the Spirit of God is explicitly said to rest permanently upon a person, we may mention again the Isaianic picture of the ideal prince.[1] Of him it is said that the Spirit of God 'shall rest upon him' (*Isa.* 11. 2). The same conception is found in the portrait of the Servant of the Lord in Deutero-Isaiah: 'I have put my spirit upon him' (*Isa.* 42. 1). With this agrees the familiar passage which our Lord quoted in reference to Himself in His sermon in the synagogue at Nazareth: 'The Spirit of the Lord God is upon me' (*Isa.* 61. 1). This is indeed the essential characteristic of the prophet, that he is one upon whom the Spirit of God rests. In the phrase of Hosea, he is 'a man of spirit (*ruach*),' or 'the man of the spirit' (*Hos.* 9. 7). So Micah describes himself as one who is 'full of strength by the Spirit of the Lord,' or, as we may translate it more literally, 'full of strength, even the Spirit of the Lord' (*Mic.* 3. 8). It is this possession of the Spirit of God which was believed to be conferred by anointing the head with oil. There is, indeed, only one passage in the Old Testament which *explicitly* states that the Spirit of God is given by anointing; but it is surely significant that it is the passage from Isaiah 61 which our Lord quotes with reference to Himself. It is, however, clearly *implied* that this is the case by the practice of anointing both kings and prophets. Thus Elijah is told: 'Elisha, the son of Shaphat of Abel Meholah, shalt thou anoint to be prophet in thy room' (1 *Kings* 19. 16). Later we read that, after Elijah had been taken away, the sons of the prophets said: 'The spirit of Elijah doth rest on Elisha' (2 *Kings* 2. 15). In this passage 'the spirit of Elijah' clearly means 'the Spirit of God which dwelt in Elijah.'[2] At the same time we see how easily arises the dangerous tendency to allow the vital distinction between the Spirit of God and the 'spirit' of man to be blurred and even obliterated.

THE CORPORATE RECEPTION OF THE SPIRIT OF GOD

There are three prophets—Ezekiel, Deutero-Isaiah, and Joel—in whom the idea of a corporate reception of the Spirit of God is

[1] The O.T. idea of the king as endowed specially by anointing with the Spirit of God may go back to the primitive Canaanitish belief that the god himself actually was identified with the king—cf. Ps. 45. 7 and see S. Mowinckel: *He That Cometh* (Blackwell 1956), pp. 78 ff.

[2] Cf. the phrase in the Book of Enoch (1 Enoch 49. 3) when it is said that in the Son of Man dwells 'the spirit of those who have fallen asleep in righteousness,' which must surely refer to the Spirit of God who indwelt the righteous departed. See Mowinckel: *op. cit.*, p. 377.

to be found. In the case of Ezekiel we have the well-known vision of the exiles in Babylon where the latter are depicted as a collection of dry bones scattered in the valley. Ezekiel prophesies unto the *ruach* (i.e. the 'wind' or the 'spirit') and says to it: 'Come from the four *ruchoth* [i.e. 'winds' or 'spirits'], O *ruach*, and breathe [or blow] upon these slain, and they shall live' (*Ezek.* 37. 9). A few verses later, this is said by God to be 'putting My *ruach* within them'—the fulfilment of the prophecy in the previous chapter: 'I will put My *ruach* within you, and cause you to walk in My statutes, and ye shall keep My judgements, and do them' (*Ezek.* 36. 27).

In this passage we see clearly the intimate connection in meaning which exists between breath, wind, and spirit in the thought of the Hebrews. The phrase 'the *ruach* of God,' in fact, covers all three.

The second passage is from Deutero-Isaiah (44. 3 ff.) and runs:

> I will pour water upon the thirsty land
> And streams upon the dry ground;
> I will pour my spirit upon thy seed
> And my blessing upon thine offspring;
> And they shall spring up like the grass,
> As willows by the watercourses.
> One shall say, I am the Lord's
> And another shall call himself by the name of Jacob;
> And another shall tattoo his hand unto the Lord
> And surname himself by the name of Israel.

Here the corporate outpouring of the Spirit of the Lord is depicted under a different figure—not as reviving corpses, but as refreshing parched land. There is, however, an important advance here on the conception of Ezekiel. Not only is the nation of Israel revivified, but the heathen also receive the benefit of this outpouring of the spirit. The conception is, in fact, similar to that found in the eighty-seventh Psalm:

> Yea, of Zion it shall be said,
> This one and that one was born there:
> And the Most High Himself shall establish her.
> The Lord shall count, when he writeth up the peoples,
> This one was born there.

All this is to be the result of the outpouring of the Spirit—a foreshadowing of the Catholic Church of Christ. Moreover, the use of the metaphor of 'pouring' the Spirit comes into use for the first time. The word used by Deutero-Isaiah (*yaçaq*) is the word regularly used for anointing, and the religious act of pouring oil; and although in the passage we are considering it is actually paralleled by the pouring of water, the allusion to oil is clearly present. And here, of course, we also find the association of *ruach* and water—a connection of ideas which was later to have such importance.

The third passage in which we read of the corporate reception of the Spirit of God is the well-known prophecy of Joel:

> And it shall come to pass afterward,
> That I will pour out my *ruach* upon all flesh;
> And your sons and your daughters shall prophesy,
> Your old men shall dream dreams,
> Your young men shall see visions.
> (*Joel* 2. 28: or 3. 1 in the Hebrew text.)

This is almost certainly the latest of the three prophecies, and in its original meaning it is set in a lower key than the magnificent prophecy of Deutero-Isaiah. But the subconscious phenomena which characterized the events of the great Day of Pentecost naturally suggested it to the mind of S. Peter as the most appropriate prophecy to quote. Moreover, by 'all flesh' Joel meant 'all Israelites,' and we know that S. Peter had not at this time appreciated the wider application of the words. We should notice that there is probably an allusion here to the passage in the Book of Numbers where Moses is represented as saying: 'Would that all the Lord's people were prophets' (*Num.* 11. 29). We observe also the recurrence of the metaphor of 'pouring.' But a different word is used here (*shaphak*). This is the normal word applied to the pouring of water. It is evident from the context that Joel, like Deutero-Isaiah, is thinking also of the outpouring of the Spirit of God as being the consummation of the process whereby drought and desolation are relieved.

These three passages are—apart from the brief reference in Isaiah 32. 15: 'until the spirit be poured upon us from on high'—the only references in the Old Testament to a corporate bestowal of the Spirit of God; but, in view of later events, they are of great importance. In point of fact they led to a revolution in the whole doctrine of the Spirit of God. Their existence is the more remarkable when it is remembered that the idea of the Spirit of God had become discredited owing to the claims and the influence of the numerous false prophets. This is clearly shown by the remarkable fact that the expression 'the spirit of God' is entirely absent from Jeremiah's writings, as it is from the Book of Deuteronomy. It required a high degree of inspiration to realize that what was required was a corporate outpouring of the Spirit of God; for only in this way could the nation be preserved from the danger of deception by the false prophets who, to use the expression of Jeremiah, 'speak a vision of their own heart' or, as Ezekiel puts it, 'follow their own spirit' (*Ezek.* 13. 3).

In the case of Joel's prophecy, the corporate outpouring of the Spirit of God was to be manifested (as has been noticed) by certain subconscious phenomena, described as the seeing of visions and the dreaming of dreams. And we know that this was precisely what happened when the Spirit came on the Day of Pentecost, however we may choose to interpret the gift of tongues—a matter which will come up for consideration later. But in whatever way we interpret these phenomena they are clearly of secondary importance, as S. Paul plainly taught: for it is not the *manner* of the coming which is of primary importance but the *results* of the coming. It is, therefore, significant that Ezekiel—ecstatic though he was—did not predict the corporate sending of the Spirit of God in this way. According to him, the effect of the sending of the Spirit of God will be to lead men to walk in His statutes, to keep and do His judgements, and to be saved from all their uncleannesses (*Ezek.* 36. 27–29).

THE FORESHADOWING OF THE NEW TESTAMENT DOCTRINE

Thus far we have been considering the essential meaning of *ruach* and, in particular, of the *ruach* of God in the Old Testament. We have seen that it is essentially the power of 'the living God,' to use the common Old Testament phrase. 'Not by might, nor by power [i.e. human power], but by My *ruach*, saith the Lord of Hosts' (*Zech.* 4. 6). But when we proceed to ask what connection there is between the phrase 'the *ruach* of God' and the Christian conception of 'the Holy Spirit,' the answer is not clear. It is easy enough, indeed, to say that, since the Hebrews became rigidly monotheistic before the end of Old Testament times, the phrase is simply and solely a periphrasis for 'God'; and that, therefore, there is no connection between the two expressions other than a purely verbal connection. And yet such a view is not entirely satisfactory, for it fails to do justice to the nature of prophecy. The root of Hebrew prophecy consists in the fact that the prophet can dip into the future: 'Coming events cast their shadows before' upon the mind of the prophet. This is because he 'stands in the council of the Lord,' to use Jeremiah's phrase (*Jer.* 23. 18). Therefore he can speak more truly than he himself can really know. The modern tag that a prophet is not a fore-teller but a forthteller is wide of the mark. We may, therefore, perhaps not be led astray entirely if we see in some, at least, of the Old Testament language about the *ruach* of God the shape of things to come.

This *unconscious* element in prophecy is nowhere more clearly illustrated than in the remark attributed to Caiaphas: 'Ye know nothing at all, nor do ye take account that it is expedient for you that one man should die for the people, and that the whole nation perish not.' The Evangelist adds the significant comment: 'Now this he said not of himself: but being high priest that year, he *prophesied* that Jesus should die for the nation; and not for the nation only, but that he might also gather together into one the children of God that are scattered abroad' (*S. John* 11. 49–52). If this prophetic foreshadowing can hold good in the case of a man like Caiaphas, how much more in the case of the true prophet!

From the nature of the case, however, this foreshadowing of the coming of the Holy Spirit was bound to be largely uncon-scious, owing to the entirely unphilosophical nature of the Hebrew mind in the Old Testament; for *full* belief in the Holy Spirit involves the metaphysical doctrine of the Trinity. Such a mode of thought was foreign to the mind of the Old Testament. There is virtually no philosophy in it. Thus it is (for example) that the Old Testament writer can speak of the *ruach* of God departing from Saul and an evil *ruach* from the Lord troubling him. He seems to be totally unaware of the difficult theological problem raised by such a statement. Clearly, therefore, it is profitless to look for anything like a *conscious* foreshadowing in the Old Testament of the Christian doctrine of the Holy Spirit.

The most we can expect to find is the use of language which, *après coup*, can be pressed into the service of the doctrine. And this is what we do find. There are, in fact, three different expressions in the Old Testament which played their part in this way. They are: the *ruach* of God, the word of God, and the wisdom of God. By far the most important of these is the first, of which we have been speaking. But the other two are not unimportant because they prepared the way for belief in the existence of distinctions within the Godhead—a necessary prerequisite for belief in the doctrine of the Trinity.

THE WORD OF GOD

The word of God is one of the commonest expressions to be found in the Old Testament, occurring no less than 394 times, according to Brown, Driver, and Briggs.[1] It is used to express three different forms of divine activity, viz. creation, providence, and revelation. As an instance of the first of these we may quote Psalm 33. 6: 'By the word of the Lord were the heavens made: and all the hosts of them by the *ruach* of His mouth.' Here we should notice the close connection which was understood to exist between the word of God and the *ruach* of God. This is not difficult to understand, for to utter a word is to send forth breath. God's breath, or *ruach*, is creative. As the same writer says later on in the same psalm: 'He spake and it was done' (*Ps.* 33. 9). Another instance of God's creative word is afforded by Genesis 1, where all is dependent upon the fiat of the word of God.

Next, we observe that the phrase 'the word of God' is used in reference to the divine providence. A good instance occurs in Psalm 148. 8: 'Storm-*ruach*, fulfilling His word.' Once more, we note the association with *ruach*. Another example is afforded by the statement that the angels fulfil God's word (*Ps.* 103. 20). A similar belief in the providential power of God's word is to be found in the well-known saying that the word that proceeds out of the mouth of God shall not return unto Him empty, but shall prosper in the thing whereto He sends it (*Isa.* 55. 11).

The use of the expression 'the word of God' to signify the idea of revelation is, of course, by far the commonest use. It is

[1] Hebrew Lexicon s.v.

superfluous to give examples. Every genuine prophet provides an instance. It should be noticed, however, that the graphic and imaginative mind of the Hebrews naturally tends to hypostatize the word of God which comes to the prophets. Thus, for example, we read: 'The word of the Lord that came to Micah the Morashtite... which he *saw*.' Moreover, this word of revelation is closely akin to *ruach*, as is abundantly clear from the numerous references to *ruach* in the Book of Ezekiel. Unfortunately, the English versions consistently misrepresent the meaning by translating it 'the spirit'; but there is no definite article in the Hebrew text. The point is that it is (so to say) *ruach*-substance which enters into Ezekiel and controls his actions and his utterances. Language of this kind unconsciously prepared the way for the Christian belief in the Holy Spirit.

THE WISDOM OF GOD

The third conception in the Old Testament which is significant for the later doctrine of the Holy Spirit is that of 'the wisdom of God.' This is found only in late books, such as Proverbs and Job, and (in the Apocrypha) Ecclesiasticus and Wisdom. It is especially in the last named that it is prominent. There the 'word of God' is mentioned only three times (*Wisd.* 9. 1; 16. 2; 18. 15) and seems to be equivalent to 'the wisdom of God':

> O God of the fathers, and the Lord who keepest Thy mercy,
> Who madest all things by Thy word, and
> By Thy wisdom formedst man. (9. 1)

It also seems to be identified in the writer's mind with the Spirit ($\pi\nu\epsilon\hat{v}\mu a$) of the Lord (1. 5–7); but he is not an exact thinker, and we need not suppose that he had consciously tried to work out the connection between these different phrases. In any case, it is clear that this is the idea of wisdom which holds the foremost place in his mind. The actual phrase 'the wisdom of God' does not occur, but the idea of it permeates the whole book. Indeed, the idea is so strongly personified that it almost amounts to hypostatization. Wisdom sits by the throne of God and is His intimate associate (9. 4, 9; 8. 3). She is an effluence from His glory, the mirror of His power, the image of His goodness (7. 25 ff.). She transforms the souls of men, bestowing on them virtues (7. 27; 8. 4–8). She guides their outward fortunes (chapter 10) and comes to dwell with them as friend (8. 2, 9). She is to be obtained from God by prayer (8. 21).

Taking a general view of the language of this kind used by the Old Testament writers—especially the later writers—and its connection with the developed New Testament doctrine of the Holy Spirit, it can be said that it prepared the way for the latter in three respects. First, as has been already said, it opened up the way for belief in the possibility of distinctions within the Godhead, and thus it foreshadowed the doctrine of the Trinity. Secondly, this use of the words *ruach* and *pneuma* provided an instrument for the development and expression of the Christian doctrine of the Holy Spirit. In both these respects we may see a providential foreshadowing of the revelation which was to come; but, of course, its meaning was entirely hidden from the users of this terminology. The doctrine of the Holy Spirit is essentially a *Christian* doctrine and could not possibly be appreciated before the rise of Christianity. To look for it in the Old Testament, therefore, is necessarily a vain quest. Thirdly, it led to the expectation that there would be an outpouring of the Holy Spirit in the last days, thus making the New Testament doctrine of the Holy Spirit 'eschatological.'[1]

---

[1] I have been sparing in the use of this ungainly word, which appears with unpleasant frequency in too many modern books of theology. But it must not on that account be supposed that I have been unmindful of the truths for which it stands. It is a pity we cannot substitute the adjective 'end-time' or 'last-time.'

PART II

THE NEW TESTAMENT DOCTRINE

THE NEW TESTAMENT DOCTRINE

IN the Old Testament, as we have seen, the phrase the Spirit (*ruach*) of the Lord or the *ruach* of God is very common. We observed that the expression 'holy *ruach*' occurs only three times, and even then with 'Thy' or 'His.' In the New Testament, Holy Spirit (*pneuma hagion*), sometimes with the definite article and sometimes without it, occurs eighty-eight times. Again, whereas in the Old Testament the phrase 'the *ruach*' is never used except to denote the wind or the breath, in the New Testament the expression 'the Spirit' occurs in at least forty-six passages, without counting the many instances in which 'spirit,' without the article, seems to stand for the working of the Spirit of God upon the spirit of man—e.g. in such phrases as 'the spirit of adoption,' or 'the spirit of meekness,' or 'the spirit of revelation.' It has been already pointed out that the English versions of Ezekiel are seriously misleading in that they repeatedly render *ruach* (without the article) as 'the spirit' instead of 'a spirit.'

These figures reveal a new world, or, as we commonly say, a new dispensation. The New Testament speaks regularly of 'the Holy Spirit,' which phrase is to be carefully distinguished from the Old Testament 'thy holy Spirit.' In like manner the common New Testament use of the phrase 'the Spirit' indicates that He is so familiar and central in Christian experience that it is sufficient thus to describe Him. He is '*The* Spirit' *par excellence*: every Christian will know who is meant. On the other hand, for a Hebrew 'the *ruach*' could only mean 'the wind' or 'the breath' (cf., for example, 1 *Kings* 19. 11).

Clearly some powerful event must have taken place to account for this decisive change. The New Testament states that this was the descent of the Holy Spirit on the Day of Pentecost, described in the second chapter of the Acts of the Apostles; and what this change meant for the disciples of Christ is revealed in all the Epistles, which are permeated with references to the Holy Spirit. We shall have to examine this language carefully later on, after we have considered the account of the Pentecostal outpouring of

17

the Spirit. But first of all it is necessary to consider our Lord's teaching about the Holy Spirit as recorded in the first three Gospels. The fewness of the relevant passages, as well as their nature, incidentally affords strong corroborative evidence of the historical worth of these Gospels; for it would have been fatally easy for their authors, writing a generation or more after Pentecost, to have put later ideas into His mouth.

OUR LORD'S TEACHING IN THE SYNOPTIC GOSPELS

There are, in fact, only eight passages in which there is a reference, or possible reference, by our Lord to the Holy Spirit. They are as follows:

(*a*) The teaching about blasphemy against the Holy Spirit (*S. Mark* 3. 28-30; *S. Matt.* 12. 31, 32; *S. Luke* 12. 10).

(*b*) The promise of the guidance of the Spirit in the coming time of persecution (*S. Mark* 13. 11; *S. Matt.* 10. 20; *S. Luke* 12. 12; cf. *S. Luke* 21. 14, 15).

(*c*) The saying about casting out evil spirits by the Spirit of God (*S. Matt.* 12. 28; cf. *S. Luke* 11. 20).

(*d*) The reference to the inspiration of Psalm 110 (*S. Mark* 12. 36; *S. Matt.* 22. 43).

(*e*) The giving of Holy Spirit in answer to prayer (*S. Luke* 11. 13; cf. *S. Matt.* 7. 11).

(*f*) The Baptismal Command (*S. Matt.* 28. 19).

(*g*) Two passages, peculiar to S. Luke; the first, the reference to Isaiah 61. 1, 2, in the sermon at Nazareth (*S. Luke* 4. 16 ff.); the second, the account of our Lord's promise of the Pentecostal outpouring (*S. Luke* 24. 49).

We begin with passage (*a*): 'Verily I say unto you, All their sins shall be forgiven unto the sons of men, and their blasphemies wherewith soever they shall blaspheme: but whosoever shall blaspheme against the Holy Spirit hath never forgiveness, but is guilty of an eternal sin: because they said, He hath an unclean spirit.' Comparing this with the Matthaean and Lucan accounts of the same incident, we should observe that in the latter blasphemy against the Spirit is explicitly contrasted with blasphemy against the Son. This excludes the common interpretation of blasphemy against the Holy Spirit as referring to the Holy Spirit

working in our Lord. It must refer to sin against the light of the
Holy Spirit in every man, i.e. the falsification of conscience: the
sin described by Isaiah as calling good evil and evil good, putting
darkness for light and light for darkness, bitter for sweet and
sweet for bitter (*Isa.* 5. 20). As our Lord said on another occasion:
'If the light that is in thee be darkness, how great is that darkness.'
This interpretation alone can explain why this sin is different from
all others and can make sense of the words in S. Mark's account
which state this but are difficult to translate. The Authorized
Version, 'is in danger of eternal damnation,' is only a paraphrase.
The Revised Version translates: 'is guilty of an eternal sin.'
Literally, 'is liable to eternal (*aionios*) judgement.' These words
are omitted by Matthew and Luke, perhaps because of the
difficulty in meaning; and yet the context makes it sufficiently
clear that they must indicate a state which knows no possibility of forgiveness, in which the salt has completely lost its
savour.

This passage is of the greatest importance for a right understanding of our Lord's teaching about the Holy Spirit. He seems
to be making here a clear reference to the light of the Holy
Spirit in the human conscience, as we call the capacity for passing
moral judgements. In other words, He clearly teaches that the
Holy Spirit is at work at the natural level in every man.
This is the clearest statement in our Lord's recorded teaching on
this subject. But many other passages presuppose this teaching.
In S. Luke our Lord says on one occasion to His hearers, 'Why
even of yourselves judge ye not what is right?' (*S. Luke* 12. 57);
and in S. Matthew there is the passage about His hearers being
able to read the face of the sky but unable to read the signs of
the times—i.e. to pass right moral judgements on the course of
events. This He calls 'hypocrisy,' which, of course, is here not
at all what we mean by the term, but the self-deception which
is the result of a perverted conscience. And all that our Lord has
to say about hypocrisy is a direct consequence of His belief that
the light of the Holy Spirit enlightens every man.

Furthermore, belief in the working of the Holy Spirit at the
natural level underlies a great deal of Christ's teaching given in
parables. The familiar description of a parable as 'an earthly story
with a heavenly meaning' may be seriously misleading; for it

suggests that a parable is an allegory. This, however, is, generally speaking, not true of Christ's parables, and if we try to interpret them all in this way we shall fail to grasp their meaning.[1] As a rule, they are not allegories but stories of ordinary decent men and women going about their daily life, and showing by virtue of their behaviour that, while 'being evil,' they nevertheless reveal the working of the natural light of the Holy Spirit which in turn reflects the character of the Heavenly Father. All this teaching—and there is a great deal of it—is *implicitly* teaching which is in close accord with what our Lord says about blasphemy against the Holy Spirit. It is precisely because the normal man and woman is entirely free from this, the final sin, that his actions are capable of reflecting something of the goodness of God. In other words, our Lord's teaching presupposes the existence of the Natural Law. It is one of the greatest weaknesses of the theology of the Reformers that their own preoccupation with sin and grace blinded them to this teaching. It is to be hoped that the time will soon come when modern theologians of the Reformation tradition will be able to remedy this unfortunate mistake.

In the last part of this book we shall see the vital importance of giving a full and frank recognition to the operation of the Holy Spirit at the natural level, in 'everyman.' The fact that the New Testament is (naturally enough) dominated by the thought of the supernatural gift of the 'Spirit of Christ,' i.e. the gift of the Holy Spirit imparting to the Church the 'unsearchable riches of Christ,' must not allow us to forget His working in the unregenerate man and woman.

We proceed to (b): 'And when they lead you to judgement, and deliver you up, be not anxious beforehand what ye shall speak: but whatsoever shall be given you in that hour, that speak ye: for it is not ye that speak, but the Holy Ghost' (*S. Mark* 13. 11; *S. Matt.* 10. 20; *S. Luke* 12. 12; cf. *S. Luke* 21. 14, 15). There is considerable probability that this verse stood in the collection of sayings known as 'Q' and, as Swete and others have remarked, we have here the germ of the Paraclete Doctrine

---

[1] See O. C. Quick: 'The Realism of Christ's Parables,' and C. H. Dodd: 'Natural Law in the Bible' (*Theology*, June 1946), reprinted in *New Testament Studies* (Manchester U.P., 1953), pp. 129 ff.

as found in the Fourth Gospel. The place which it occupies in S. Mark's Gospel is the so-called 'Little Apocalypse.' *As it stands* this discourse may well consist of a later 'writing up' of material, collected from different sayings of our Lord, spoken at different times. But even if this is the case, there is no sound reason for doubting that the sayings are genuine sayings of our Lord. It is in any case highly probable that he did give this kind of teaching about the sending of the Paraclete, as recorded in the Fourth Gospel; and, granting this, there is no reason to question the authority of the present saying. But what is most remarkable about it is that, though its substance is identical in all three Synoptic Gospels, the actual wording shows considerable variety, so that it is difficult to believe that either S. Matthew or S. Luke have here copied S. Mark or have drawn upon a common written source—Q or any other. However that may be, there is a significant difference of phrasing between the Matthaean account and that of the other two Gospels. The former refers to 'the Spirit of your Father' instead of using the expression 'the Holy Spirit' which occurs in S. Mark and S. Luke. This is clearly reminiscent of the words attributed to our Lord in the Fourth Gospel: 'When the *Paraclete* is come, whom I will send unto you from the Father, even the Spirit of truth, who proceedeth from the Father, He shall bear witness of Me' (*S. John* 15. 26). The Matthaean phrase, 'the Spirit of your Father,' reads like an abbreviated recollection of the words ascribed to our Lord by S. John, and may reasonably be accepted as corroborative evidence for the authenticity of that saying.

The third passage (*c*) is as follows: 'But if I by the Spirit of God cast out devils, then is the kingdom of God come upon you' (*S. Matt.* 12. 28). In the Lucan version of this saying, we read for 'the Spirit of God' the expression 'the finger of God.' Assuming, as we may, that these two expressions both mean the same thing, viz. 'by the power of God,' this passage throws no light on the Christian doctrine of the Spirit. In it our Lord is merely using the current Jewish terminology.

The fourth passage (*d*) is that in which our Lord refers to the inspiration of Psalm 110, when He says that in that psalm David spoke ἐν Πνεύματι (*S. Matt.* 12. 43) or ἐν τῷ Πνεύματι τῷ Ἁγίῳ

(*S. Mark* 12. 36). Here, as Swete[1] says, he uses the 'formula of the pious Jew of his own time' to refer to inspiration, and, once again, the passage throws no fresh light on the Christian doctrine of the Spirit.

The fifth passage (*e*) is that which, in the Lucan version, relates that our Lord says that the Father will give 'Holy Spirit' to them that ask Him (*S. Luke* 11. 13). S. Matthew (7. 11) has 'give good things' and this is surely more likely to be the original version. If 'Holy Spirit' stood in the original, it is most improbable that it would have been changed to 'good things,' whereas the reverse process, in view of the obvious fondness of the third Evangelist for bringing in the Holy Spirit, is fully intelligible. This being the case, this passage can add nothing relevant to our purpose.

The next passage for consideration (*f*) is peculiar to the first Gospel. It is the well-known command to baptize: 'Go ye therefore, and make disciples of all the nations, baptizing them into the name of the Father, and of the Son, and of the Holy Ghost.' Critics have been inclined to make heavy weather of this passage and to assert that it is the result of reading back the liturgical practice of the second-century Church into our Lord's day, arguing that it is impossible to hold that He spoke in such terms. We need not here enter into the vexed question as to whether εἰς τὸ ὄνομα should be rendered, as in the Revised Version, 'into the name,' or, as in the Authorized Version, 'in the name.' In any case, the New Testament clearly regards baptism as being 'into Christ,' i.e. as in some way effecting what we should call 'a mystical union' with Him. Furthermore, this question is not really relevant to the matter with which we are now concerned, viz. whether our Lord could have used on this occasion the trinitarian formula. There are two objections commonly alleged against His having done this. The first is that we are repeatedly told in the New Testament that individuals were baptized in the name of the Lord Jesus, or into Christ, and consequently it is difficult to suppose that a trinitarian formula was used, as it must have been if Christ had specifically ordered it. In reply it may be pointed out that it is quite possible that the reference to baptism in Christ's name is merely a compendious way of referring to

---

[1] H. B. Swete: *The Holy Spirit in the New Testament*, p. 121.

trinitarian baptism. For we have clear evidence of this usage from the *Didache*, where in chapter seven baptism in the name of the Trinity is enjoined, and in chapter nine baptism is said to be 'in the name of the Lord.' Moreover, we ourselves nearly always refer to trinitarian baptism as 'Christian Baptism.' Another way of meeting this difficulty is to suppose that the passage in S. Matthew 28 is not to be understood as enjoining the use of a *formula* for baptism but, in the words of Bishop Chase, as describing 'what baptism essentially is.'

The second objection is that the words look far too much like a later liturgical formula for us seriously to suppose that they can have been uttered by our Lord. But we have to reckon with the fact that there are many passages in the New Testament which are fully trinitarian in principle, and presuppose such a belief as is expressed by this formula. Consider, for example, such a passage as: 'Through Him [i.e. Christ] we both [Jews and Greeks] have our access in one Spirit unto the Father' (*Eph.* 2. 18). How are we to understand that Jews, who are rigid monotheists, came to think so soon in these terms,[1] unless our Lord had given clear teaching to this effect? Granting the substantial accuracy of S. Matthew 28. 19, we have an explanation of all this language. Otherwise we have not.

Taking a broad view of this passage, therefore, we seem to be justified in claiming that it reveals our Lord's authority for the undeniable belief of the early Church in the Holy Spirit, as on an equality with the Father and the Son. Such a passage, of course, does not throw any fresh light upon the person and work of the Holy Spirit, but it lays the foundations on which those doctrines must be built, and in fact were subsequently built.

This brings us to (*g*), the last two of the Synoptic passages which have any bearing on our Lord's teaching on the Holy Spirit, both of them peculiar to S. Luke.

The first is the account of our Lord's sermon at Nazareth, following upon His temptation (*S. Luke* 4. 16–30). He opens the roll of the book of the prophet Isaiah which was handed to Him and begins to read at the sixty-first chapter: 'The Spirit of the

---

[1] Compare also the following passages: 2 Thess. 2. 13 ff.; 1 Cor. 12. 4 ff.; 2 Cor. 13. 14; Eph. 3. 14 ff.; Eph. 4. 3 ff.; 1 S. Pet. 1. 2; 1 S. John 3. 23 f.; S. Jude 20 f.; Heb. 6. 4 ff.; 1 S. John 4. 2.

Lord is upon Me, because He hath anointed Me to preach good tidings to the poor. . . .' Some critics are inclined to see in this passage a Lucan imaginative picture of the significance of our Lord's ministry rather than a sober historical account of what He actually said and did. It is argued that the Evangelist having just previously said that our Lord was 'full of the Holy Spirit' (*S. Luke* 4. 1), proceeds to paint an imaginative picture to illustrate the fact that Spirit-filled Christ is inaugurating the Messianic Age. Possibly this is the case; but it is also possible that S. Luke is, in fact, recording what happened. There is certainly nothing improbable in assuming this to be so. But the matter is of no importance from the point of view of our present inquiry. Whether the incident is historical or Evangelist's comment, its meaning is clear; it indicates the belief that our Lord's coming means the ushering in of the Messianic Age, and the fulfilment of prophecy. To use the fashionable jargon, the passage is eschatological.

The second of the passages peculiar to S. Luke is as follows: 'And behold, I send forth [ἐξαποστέλλω] the promise of My Father upon you: but tarry ye in the city, until ye be clothed with power from on high' (*S. Luke* 24. 49). There is here a clear allusion to the forthcoming Pentecostal outpouring, which S. Luke was to record fully in the Acts. It is described in the phrase 'the promise of My Father' (ἡ ἐπαγγελία τοῦ πατρός μου). This may be an allusion to Old Testament prophecies, but is surely more naturally taken to imply the promise of the Father which He had previously mentioned. This is clearly stated to be the case in the Acts, when the same expression occurs again: 'the promise of the Father, which, said He, ye heard from Me' (*Acts* 1. 4). Our minds go back to the saying which we have already considered under (*b*). Thus, even leaving out of account the Johannine teaching (which we shall shortly have to consider), there is ground in the Synoptic tradition for such an interpretation. The similarity between the phrase 'the promise of My Father' and 'the Spirit of your Father' (*S. Matt.* 10. 20) should be carefully noted.

No reference is made in this passage to baptism, but it may be pointed out that, if we compare the setting in which it stands with S. Matthew 28. 19, there is a clear resemblance between the two passages. In S. Luke 24. 47 we read: 'That repentance and remission of sins should be preached in His name unto all the nations, beginning from Jerusalem.' In both passages we have the identical expression 'all the nations' (πάντα τὰ ἔθνη), and the mention of repentance and remission of sins is a clear allusion to baptism, which in the New Testament is regularly associated with them. Thus these two passages—the Matthaean and the Lucan—tend to support each other.

This brings us to the question which is often asked—Why do the Synoptic Gospels say so little about the Holy Spirit, or, rather, why does our Lord say so little about Him? Some scholars have argued that the reason for this is that in Jewish thought 'the general gift of the Spirit belongs to the time of the vindication and manifestation of the Messiah and the Messianic Kingdom.'[1] And this is doubtless true so far as the supernatural manifestation of the Spirit in the Church—which is the Messianic community—is concerned. But, as we shall see, we must by no means overlook the very important fact that our Lord presupposes in much of His teaching the fact of the natural operations of the Holy Spirit, working in every man and in every place. We must not overlook this presupposition (silent for the most part) of our Lord's teaching. Nor, as I think, are we entitled to write off as a 'community product' pure and simple the profound teaching of the Last Discourses in S. John's Gospel—a matter which will engage our attention shortly.

Surveying as a whole the references in the first three Gospels to our Lord's teaching about the Holy Spirit, we must, I think, be impressed by two characteristics which they bear. The first is the highly restrained nature of the account, which would surely have been very different if the Evangelists had read back into our Lord's teaching the post-Pentecostal experience of the Church. We can guess, perhaps fairly accurately, what it would have been like by considering the references constantly made to the Holy Spirit by the Evangelists themselves. Thus, for example, the narratives relating the story of our Lord's conception, birth, and childhood in S. Luke's Gospel are full of references to the Holy Spirit and 'the Spirit,' which plainly reflect the later Christian experience. S. Matthew's narrative does not cover the same

[1] C. K. Barrett: The Holy Spirit and the Gospel Tradition (S.P.C.K. 1947), p. 159.

ground, but he also has at least two references which reflect back Christian doctrine. In both cases, the language employed goes far beyond the Old Testament usage, though our familiarity with the former may to some extent blind us to this.

The second characteristic of our Lord's recorded Synoptic teaching about the Spirit is that all three Gospels relate the incident which reveals most clearly His teaching about the natural, as contrasted with the supernatural, operations of the Spirit. This is especially important because in the rest of the New Testament there is no direct emphasis upon this aspect of the Holy Spirit's work. 'The light that lighteneth every man' is ascribed by the fourth Evangelist to the *Logos* and not to the Spirit, in the solitary reference which he made to it. There could hardly be a clearer proof that the teaching of the Lord in this matter has been faithfully transmitted by the Evangelists.

THE TEACHING OF S. JOHN THE BAPTIST

Something must be said now about the teaching which S. John the Baptist is alleged to have given about the coming baptism with Holy Spirit. As is well known, there is an important difference between the Marcan account and the accounts in S. Matthew and S. Luke. In the former, John is reported to have said of the Coming One: 'He shall baptize you with Holy Spirit' (ἐν Πνεύματι Ἁγίῳ) (*S. Mark* 1. 8), whereas S. Matthew and S. Luke read: 'He shall baptize you with Holy Spirit and with fire' (*S. Matt.* 3. 11 and *S. Luke* 3. 16). Some critics have argued that the reference to the Holy Spirit in these passages must be a reading back of later ideas into John's words, and that what he really foretold was baptism with fire. The basis of this argument is claimed to be the passage in Acts 19. 1–7, when S. Paul inquires of 'certain disciples' at Ephesus: 'Did ye receive the Holy Ghost when ye believed?' and their reply: 'We have not so much as heard whether there be any Holy Ghost.' This argument is, to say the least, shaky for more reasons than one. In the first place, it depends upon a doubtful rendering of the Greek, in which the reply to S. Paul's question Ἀλλ' οὐδὲ εἰ Πνεῦμα Ἅγιόν ἐστι is translated: 'We have not so much as heard whether there be any Holy Ghost.' But this is a much less probable rendering than that of the Revised Version: 'We did not so much as hear whether the Holy Ghost was given.' This brings it into line with what is unquestionably the correct rendering of the parallel passage in S. John 7. 39: οὔπω γὰρ ἦν Πνεῦμα ὅτι ὁ Ἰησοῦς οὔπω ἐδοξάσθη; 'for the Spirit was not yet given; because Jesus was not yet glorified.' Moreover, it is quite incredible that devout Jews could ever have said that they had not heard of Holy Spirit. In fact, we know from S. Peter's speech on the Day of Pentecost, when he at once called to mind the prophecy of Joel, that this was not the case.

In the second place, apart from these considerations, if the reference to Holy Spirit in S. Mark 1. 8 is omitted, the whole passage becomes meaningless. It would have been quite different if the Marcan account of S. John the Baptist's words had read, with S. Matthew and S. Luke, 'with Holy Spirit and with fire.'

It may be noticed in passing that this passage makes it very difficult to accept the theory which some are maintaining to-day, that the teaching of the New Testament is that the Holy Spirit is given in water-baptism apart from the laying on of hands. For S. Paul's next question, after the Ephesian disciples had said that they had not heard whether the Holy Spirit had been given: 'Into what then were ye baptized?' on the face of it would seem to imply that the Holy Spirit was given through water-baptism. But when we go on to read that, after water-baptism, S. Paul laid his hands upon them and 'the Holy Spirit came on them,' it becomes quite clear that 'baptism' in S. Paul's question *must* refer to the double rite of water-baptism and the laying on of hands. If this is the case here, there is at least a likelihood that it is the case elsewhere in the New Testament, unless the context actually forbids such an interpretation. We shall have to examine this question more fully later.

THE JOHANNINE TEACHING ABOUT THE HOLY SPIRIT

Here we enter upon a field of decisive importance for the understanding of the New Testament doctrine of the Holy Spirit, but unquestionably it is one which has been bedevilled by a great deal of controversy. There are some scholars who are prepared to maintain that, despite the obviously 'theological' nature of this

Gospel and the fact that much of it represents 'Evangelist's comment' rather than an accurate record of historical events, there is, nevertheless, a good deal of genuine historical reminiscence, some of it of the greatest value. On the other hand, there are others who are unwilling to admit that the Fourth Gospel contains any narrative at all which can seriously claim to be used as evidence of our Lord's actual teaching. Plainly it is impossible for us to debate this big question here. It must suffice if I say that I am satisfied, in my own mind, that the former group of scholars are nearer the truth than the latter, and that I shall therefore not hesitate to accept (for example) the Last Discourses as representing with substantial accuracy our Lord's teaching about the Holy Spirit. But even if it were to be conceded that this teaching represents not what our Lord said but what a great Christian theologian taught—under the guidance of the Holy Spirit—at the end of the first century A.D., it would not follow that it is untrue. Indeed, I suppose that nobody who would call himself a Christian would assert this.

Nevertheless, if we are able to find genuine historical reminiscence in the Fourth Gospel, we shall find a greater satisfaction, and, for my part, I see no reason why we should not. Thus, for example, we have already noticed that, in the Synoptic tradition, there is clear evidence that our Lord did promise the disciples that they would have the special presence of the Spirit of the Father. It is, therefore, entirely in keeping with this that just before the Crucifixion He should have delivered privately to the disciples the Last Discourses in the Upper Room, substantially as they are reported by the Evangelist. Indeed, it is hard to think that this wonderful teaching could possibly have any other source than our Lord Himself.

Turning, then, to the evidence of this Gospel, we notice that the teaching about the Spirit falls into two broad divisions: (a) the teaching in the first half of the book, and (b) the teaching of the Last Discourses and the post-Resurrection appearances. It will be convenient to consider the material in this way.

First of all, let us briefly consider what the Fourth Evangelist has to tell us about our Lord's baptism by S. John. It will be convenient to have the whole passage before us:

'On the morrow he seeth Jesus coming unto him, and saith,

Behold, the Lamb of God, which taketh away the sin of the world! This is He of whom I said, After me cometh a man which is become before me. And I knew Him not; but that He should be made manifest to Israel, for this cause came I baptizing with water. And John bare witness, saying, I have beheld the Spirit descending as a dove out of heaven; and it abode upon Him. And I knew Him not: but He that sent me to baptize with water, He said unto me, Upon whomsoever thou shalt see the Spirit descending, and abiding upon Him, the same is He that baptizeth with the Holy Spirit (ἐν Πνεύματι ʾΑγίῳ). And I have seen, and borne witness that this is the Son of God' (S. John 1. 29–34).

I would begin by saying that all this reads like a transcript from real life. There is, in fact, a good deal of similar material to be found in the first two chapters of the Gospel.[1] We may, therefore, accept it as such, especially as, if we so interpret it, it throws light on the meaning of the Synoptic narrative. It claims to give a straightforward account of what S. John the Baptist saw and thought when he baptized our Lord. He tells us that he had been forewarned by God that the man upon whom he should see a dove descending was He that should baptize with Holy Spirit. It must be emphasized, as Bernard points out, that the word which the Evangelist uses for 'saw' (θεάσθαι) always refers to literal seeing and 'is never used in New Testament of spiritual vision.'[2] He, therefore, intends us to believe that a dove did literally descend upon our Lord, and that the Baptist had previously been taught to regard this as 'a sign' that here was the Promised One, who should baptize with the Spirit. This is entirely in accordance with the mind of the Old Testament prophets, and is reminiscent in particular of the sign which Elijah gave to Elisha (2 Kings 2. 10). Moreover, this confirms the very explicit language of S. Luke that the Spirit 'descended in a bodily form, as a dove' (S. Luke 3. 22). In view of this evidence it is difficult to understand why anybody should think himself justified in regarding the incident as a subjective 'vision.'

However we may choose to explain it, the dove arrived,[3] and

---

[1] Those who are inclined to question this will, I think, be reassured if they read the essay on The First Days of Our Lord's Ministry in F. J. Badcock's Reviews and Studies (Longmans 1925). This valuable book is too little known.

[2] J. H. Bernard: S. John (I.C.C.), Vol. I, p. 48.

[3] 'All these evangelists . . . agree in recording that a dove alighted upon Jesus when presenting Himself for baptism' (Bernard: op. cit.).

the sign was read by the Baptist: 'Here is He who will baptize with Holy Spirit, as was foretold by the Old Testament prophets.' Thus is confirmed the accuracy of the reference to baptism by the Spirit in the first three Gospels, which all also record the appearance of the dove. There is definite evidence that the rabbis interpreted the reference to the Spirit of God brooding on the waters in the first chapter of Genesis as alluding to a dove. Hence the symbolism is not unintelligible. Moreover, the dove was the only bird included in the Old Testament sacrificial system, and we know that our Lord viewed baptism[1] sacrificially. Those critics who assert that S. John Baptist foretold only that our Lord would baptize with fire do not tell us what place the dove symbol can have in such a scheme of thought. They have conveniently forgotten that. I would venture to claim, therefore, that if we are prepared to trust the historicity of this passage (along with some other parts, at least, of the first two chapters of the Gospel) we are enabled to see more clearly than is otherwise possible the inner meaning of the fuller descriptions of the event to be found in the first three Gospels. Our Lord is being called to His Messianic office, and the inauguration of His work is accompanied by the descent of the Holy Spirit upon Him. At the time of our Lord's baptism by S. John this was not understood at all; and we know that for the author of the first Gospel the event seems to have been a stumbling-block ('I have need to be baptized of Thee, and comest Thou to me?' says S. John the Baptist in the Matthaean narrative). But the writer of the Fourth Gospel sees clearly into the meaning of the event.

We proceed next to consider the group of passages in the first half of the Gospel which claim to record our Lord's teaching about the Holy Spirit. There are three such passages. Two of them purport to record teaching given privately to individuals— to Nicodemus (chapter 3) and to the Woman of Samaria (chapter 4). The third contains an account of teaching given publicly and emphatically[2] at the Feast of Tabernacles (chapter 7). It will be convenient to take this first. It was as follows: 'Now on the last day, the great day of the feast, Jesus stood and cried, saying, If any man thirst, let him come unto Me, and drink. He that

---

[1] S. Luke 12. 50.
[2] Our Lord adopts an unusual posture for a teacher: He stood, *and* shouted.

believeth on Me, as the scripture hath said, out of his belly shall flow rivers of living water. But this spake He of the Spirit, which they that believed on Him were to receive: for the Spirit was not yet given; because Jesus was not yet glorified.'

The punctuation and exact interpretation of this passage are uncertain. In the Revised Version quoted above, our Lord is made to reiterate what He is reported to have said to the Woman of Samaria: 'The water that I shall give him shall become in him a well of water springing up into eternal life.' And the meaning of this saying is here further elucidated. It is made clear by the comment of the Evangelist: 'But this spake He of the Spirit' (S. John 7. 39). This interpretation gives an excellent sense, viz. that the individual believer who shall possess the Holy Spirit will naturally and inevitably be a missionary, communicating the gift to others. But there is a formidable objection to it and that is that there is no passage in the Old Testament scriptures which says that out of the belly of the believer there shall flow rivers of living water. Our Lord had indeed said this— or something like it—to the Samaritan woman, but nothing resembling it is to be found in the Old Testament. It is hard, therefore, to believe that He could have asserted in this way that such a scripture was being fulfilled. It looks as if there has been some failure to report accurately what He did say.

An ingenious suggestion which, if correct, solves the difficulty was made by Burney.[1] He points out that in unvocalized Aramaic (in which language it may be presumed that our Lord was speaking) 'belly' and 'fountain' are identical, and hence he suggests that what our Lord really said was not 'out of his belly' but 'out of the fountain.' In this case, as many of the Fathers supposed, the words 'he that believeth in Me' should be taken with what precedes and not with what follows. The passage will then run:

> If any man thirst, let him come unto Me,
> And let him drink that believeth on Me.
> As the Scripture hath said,
> Out of the fountain shall flow rivers of living water.

In this case the last line contains a general allusion to Ezekiel 47. 1-12, taken up by Joel 3. 18, and Zechariah 14. 8, where the

---

[1] In his book, *The Aramaic Origin of the Fourth Gospel* (1922), p. 109.

fountain of living waters is foretold.[1] The only remaining difficulty is that 'the' must be substituted for 'his' before 'belly.' But it is easy to see that if 'belly' was read by mistake for 'fountain' it would have been necessary to change 'the belly' into 'his belly.'

If the passage is read in this way, the Evangelist's comment in the next verse (*S. John* 7. 39) follows on quite naturally: 'But this spake He of the Spirit, which they that believed on Him were to receive: for the Spirit was not yet given; because Jesus was not yet glorified.' That those who believe in our Lord were to receive the Spirit would be clear to all who accepted the testimony of the Forerunner. The fact that the Spirit could not be given until after the Ascension would be appreciated by those who were acquainted with the teaching of the Last Discourses, which is here anticipated by the Evangelist's comment. He apparently does not think it necessary to state at this point in his narrative the reason for this. The Greek οὔπω γὰρ ἦν Πνεῦμα can obviously not be taken literally, but, as we saw in dealing with the passage in Acts 19, clearly requires the word 'given' to be supplied.

The foregoing interpretation of this passage is rendered more probable when it is remembered that it brings it into line with the tradition whereby Christ is regarded as the spiritual Rock, from which flows the life-giving stream (cf. 1 *Cor.* 10. 4).[2] It seems to be to this that S. Paul is alluding when he says that 'we were all made to drink of one Spirit' (1 *Cor.* 12. 17). Thus there seems here to be a very close correspondence between the Johannine and Pauline doctrine of the Holy Spirit.

This brings us to the consideration of the discourse with Nicodemus (*S. John* 3. 1–15) and the discourse with the Woman of Samaria (*S. John* 4. 1–42). It will be profitable if we can consider them in close proximity; for although they obviously differ in many ways (one of them being directed to an educated man, and the other to an unsophisticated woman), so far as the doctrine, or implied doctrine, of the Holy Spirit is concerned,

---

[1] In Ezek. 47 we have the famous vision of the living waters flowing from the Temple at Jerusalem. This is taken up by Joel who says briefly: 'A fountain shall come forth from the house of the Lord, and shall water the valley of acacias'; and this, again, in Zech. 14, becomes, 'living waters shall go down from Jerusalem. . . .'

[2] It is at least possible that in the famous commission to S. Peter in S. Matt. 16. 19, 'upon this rock' may refer to our Lord Himself, and not S. Peter. Many of the Fathers so interpret it, and it gives an excellent sense.

there is a close resemblance between them. Our Lord, then, confronts Nicodemus with the doctrine of the new birth. We need not spend time in debating whether ἄνωθεν is to be rendered 'again' or 'from above.' The meaning is substantially the same in either case. And we may postpone for the time being the consideration of the reference to 'water' (in 3. 5). Let us concentrate our attention on the indubitable fact that our Lord here enunciates a spiritual law, which is based upon the general principle that like begets like. 'That which is born of the flesh is flesh, and that which is born of the Spirit is Spirit.' Here He is merely giving another instance of what He had previously said according to the Synoptic tradition: 'Do men gather grapes of thorns or figs of thistles?' The enunciation of this principle in S. John 3. 6 has the ring of authenticity about it. There is no intention to belittle the flesh here, or assuredly the writer who had just said 'the word became flesh' could never have quoted the saying. Our Lord is merely adopting the recognized Hebrew idiom whereby there is a fundamental distinction between Spirit which is God's essence and flesh which is man's essence,[1] and proceeding to argue on that basis. It clearly follows that man, who is *per se* flesh, needs the quickening power of God who is *Spirit*. This power our Lord claims to impart, in accordance with the prophecy of the Baptist. What He is saying to Nicodemus is simply a fulfilment of that prophecy. He warns him that this may seem hard to understand, but, bringing into use the double meaning of *ruach*, He points out that, since it is impossible ever to understand fully the movements of the *wind*, Nicodemus should not boggle at the mystery of the *Spirit*.

According to the best text of verse 5 (though not of verse 8) we should undoubtedly read 'born of water and the Spirit.' Where did that additional phrase 'of water' come from? It certainly could not have come from John the Baptist, because he had explicitly contrasted baptism with water and baptism with the Spirit. There are those who claim that it comes from the practice of the early Church. The possibility of this cannot be excluded; nor, on the other hand, can the possibility be excluded

---

[1] See Isa. 31. 3 and what is said above on page 5.

that our Lord said this. It certainly would not be surprising if He did, in view of the fact that water and spirit were so closely associated in our Lord's mind, in accordance with the Old Testament tradition. In fact, what needs to be explained is really not why 'water' is mentioned here, but why the Baptist separated 'water' and 'spirit.' We are apt to read his words as if they put the two conceptions into opposition. Yet S. John need not have implied this. All that he may have meant is that water-baptism is the first stage leading to water-spirit baptism. In accordance with the regular Semitic idiom, he makes an emphatic statement by means of a negation.[1]

We pass on to the discourse with the Woman of Samaria (S. John 4. 1–42). Here we have in a different form the contrast between 'flesh' and 'spirit.' This time it is given in the contrast between ordinary water and 'living water,' which in the prophetic teaching symbolizes the Spirit. This is the clue to the understanding of the passage which is too often misunderstood: 'God is a Spirit: and they that worship Him must worship in spirit and in truth' (ἐν πνεύματι καὶ ἀληθείᾳ). We should almost certainly render this, 'God is Spirit,' in accordance with R.V. margin.[2] This is simply a straightforward statement of what would be a commonplace to a Jew, and presumably to a Samaritan also. The rest of the sentence, therefore, must not be taken to mean merely that God demands sincere and genuine worship. It means that God, being Spirit, can be rightly worshipped only 'in the Spirit,' or, as Christians come later to say, 'in the Holy Spirit.'[3] The fact that this latter phrase is not put by the Evangelist into our Lord's mouth may perhaps have some force in corroborating that he is recording an actual conversation with some pretence of accuracy. In fact, our Lord is really saying in other words to this woman what He had said to Nicodemus. For if God demands worship 'in the Spirit' this clearly involves

---

[1] Thus our Lord says: 'I came not to call the righteous, but sinners' (S. Mark 2. 17). Clearly He does not mean that He has no interest in 'the righteous men.' He came to save all men. This is merely an emphatic way of saying that He is chiefly concerned with leading sinners to repentance. See A. Guillaume: Prophesy and Divination (Longmans 1925). There is also doubtless a rebuke here to the self-righteous Pharisees.

[2] So also the recent American Standard Version.

[3] There is a good discussion of the meaning of this passage (which has been so frequently completely misunderstood to mean that true worship can be offered anywhere and by anybody) in G. S. Hendry, The Holy Spirit in Christian Theology (S.C.M. Press 1957), pp. 31 and 32.

the doctrine of the new birth, since that which is born of the flesh is flesh and that which is born of the Spirit is Spirit. But the woman fails to grasp His meaning as completely as Nicodemus had done. She could no more understand the doctrine of the Spirit under the figure of living water and living worship than Nicodemus could do under the image of the new birth. This is not surprising. What is perhaps surprising is that our Lord should have expected them to understand. Some critics will say that this shows that the two incidents are completely unhistorical and must be symbolically understood. And yet somehow they read like transcripts from life, especially the second discourse, where we appear to have a *compression* of a much longer conversation. May our Lord not have 'tried out' this kind of teaching on occasion to see how it would go down? However this may be, we know that He was later going to give it privately and at length to the disciples, if we may trust the substantial historicity of the Last Discourses in the Fourth Gospel.

THE LAST DISCOURSES IN S. JOHN'S GOSPEL

We now come to what must be described as the classical statement of the person and work of the Holy Spirit, which we find in the Last Discourses, to which is added as an appendix the charge to the Apostles on the evening of Easter Day. It will be convenient to have the relevant passages before us:

'If ye love Me, ye will keep My commandments. And I will pray the Father, and He shall give you another Comforter (Παράκλητος), that He may be with you (μεθ' ὑμῶν) for ever, even the Spirit of truth (τὸ πνεῦμα τῆς ἀληθείας): whom the world cannot receive; for it beholdeth Him not, neither knoweth Him (οὐ θεωρεῖ οὐτό, αὐδὲ γινωσκει); for He abideth with you, and shall be in you (ὅτι παρ' ὑμῖν μένει, καὶ ἐν ὑμῖν ἔσται).[1] I will not leave you desolate (ὀρφανούς): I come to you' (S. John 14. 15–18).

'These things have I spoken unto you, while yet abiding with you (παρ' ὑμῖν). But the Comforter (Παράκλητος), even the Holy

[1] There is a well-attested variant reading ἐν ὑμῖν ἐστιν 'is in you,' which, being the harder reading, some critics are inclined to accept as genuine. In this case, we seem compelled to render the present tenses proleptically as futures (see Bernard, S. John, I.C.C., p. 546), for the whole context makes it clear that our Lord is contrasting a present condition with one in the future.

Spirit (τὸ Πνεῦμα τὸ ʺΑγιον), whom the Father will send in My name, He shall teach you all things, and bring to your remembrance all that I said unto you' (S. John 14. 26).

'But when the Comforter (Παράκλητος) is come, whom I will send unto you from the Father, even the Spirit of truth, which proceedeth from the Father (ὃ παρὰ τοῦ πατρὸς ἐκπορεύεται), He shall bear witness of Me: and ye also bear witness, because ye have been with Me from the beginning' (S. John 15. 26).

'Nevertheless I tell you the truth; it is expedient for you that I go away: for if I go not away, the Comforter (Παράκλητος) will not come unto you; but if I go, I will send Him unto you. And He, when He is come, will convince (ἐλέγξει) the world in respect of sin, and of righteousness, and of judgement: of sin, because they believe not on Me; of righteousness, because I go to the Father, and ye behold Me no more; of judgement, because the prince of this world hath been judged. I have yet many things to say unto you, but ye cannot bear them now. Howbeit when He, the Spirit of truth, is come, He shall guide you into all the truth: for He shall not speak from Himself; but what things soever He shall hear, them shall He speak: and He shall declare unto you the things that are to come. He shall glorify Me: for He shall take of Mine, and shall declare it unto you. All things whatsoever the Father hath are Mine: therefore said I, that He taketh of Mine, and shall declare it unto you. A little while, and ye behold (θεωρεῖτέ) Me no more; and again a little while, and ye shall see Me (ὄψεσθέ με)' (S. John 16. 7–16).

'And when He had said this, He breathed (ἐνεφύσησεν) on them, and saith unto them, Receive ye the Holy Ghost (Λάβετε Πνεῦμα ʺΑγιον): whose soever sins ye forgive, they are forgiven unto them; whose soever sins ye retain, they are retained' (S. John 20. 22, 23).

Let us begin our consideration of these passages by dealing with the word Paraclete (ὁ Παράκλητος). As is well known, this word in both the Authorized and the Revised Versions of the New Testament is rendered 'Comforter,' the Revised Version margin reading 'or Advocate, or Helper, Gr. Paraclete.' Apart from these last discourses, when it occurs three times, it is used in only one other place in the New Testament, in 1 S. John 2. 1, when it is rendered 'Advocate,' the Revised Version margin reading 'or

Comforter, or Helper, Gr. Paraclete.' The passage is as follows: 'If any man sin, we have an advocate with the Father, Jesus Christ the righteous.'

To decide upon a satisfactory rendering of this word is not easy. On the linguistic side, the form *Parakletos* suggests a passive meaning, and this would exclude 'Comforter' which has an active sense. This interpretation of the word receives unjustifiable support from the familiar, but inaccurate, rendering of ὀρφανούς by 'comfortless' in the Authorized Version of verse 18. Probably this translation should, therefore, be rejected; but there is much to be said for 'Advocate,' which certainly fits the passage in 1 S. John 2. 1, and for 'Helper,' literally 'one who is called to one's side.' There is also something to be said for the translation 'interpreter,' for it should be noted that the Targum on Job 33. 23 renders the Hebrew מֵלִיץ or interpreter as פַּרְקְלִיטָא, i.e. Paraclete.

Perhaps the best solution is to retain the word Paraclete, and try to fill in the meaning from what we are told about His functions in these passages. It should not be forgotten that our Lord was, after all, not addressing His disciples in Greek, but in Aramaic, so that we should not pay too much attention to the etymology of the Greek word. As we do not know what was the Aramaic original, we seem to be on the safest ground if we try to deduce the meaning of this word from what our Lord tells us about the functions of the Paraclete. He tells us that (*a*) He is the Spirit of truth—τὸ πνεῦμα τῆς ἀληθείας (this must mean that in some sense He is a teacher of the truth); (*b*) He will abide in the disciples (plural); (*c*) He will in some sense bring our Lord back to His disciples; (*d*) He will teach them by bringing to remembrance what our Lord had said, and (it is implied) they will have forgotten; (*e*) He will bear witness to Christ, who is the truth (cf. S. John 14); (*f*) He will have a task to fulfil, not only to the disciples, but also to the world, viz. to convince it of the meaning of sin—as manifested by the life of Christ—and of judgement—the inevitable result of bringing sin and righteousness face to face; (*g*) He will progressively lead them into all truth.

Those several points may be said to summarize the work of the Paraclete, when He is come. Throughout He is spoken of in fully personal terms—as personal as those applied to our Lord Himself. He is another Paraclete (ἀλλός Παράκλητος); that is to say, he takes the place of our Lord, and if He was less than personal this could not be. In Him, in fact, our Lord will return invisibly to the disciples. The very fact that Christ is thus invisibly to be brought before His disciples will, it is implied and even stated, bring a full revelation of His Person and teaching. The Paraclete will bring to remembrance things which the disciples had forgotten, because, as we should say, they had 'repressed' them. When we come to deal with the evidence of the Acts of the Apostles, we shall see how true this turned out to be. Indeed, the story in the Acts is a striking commentary on the truth of this teaching in the Last Discourses. Of course, it is possible to argue that the latter must represent a reading back of later experiences into the words of Christ. It is possible that this may be true in some degree; but the account in the Acts is certainly easier to understand and accept, if some such teaching as is contained in the Last Discourses was, in fact, given by our Lord before the Ascension. Indeed, the whole of the remainder of what the New Testament says about the Holy Spirit is a commentary on this teaching in the Last Discourses.

We have now to deal with what we have described as a kind of appendix to the teaching in the Last Discourses—the scene on the evening of Easter Day. I think that it is important to regard it as an appendix, and to remember that it is the work of the same hand as that which has recorded the Last Discourses. We shall see the reason for this in a moment. We read that the Risen Lord appeared among the disciples, and after giving them the ordinary salutation, He showed them His hands and His side, as a proof of His identity, and added, 'As the Father hath sent Me, even so send I you.' It is probable, though not quite certain, that these words and the charge following were addressed to the 'twelve' only, Judas having gone to his own place, and Thomas being also absent (verse 24).[1] Then our Lord breathed on them (ἐνεφύσησεν, cf. *Gen.* 2. 7) and said, 'Take Holy Spirit: whose soever sins ye forgive, they are forgiven unto them; whose soever sins ye retain, they are retained.'

The relation between this account and the account of the

[1] Cf. S. John 17. 18.

outpouring of the Holy Spirit at Pentecost in Acts 2 has been much discussed. Some scholars, following Westcott, have seized upon the fact that the anarthrous expression 'Holy Spirit' is used here, and not 'The Holy Spirit,' and argued in favour of a distinction between receiving a gift of the Spirit (without the article) and receiving the Spirit Himself (when the article is used). Westcott maintained that the same held true of the passage in S. John 7. 39: οὔπω γὰρ ἦν Πνεῦμα, 'Spirit was not yet.' But, as Bernard has pointed out, it is hard to maintain such a distinction in the last named passage, because it is said just previously 'He spake of the Spirit (περὶ τοῦ Πνεύματος) whom they who believed on Him were to receive: for Spirit was not yet.' Bernard argues correctly that 'we should expect, if the proposed rule about the article were sound, that at its first occurrence in this verse πνεῦμα should be without it.'[1]

Another way out of the difficulty is to adopt the drastic expedient of accepting the Johannine account as the true version of the coming of the Comforter and rejecting root and branch the Lucan tradition, whereby He came fifty days after Easter, and ten days after the Ascension, which, on this theory, took place on Easter Day. The argument for this is to say that Luke invented his chronological scheme in order to conform his narrative to rabbinical patterns,[2] the Feast of Pentecost being regarded as the anniversary of the giving of the Law on Sinai and the founding of the 'church in the wilderness' (Acts 7. 38).

To this view there are three serious objections, which cumulatively are, I think, fatal. (1) Luke is less influenced by rabbinical thought than any of the other Evangelists, as Dr. Daube has shown.[3] A priori it is most unlikely that he should have constructed such a scheme. (2) If he had done so, it would have violated his declared purpose 'to trace the course of all things accurately' and to write 'in order' (καθεξῆς—a Lucan word, which appears to refer to chronological order here, as it evidently does in Acts 11. 4 and 18. 23). (3) In the Last Discourses it is clearly implied, if not actually stated, that the Paraclete would not come until our Lord had departed (S. John 16. 7). The theory is highly improbable and is unlikely to stand the test of time.

[1] Bernard: op. cit., p. 284.   [2] A. Richardson, op. cit., pp. 118, 119.
[3] D. Daube: The N.T. and Rabbinical Judaism (The Athlone Press 1956), passim.

The most probable solution is to say, with Swete (*op. cit.*, p. 167)
that this incident is to be interpreted proleptically. As we have
already seen, the Evangelist says (*S. John* 7. 39) that the Holy
Spirit was not yet (given) because Jesus was not yet glorified.
By this it is clearly implied that He *could* not be given until then.
If the retort is made that this only means that He could not be
given until after the Crucifixion, which is regarded by the Fourth
Evangelist as our Lord's 'glorification' (*S. John* 12. 23, 24), it has
already been pointed out that it is also implied in S. John 16. 7
that the Paraclete could not come until our Lord had gone away.
It is surely incredible that the Evangelist, who has so recently
quoted that saying of our Lord, should shortly afterwards proceed
to describe the coming of the Holy Spirit before our Lord *had*
finally departed. We should probably understand the whole
action proleptically. In doing so, indeed, we have a parallel in
the Last Supper. This could not be a Eucharist, in the full sense,
before our Lord had passed through death and risen again. Until
then the bread and the wine could only proleptically be called
His Body and His Blood. Likewise here our Lord bestows the
authority of the Spirit upon the Apostles for binding and loosing,
an authority which could not, so to say, 'come to life' until after
Pentecost. Nor is there any evidence that it did so.

Surveying as a whole the teaching about the Holy Spirit as
recorded in the latter part of this Gospel, we see how completely
it represents a new departure. The Paraclete is, in fact, very
different from the *ruach* of the Old Testament. There we have
something like an impersonal force, gradually being elevated
towards the level of moral personality. Here we have from the
first a fully Personal Being, who is not only conceived as power,
but also as light. No doubt this latter idea was foreshadowed in
the Old Testament since 'fire' as well as 'wind' was a traditional
symbol of the Spirit. Presumably this conception went back
originally to the theophanic interpretation of the thunderstorm.
But the light which the Spirit of truth, the Paraclete, will bring
is as a clear and steady flame in contrast with the fitful flashes of
the lightning. The latter can lighten the landscape brilliantly for
a split second and then all is darkness; the Paraclete will bring the
abiding light of God into the whole Body of Christ. So our
Lord foretold, and so history has shown, as we shall see.

Why, then, we must inquire, could not the Paraclete come until the Lord had gone? This question presses for an answer, and it must not be shirked. Perhaps the solution of the difficulty is to be found in the fact that during our Lord's Incarnate life He was necessarily restricted by spatial conditions. It was of the very essence of the Incarnation that the infinite God should thus by His own will be limited. But after our Lord had ascended, God could come back in the person of the Holy Spirit, who would not be thus limited, but could be supernaturally present wherever the members of the Body of Christ might be. This time God would come as the light, which, invisible itself, makes all other things visible. Thus the invisible Holy Spirit reveals the meaning of the life and teaching of the Christ. As Swete has said, 'Then for the first time the vision of a sinless humanity burst upon the world with the results that we know, changing both the conception which men had formed of the person of Jesus, and the standards of human conduct.'[1] Nor, we must add, has this revelation ceased. The Holy Spirit will never cease to 'take of the things of Christ' and reveal them to the Spirit-bearing Body, which is the Church, bringing out of His store 'things new and old.'

THE HOLY SPIRIT IN THE ACTS OF THE APOSTLES

We now come to the historical account of the 'coming' of the Spirit on the Day of Pentecost, and the story of the first days of the Spirit-filled and Spirit-illumined Church. We must begin by carefully considering the account in the second chapter of the Acts. In the Revised Version it reads as follows:

'And when the day of Pentecost was now come, they were all together in one place. And suddenly there came from heaven a sound as of the rushing of a mighty wind, and it filled all the house where they were sitting. And there appeared unto them tongues parting asunder, like as of fire; and it sat upon each one of them. And they were all filled with the Holy Spirit, and began to speak with other tongues, as the Spirit gave them utterance.

'Now there were dwelling at Jerusalem Jews, devout men,

---

[1] Swete: *op. cit.*, p. 159.

from every nation under heaven. And when this sound was heard, the multitude came together, and were confounded, because that every man heard them speaking in his own language. And they were all amazed and marvelled, saying, Behold, are not all these which speak Galilaeans? And how hear we, every man in our own language, wherein we were born? Parthians and Medes and Elamites, and the dwellers in Mesopotamia, in Judaea and Cappadocia, in Pontus and Asia, in Phrygia and Pamphylia, in Egypt and the parts of Libya about Cyrene, and sojourners from Rome, both Jews and proselytes, Cretans and Arabians, we do hear them speaking in our tongues the mighty works of God. And they were all amazed, and were perplexed, saying one to another, What meaneth this? But others mocking said, They are filled with new wine.

'But Peter, standing up with the eleven, lifted up his voice, and spake forth unto them, saying, Ye men of Judaea, and all ye that dwell at Jerusalem, be this known unto you, and give ear unto my words. For these are not drunken, as ye suppose; seeing it is but the third hour of the day; but this is that which hath been spoken by the prophet Joel;

> And it shall be in the last days, saith God,
> I will pour forth of My Spirit upon all flesh:
> And your sons and your daughters shall prophesy,
> And your young men shall see visions,
> And your old men shall dream dreams:
> Yea, and on my servants and on my handmaidens in bondage
> Will I pour forth of my Spirit; and they shall prophesy.
> And I will show wonders in the heaven above,
> And signs on the earth beneath;
> Blood of fire and vapour of smoke:
> The sun shall be turned into darkness,
> And the moon into blood,
> Before the day of the Lord come,
> That great and notable day:
> And it shall be, that whosoever shall call on the name of the
>   Lord shall be saved.'

According to the author of Acts, the disciples had been explicitly prepared by Christ for a baptism with the Holy Spirit

(ἐν Πνεύματι ʿΑγίῳ)[1] in the near future, and had been told that
when the Holy Spirit had come upon them (ἐπελθόντος τοῦ ʿΑγίου
Πνεύματος) they should receive power (δύναμις).[2] Here we have
the fulfilment of the promise which, as we have seen there is
good reason to believe, goes back to the pre-Resurrection teaching of our Lord. In this account certain things are reasonably
clear even if the precise nature of the speaking with tongues is
obscure. It will be convenient to leave the latter for consideration
at the end, and to begin by dealing with the matters which are
clear, assuming, as perhaps we may,[3] the substantial historical
accuracy of the narrative.[4]

AT PENTECOST ALL BELIEVERS WERE FILLED WITH THE SPIRIT

In the first place, it is clear that the author regards the essential
meaning of the event to be the 'filling' of the little company of
believers with the Holy Spirit. He says (καὶ ἐπλήσθησαν πάντες
Πνεύματος ʿΑγίου) 'and they were all filled with Holy Spirit.'
This expression 'to be filled with Holy Spirit' is of decisive importance and is entirely new. It does not occur once in the Old
Testament. The only previous occasion of its use is by the same
writer in his account of our Lord's baptism, where we read of
'Jesus, full of Holy Spirit' (S. Luke 4. 1), returning from the river
Jordan. It would appear, therefore, that the writer intends to
suggest that the members of the infant Church were by this
momentous event lifted up to a new and supernatural level, the
level of the Spirit-filled humanity of the Incarnate Lord. In other
words, as S. Paul was to say, here was 'a new creation,' or, as
the Fourth Gospel put it, 'a new birth.' That is to say, the
prophecy of the Baptist was hereby fulfilled. The Church was
'baptized with Holy Spirit.' And this interpretation is borne out
by the fact that the expression 'full of' Holy Spirit is thereafter
of frequent occurrence. Thus we are told in chapter 6 that the
seven are 'full of the Spirit' (πλήρεις Πνεύματος) and here the
omission of the adjective 'holy' is most significant. It suggests

---

[1] Acts 1. 5.   [2] Acts 1. 8.

[3] Some decisive event is clearly required to bring about the complete change of terminology already mentioned. If this present story is entirely unhistorical, the change is
inexplicable.

[4] It is clearly too big a subject to be treated here.

that the presence of the Holy Spirit was by this time so over-whelmingly obvious to all concerned that the epithet 'Holy' was almost redundant. There was for them only one Spirit, the Holy Spirit. Again, we read that both Stephen and Barnabas were filled with Holy Spirit; and subsequently we are told that all the disciples were filled 'with joy and Holy Spirit' (*Acts* 13. 52).

It is explicitly stated that this decisive experience could not come to pass so long as our Lord was visibly present among them; but we are left to guess what the reason for this can be. This is a point to which we shall have to return later in this book. For the present it is enough to appreciate the fact that herein lies the essential meaning of the events which occurred in the Day of Pentecost.

PENTECOST WAS THE FULFILMENT OF PROPHECY

We pass on to consider a second point which the narrative makes clear, viz. that the occurrence was the fulfilment of prophecy. It was, at any rate, quite clear to S. Peter that here was the fulfilment of the prophecy of Joel, who foretold a state of affairs in which there would be something like the condition which Moses had indicated when he said 'Would God that all the Lord's people were prophets' (*Num.* 11. 29). This, indeed, is only another way of saying that all the Lord's people should be full of Holy Spirit. For though, as we have seen, the actual phrase 'to be full of the Spirit of the Lord' is not pre-Christian, the idea underlying it is very close to the highest conception of prophecy as (for example) it is represented in the saying of Micah, 'But truly I am full of power by the Spirit of the Lord' (*Mic.* 3. 8).

We can, of course, only guess whether this application of the prophecy of Joel was 'a sudden inspiration' which came to Peter, or whether our Lord had explicitly prepared the mind of the disciples by referring to this passage. Probably the latter is the case, for there is reason to think that this passage was an early Christian *testimonium*.[1] In any case, the matter is not one of great importance, since the subsequent narrative makes it quite clear that there is a strong emphasis on Christian prophecy in the whole of the Acts, and, indeed, in the whole of the New

[1] See C. H. Dodd: *According to the Scriptures* (Nisbet 1952), p. 47.

Testament. The first Christians were fully conscious that they 'stood in the council of the Lord,' to use the phrase of the prophet Jeremiah (*Jer.* 23. 18). They were not only Spirit-filled, but Spirit-guided. And they were conscious that in this there were some among them who stood above the rest of their brethren and they were called *par excellence* 'prophets.' It was not easy for all believers to remain at that high level, and later on we find S. Paul telling the Ephesians to be 'filled with the Spirit' (*Eph.* 5. 18). Those who were designated 'prophets' ranked in the public estimation second only to the Apostles themselves,[1] though we must be careful to avoid the hasty assumption which has too often been made, that in New Testament times there was a primitive 'charismatic' ministry of Apostles, prophets, and teachers which was subsequently replaced by the threefold ministry of bishops, priests, and deacons.[2] The situation seems rather to have been that in the earliest days of the Church the settled threefold ministry was gradually being developed under the guidance of the Holy Spirit, speaking through the New Testament prophets. There is quite a respectable amount of evidence to indicate this. Thus, for example, S. Paul reminds the Ephesian 'elders' that it was the Holy Spirit who had made them 'overseers' of the flock (*Acts* 20. 28) even as He had testified unto S. Paul 'in every city' (*Acts* 20. 23). It was while the infant Church was worshipping under the inspiration of the Holy Spirit that He told them to 'separate Me Barnabas and Saul for the work whereunto I have called them.' In like manner, we are told that Timothy's ordination was bound up with prophecy (1 *Tim.* 4. 14; cf. 1. 18).

In course of time a tension grew up between the prophetic ministry and the ordered ministry, and this came to a head in the schism of Montanism. But while this tension has been and still is a constant tension, it should be remembered that it is not one which should lead to rupture and weakness but rather to unity and strength. There is no essential antithesis between prophecy and 'law.' Moses the lawgiver was also a prophet. In like manner, Ignatius, the strong upholder of early monepiscopacy, was also a prophet (cf. *Ep. ad Philadelph.* 7). Thus we sing in the

---

[1] See 1 Cor. 12. 28; Eph. 5. 4, 11.
[2] See J. Armitage Robinson in *The Early History of the Church and Ministry*, ed. Swete (Macmillan 1918), pp. 60 ff.

ancient Christian hymn: 'The glorious company of the Apostles praise Thee: The goodly fellowship of the Prophets praise Thee.' This is a point to which we shall have to return later.

PENTECOST BOTH AN INDIVIDUAL AND A CORPORATE EXPERIENCE

The third point which is clear in the account of the Pentecostal outpouring of the Spirit is that it was an experience at one and the same time individual and corporate. The 'tongues parting asunder, like as of fire . . . sat upon each one of them' (*Acts* 2. 3). Nothing could be plainer than the intensely individual nature of this experience. It is quite needless to labour this matter. On the other hand, the subsequent narrative makes it equally clear that a new sense of fellowship was created, which soon came to be known as 'the *koinonia* of the Holy Spirit' (2 *Cor.* 13. 10). This *koinonia*, or fellowship, was a new and unique experience. The infant company of believers 'were of one heart and soul' (*Acts* 4. 32), and it was this which led to the act of the sharing of goods, which is sometimes misleadingly described as 'an experiment in communism.' It was neither an experiment, nor was the resulting state of affairs in any essential analogous to what we now know as communism. It was simply a spontaneous manifestation of what S. Paul calls the oneness of the Spirit, i.e. the oneness created by the Holy Spirit (ἡ ἑνότης τοῦ Πνεύματος).

It is probable that this supernatural society was known as 'The Fellowship.' In the best text of Acts 2. 42 we read: ἦσαν δὲ προσκαρτεροῦντες τῇ διδαχῇ τῶν Ἀποστόλων καὶ τῇ κοινωνίᾳ τῇ κλάσει τοῦ ἄρτου καὶ ταῖς προσευχαῖς, and this should probably be translated, 'And they continued steadfastly in the teaching of the Apostles and in the Fellowship, in the breaking of the loaf, and in the prayers.' The significance of the one loaf here should not be overlooked. We learn from the *Didache*, that puzzling but undoubtedly primitive Christian writing, that as the unity of the loaf was derived from the ears of corn scattered on the hillside, so it was that the Church was gathered into the kingdom. And it was probably from the fact that this Eucharistic loaf was by our Lord designated as His Body that the Church came to be known as the Body of Christ. This is the simplest explanation of what is an entirely new meaning for the Greek word *soma*.

'We being many,' says S. Paul, 'are one loaf, one body, for we all partake of the one loaf.'[1]

It may have been some little time before this *koinonia* of the Spirit was first called 'the Church' (ἡ ἐκκλησία). It is perhaps significant that in the first passage in the Acts of the Apostles in which the word 'Church' occurs, it is not part of the true text, which runs: ὁ δὲ Κύριος προσετίθει τοὺς σωζομένους καθ᾽ ἡμέραν ἐπὶ τὸ αὐτό.[2] It is not grammatically easy to make sense of this passage as it stands. The phrase ἐπὶ τὸ αὐτό literally means 'together,' as, for instance, in Acts 1. 15, 'The number of names together (ἐπὶ τὸ αὐτό) was about a hundred and twenty.' This passage literally means, 'The Lord added together daily those who are being saved.' The sense clearly demands the addition of 'to the Church' or some such phrase. And this we find in the Western text. In any case, the conception of the *koinonia* of the Spirit clearly underlies the passage, by whatever name it may be called. It is clear that the effect of the descent of the Spirit is to create that corporate society, which very soon came to be known universally as the Church.

THE DESCENT OF THE SPIRIT BROUGHT POWER AND ILLUMINATION

The fourth and last main point which is clear from the story of Pentecost is that the descent of the Spirit brought not only power (δύναμις) but also illumination. In what did the power consist? As everybody knows, it was first dramatically presented in the manifestations of the Day of Pentecost, and in the utterances of Christian prophets. But it did not take long for the leaders of the Church to realize that the power of the Holy Spirit was pre-eminently moral power—i.e. power to reproduce the Christ-like character. Paul was soon to write: '*Agapē* never faileth: but whether there be prophecies, they shall be done away; whether there be tongues, they shall cease' (1 *Cor.* 13. 8). The provision of this moral power was the supreme miracle of

---

[1] 1 Cor. 10. 17. The theory put forward by W. D. Davies in *Paul and Rabbinical Judaism* (S.P.C.K., 1948, p. 53) that the idea of the Church as the body of Christ is derived from the rabbinical notion of the unity of mankind in Adam breaks down at the critical point because he produces no evidence to show that the rabbis ever called mankind 'the body of Adam.' Nor do the analogous phrases 'the body of Israel' and 'member of Israel' seem to occur.

[2] Acts 2. 47.

Pentecost. The cynical Bernard Shaw may have said, 'The trouble with Jesus Christ was that He had disciples,' but the fact is that the true disciples of Christ have been His glory. He alone, among all the great ones of the earth, has possessed the power to reproduce His likeness in His followers. This has come to pass, and continually comes to pass, through the agency of the Holy Spirit. There is a striking family likeness among all true disciples of Christ.

It is not surprising that in the very early days of the Church there should have been some who were more attracted by the more 'showy' manifestations of the Spirit's indwelling—what came to be called τὰ πνευματικά, 'spiritual gifts.' A glaring instance of this is provided by Simon Magus. The effect of the coming of the Spirit seems to have been a heightening of the natural gifts possessed by a person; and, of course, there was the strange 'gift of tongues' which we shall have to consider shortly. But as time went on, it became abundantly clear that the essential δύναμις, or power, imparted by the Holy Spirit was the power to live the Christlike life.

THE ILLUMINATION OF THE PARACLETE

Closely connected with the moral power of the Holy Spirit was the illumination of mind which the Spirit brought. Apart from this the moral power would have been blind. Indeed, the two qualities of power and illumination are strictly inseparable. Our Lord had promised this illumination in what He had said about the coming Paraclete; and it seems probable that S. Luke in the account which he gives of the illumination brought to the disciples by the Holy Spirit is thinking specifically of Him as the Paraclete. This comes out, as we shall see, in the way in which he uses the word *paraklesis* and its cognates.

It is important to realize that the infant Church was faced by certain practical questions which demanded for their solution not only freedom from prejudice but also sound judgement. The first and foremost of these was whether or not Gentiles were to be admitted to the Church, and, if so, on what terms. During His earthly ministry our Lord had confined His mission to Jews, the reason for this apparently being that, in fulfilling the role of the Suffering Servant of 2 Isaiah, it was by His death that the Gentiles were to be gathered in.[1] He had, indeed, by His teaching prepared the way for this step, but at the same time He had not Himself proclaimed the Gospel to the Gentiles. Thus, for example, His abolition of the distinction between clean and unclean foods by implication meant the abolition of the distinction between the circumcised and the uncircumcised. This teaching had been given plainly to the disciples, but it was so unpalatable that it had not been assimilated. In modern psychological terminology, it had been suppressed. This is quite clear from the dream which S. Peter is recorded in the tenth chapter of Acts to have had—a dream in which he saw a great sheet let down from heaven containing all manner of 'unclean' animals, and he himself was bidden by a voice to 'kill and eat.' Our Lord's teaching had plainly been working below the surface of his mind. It would seem probable that the coming of the Holy Spirit had freshly stimulated him to face this teaching; for the fact that it was the subject of this dream makes it probable that it was a problem which had been consciously troubling him and on which he had been brooding. Indeed, in the account of the incident which he gave subsequently to the Church in Jerusalem he stated explicitly that, as soon as he had received the messengers from the Gentile Cornelius, the Spirit bade him go with them, 'making no distinction' (*Acts* 11. 12). It is quite true that, as a result of human weakness, S. Peter subsequently went back on this guidance. Nevertheless, we see clearly here the illuminating power of the Holy Spirit.

The problem, however, had not been solved yet. The terms of admission of the Gentiles had still to be settled. And here we see, once more, the clear shining of the light of the Holy Spirit in the famous Apostolic Decree of Acts 15, which went forth explicitly on the authority of the Holy Spirit: 'It seemed good to the Holy Spirit and to us' (*Acts* 15. 28). This is not the place to discuss the question as to whether this is a fourfold decree, forbidding idolatry, murder, fornication, and eating the flesh with the blood, or whether we should follow the Western text and omit 'things strangled.' In the latter case, the decree forbids the three major sins of idolatry, murder, and fornication; and there

[1] Isa. 53. 10, 11.

is some evidence to show that this is the pattern of a good deal of New Testament ethical teaching.[1] In the former case, the decree amounts to saying that it is sufficient if Gentile believers adhere to the standard of the primitive Noachian code, which, the Rabbis taught, antedated the covenant with Abraham.[2] From our present point of view, the difference between the two interpretations of the decree is unimportant. The point is that the Apostles and elders, by the aid of the light of the Holy Spirit, unanimously pronounce that Christianity is to be a Catholic or Universal religion, free from the restrictions of Judaism. It is significant that we are told that when the Gentiles were informed of the decision, 'they rejoiced for the consolation,' ἐχάρησαν ἐπὶ τῇ παρακλήσει (Acts 15. 31). Moreover, we go on to read that 'Judas and Silas, being themselves also prophets, exhorted (παρεκάλεσαν) the brethren with many words and confirmed them.' When it is remembered that on several occasions S. Luke uses the word paraklesis and the cognate verb parakaleo in connection with the work of the Holy Spirit, one is perhaps justified in seeing here an allusion to the teaching about the Paraclete.[3] The renderings 'comfort' and 'exhortation' are apt to be rather misleading and to obscure the allusion, but it is not easy to find a suitable alternative: 'comforted' is certainly more accurate than 'exhorted.'

If the suggestion that S. Luke is here alluding to our Lord's teaching about the Paraclete is true, this will help to show the falsity of the claim which is sometimes made that the Lucan conception of the Holy Spirit is sub-personal. Thus Professor Lampe refers to 'Luke's rather undeveloped *ruach* conception of the Spirit' in which, he says later, 'there is little appreciation of the Spirit as personal.'[4] It is, of course, true that in the Acts there is no developed theology of the Spirit; but if it is a trustworthy historical document at all we should not expect to find anything of the kind. On the other hand, it is difficult to believe that S. Luke had the slightest doubt as to the fully personal nature of the Spirit. Apart from these possible allusions to the Paraclete,

---

[1] E. G. Selwyn: *I Peter*, pp. 369 ff.
[2] See Strack-Billerbeck on Rom. 2. 14.
[3] The passages are: Acts 9. 31 and 15. 31 (*paraklesis*), cf. S. Luke 2. 25; Acts 11. 23, 24; 15. 32 (*parakaleo*).
[4] Lampe: *The Seal of the Spirit*, pp. 50 and 53.

we are told that the Spirit gave clear personal guidance to the leaders of the infant Church again and again. 'Separate Me Barnabas and Saul,'[1] He is reported to have said. Again, we are told that Paul and Silas were 'forbidden of the Holy Spirit to speak the word in Asia';[2] and that, when they assayed to go into Bithynia 'the Spirit of Jesus suffered them not.'[3] There is nothing sub-personal in such language as this.

It should be carefully noted that in all this there is no suggestion of the modern belief that the mind of the Spirit is likely to be found in the vote of the majority. According to the New Testament it is expressed in something which is quite different, viz. unanimity (*Acts* 15. 25; cf. 4. 32). The assumption—derived from our modern democratic environment—that a majority is more likely to be right than a minority finds no support in Holy Scripture. On the contrary, when unanimity is not found, the Scripture suggests that the mind of the Spirit is more likely to be found in a minority. After all, the Faith began with a single individual, 'faithful Abraham,' and was preserved through the history of Israel by a minority, the remnant, until the crucial moment in history—crucial in every sense of the word—when again it was preserved by a single Individual in the Garden of Gethsemane. And a similar story has been told many times over since then. Unanimity, whether vocal or a silent *consensus fidelium*, is one thing; a majority vote, even an overwhelming majority, is something entirely different. We must not claim the authority of the Holy Spirit for this, even when the majority is the majority vote of bishops.

THE TEACHING OF ACTS CONCERNING THE HOLY SPIRIT IN BAPTISM AND CONFIRMATION

This is, perhaps, the most convenient point at which to examine the evidence of the Acts concerning the connection between the Holy Spirit and the ceremonies of water-baptism and the laying on of hands, or confirmation, because those who seek to maintain that S. Luke's conception of the Holy Spirit is different from that of other New Testament writers, and especially of S. Paul, have used this supposed difference to 'denigrate' con-

---

[1] Acts 13. 2.   [2] Acts 16. 6.   [3] Acts 16. 7.

firmation. It is argued that the commonly accepted understanding of the incidents of the conferring of the Holy Spirit by
the laying on of hands, following water-baptism, by S. Peter
and S. John in the case of the Samaritans (*Acts* 8) and by S. Paul
(*Acts* 19) in the case of the Ephesians, have no reference to what
we understand by Confirmation. They are (it is argued) rather
to be explained as entirely exceptional instances whereby S. Luke
represents the Spirit being given for purposes of evangelization
at certain decisive stages of the spread of the Gospel. First,
Jerusalem, on the Day of Pentecost; then Samaria (*Acts* 8. 12 ff.);
then Ephesus, representing 'the uttermost parts of the earth'
(*Acts* 19. 14). That S. Luke probably had this threefold scheme in
mind is not to be denied, but unfortunately for this particular
interpretation of the evidence, the conferring of the Spirit at
Pentecost is not associated by him with the laying on of hands.
It is, therefore, difficult to see why the latter should have been
introduced in the other two instances regarded as typical by S.
Luke, if that was how he understood the rite.

The position which we are examining is supported by the
alleged inconsistency of the evidence of the Acts with itself. It
is argued that, apart from the two cases mentioned in Acts 8
and 19, the evidence of the book suggests that the Holy Spirit is
conferred by water-baptism. Consequently (it is claimed), it is
impossible to acquit S. Luke of inconsistency, if he teaches that
He is given by what we should call Confirmation. But a careful
examination of the relevant evidence does not point to any such
inconsistency. Nowhere does S. Luke explicitly state that the
Holy Spirit is given by water-baptism. The position is merely
that in certain passages he mentions water-baptism without any
reference to its being followed by the laying on of hands. There
is no single passage in which he *unequivocally* asserts that water-
baptism alone confers 'the gift of the Spirit.' We must briefly
consider the evidence, which is as follows:

1. We must consider Acts 2. 38 which reads: 'Repent ye, and
be baptized every one of you in the name of Jesus Christ unto the
remission of your sins; and ye shall receive the gift of the Holy
Ghost.' This passage is the foundation on which those who
advocate the theory that water-baptism conveys the gift of the
indwelling Spirit build their argument. We must, therefore,

examine it carefully, and we begin by asking what it *necessarily* implies. The answer seems to be that it necessarily implies only that water-baptism conveys the remission of sins, but it *might* imply that the reception of the gift of the Holy Ghost synchronizes with this. The point which has to be settled is whether or not this is, in fact, the meaning of the passage. It cannot be taken for granted, as is too often the case.

The obvious way of discovering what is meant is to inquire what the word 'gift' as applied to the Holy Spirit means elsewhere in the Acts. There are, in fact, three passages in which it is so used, but none of them refers to water-baptism. They are: Acts 8. 20, 10. 44–48, 11. 15–17. The first of these reads: 'But Peter said unto him [Simon Magus], Thy silver perish with thee, because thou hast thought to obtain the gift of God with money.' Here the reference is unequivocally to the power to confer the gift of the Spirit through the laying on of hands (verse 17). The second and third passages both refer to the illapse of the Spirit on the Gentiles *apart from water-baptism*. The former passage is as follows: 'While Peter yet spake these words, the Holy Spirit fell on all them which heard the word. And they of the circumcision which believed were amazed, as many as came with Peter, because that on the Gentiles also was poured out the gift of the Holy Ghost. For they heard them speak with tongues, and magnify God. Then answered Peter, Can any man forbid the water, that these should not be baptized, which have received the Holy Ghost as well as we?' In this passage the two phrases 'was poured out the gift of the Holy Ghost' and 'have received the Holy Ghost' clearly bear the same meaning. Elsewhere in the Acts 'to receive the Holy Ghost' is the phrase used in 8. 15, 17 and 19. 2 for what we should call Confirmation. S. Luke, therefore, appears to think of this illapse on the Gentiles as a 'confirmation' which precedes water-baptism instead of following it. Hence the force of S. Peter's remark suggesting water-baptism as the next step. The two parts of the rite are not to be disjoined.

The third passage (*Acts* 11. 15–17) is S. Peter's later account of the event which has just been described. It is as follows: 'And as I began to speak, the Holy Ghost fell on them, even as on us at the beginning. And I remembered the word of the Lord, how that He said, John indeed baptized with water; but ye shall be baptized with the Holy Ghost. If then God gave unto them the like gift as He did also unto us, when we believed on the Lord Jesus Christ, who was I, that I could withstand God?'

The interesting point about this passage is that S. Peter thinks of the illapse of the Spirit as a 'baptism.' If this account stood by itself, we should have supposed that he thought water-baptism to be unnecessary in the circumstances; but the original account makes it clear that he did not think this. What this passage seems to show, therefore, is the close connection which existed in the minds of the Apostles between water-baptism and the gift of the Spirit either through a supernatural illapse of the Spirit or through the laying on of the Apostles' hands. But what neither this passage, nor either of the other two which we have just considered, demonstrates, or even suggests, is that water-baptism *per se* was believed to bestow the gift of the Spirit. It is, therefore, to say the least, precarious to interpret Acts 2. 38 as if it must mean this. That is to beg the question at issue.

2. We have the evidence of Acts 8. 12 ff. when we are told that the Samaritans, baptized by Philip the Evangelist, received the Holy Spirit through the laying on of the Apostle's hands.

3. There is the incident of Cornelius and his friends in Acts 10. 44 ff. Here the Holy Spirit descends upon S. Peter's Gentile hearers as he is speaking to them. Whereupon they at once receive water-baptism. The occasion is plainly unique—a Gentile Pentecost. But it must be pointed out, again, that as far as it goes, the evidence does not suggest that water-baptism confers the gift of the Spirit; and it is clearly incompatible with the doctrine that the essence of water-baptism is the bestowal of that gift.

4. Next comes the incident at Ephesus, where those 'disciples' who had received only S. John's baptism received Christian baptism, followed by the laying on of hands and the gift of the Spirit. The passage is as follows: 'And it came to pass, that, while Apollos was at Corinth, Paul having passed through the upper country came to Ephesus, and found certain disciples: and he said unto them, Did ye receive the Holy Ghost when ye believed? And they said unto him, Nay, we did not so much as hear whether the Holy Ghost was given. And he said, Into

what then were ye baptized? And they said, Into John's baptism. And Paul said, John baptized with the baptism of repentance, saying unto the people, that they should believe on Him which should come after him, that is, on Jesus. And when they heard this, they were baptized into the name of the Lord Jesus. And when Paul had laid his hands upon them, the Holy Ghost came on them; and they spake with tongues, and prophesied. And they were in all about twelve men' (*Acts* 19. 1–7). S. Paul's question to these disciples is important to notice. As Bishop F. H. Chase wrote: 'There is nothing in the narrative to lead us to suppose that he followed at Ephesus a course which he did not follow elsewhere. It was natural to him to ascertain whether such converts as he found in this place or that had received the grace of Confirmation. It is equally clear from the history that it was his regular practice to confirm by the laying on of hands those who had been baptized. Further, the question reveals what was commonly but not universally the case in the Apostolic Age with those who had been baptized. It was to be hoped, but it was not assumed, that they had received the Holy Ghost. If they had not, the explanation might lie in the fact that they owed their conversion to an Evangelist who had authority to baptize but not to confirm (cp. 8. 12, 14 ff.).'[1]

5. There is the case of the baptism of the Ethiopian eunuch by Philip the Evangelist (*Acts* 8. 38). It is pointed out that there is no reference here to the 'confirmation' of the eunuch. That is true but not surprising, since the evidence of the Acts is that Philip had no authority to confirm (see *Acts* 8. 14). Nor is there any suggestion that the eunuch received the Holy Spirit when he was baptized. There is, indeed, a later text in which we read: 'Holy Spirit fell upon the eunuch, and the angel of the Lord caught away Philip' for 'the Holy Spirit caught away Philip.' But even this does not suggest that the gift of the Spirit synchronized with water-baptism, but rather the reverse.

6. There remain the accounts of the water-baptism of Lydia and her household (*Acts* 16. 15); the Philippian jailer (16. 33); and the Corinthians (*Acts* 18. 8). In none of them is there any mention at all of the Holy Spirit, whether given by water-baptism

---

[1] F. H. Chase: *Confirmation in the Apostolic Age*, p. 32. See the whole passage dealing with the evidence of the Acts, *op. cit.*, pp. 22–34.

or by the laying on of hands. It is clearly impossible to assume from them, therefore, that S. Luke held that the Holy Spirit is given through water-baptism. And to argue that the laying on of hands was never received by these converts is a most insecure argument from silence. These passages prove nothing either way.

There is one further point of some importance. It is generally agreed that the practice of Christian baptism has been influenced by what took place at our Lord's baptism. S. Luke's account of the latter states explicitly that the Holy Spirit came upon Him *after* He had been baptized (*S. Luke* 3. 21). S. Mark and S. Matthew indicate the same thing when they state that this happened when He 'went up,' a technical rabbinical term (in which S. Luke, as usual, was not interested or deliberately eschewed), 'out of the water' (*S. Matt.* 3. 16; *S. Mark* 1. 10). As Dr. Daube says, in drawing attention to this, the baptism and the descent of the Spirit 'are two different things however closely linked.'[1] *A priori*, therefore, we should have expected that, in the practice of Christian initiation, the gift of the Spirit would follow and not synchronize with the baptism in water. This fully explains the association of the metaphor of anointing with the gift of the Spirit (cf. *S. Luke* 4. 18; *Acts* 4. 27, 10. 38); but why it should have been associated with the laying on of hands (which plays no part in our Lord's baptism or in the Jewish baptism of proselytes) has so far not been explained. But this does not alter the indubitable fact that it was so; and, of course, there was the precedent of Moses and Joshua (*Deut.* 34. 9).

The upshot of this discussion, therefore, is that there is no fundamental inconsistency in S. Luke's evidence about the bestowal of the Holy Spirit upon individuals. The instances of Pentecost and the Gentile Pentecost at Caesarea are plainly unique. Nothing, therefore, can safely be concluded from them as to S. Luke's attitude to Confirmation. But they certainly do not suggest, still less do they prove, that the Holy Spirit was believed to be given by water-baptism *alone*. For the rest, the argument is one from silence, and without substance. Moreover, as we shall see, there is no real ground for the contention that

---

[1] D. Daube, *op. cit.*, p. 243.

S. Paul held a different doctrine. Taken as a whole, the New Testament evidence is remarkably consistent. It is hard not to think that some who deny that there is scriptural warrant for Confirmation are influenced more by the desire for reunion with Christian bodies which reject that rite than by the New Testament evidence.[1]

THE MEANING OF THE GLOSSOLALIA

We now come to the question of the Speaking with Tongues. Three specific instances of this are recorded in the Acts. There is, first, the original speaking on the Day of Pentecost (chapter 2). Secondly, we are told that when the Holy Spirit descended upon those Gentiles to whom S. Peter was speaking at Joppa they were heard 'to speak with tongues and magnify God' (*Acts* 10. 46). Finally, we are told that after S. Paul had laid his hands upon the Ephesians who had been baptized into John's baptism 'the Holy Ghost came on them; and they spake with tongues, and prophesied' (*Acts* 19. 6). In trying to discover the essential meaning of this phenomenon, the first of these three instances is of primary importance; for it is clear that in all subsequent cases imitation (whether conscious or unconscious) of the first glossolalia is likely to have been an important factor in producing the phenomenon. We shall, therefore, concentrate our attention on the account in the second chapter of the Acts.

It is clear, if we are to trust our sources, that the disciples were 'on the tiptoe of expectation.' Our Lord had led them to expect shortly the coming of the Paraclete, and all the evidence suggests that they would experience a sudden descent of the Spirit. This being the case, plainly there would have to be some unmistakable outward sign of His coming, and the obvious outward signs would be the manifestation of the traditional symbols of the Spirit of God—wind and fire. And, however we may precisely interpret the manifestation of these symbols, such proved to be the case. S. Luke tells us that there was a sound, like a rushing

---

[1] It is perhaps necessary to emphasize that it is no part of our thesis to say that water-baptism is 'a mere preliminary' (Alan Richardson, *op. cit.*, p. 357) to the bestowal of the gift of the Spirit, but that the latter is associated with the second half of a twofold rite, consisting of water-baptism and laying on of apostolic hands, and/or anointing. To speak of anointing with water is surely an impossible usage.

wind, and that there was a vision (ὤφθησαν αὐτοῖς) of tongues as of fire sitting upon each of them. And then it was that they began to speak with other tongues (ἑτέραις γλώσσαις) as the Spirit gave them utterance. This presumably means that some of them gave expression to these 'tongues,' whatever they were, and some did not. It is possible that only the Apostles did so, for otherwise how should the remark have been made, 'Are not all these which speak Galilaeans?' This could hardly have been said if there had been a glossolaly from the disciples indiscriminately, since they were presumably *not* all Galilaeans. Furthermore, we are told that when S. Peter made his defence, he stood up 'with the eleven' (verse 14).

It is now generally agreed by scholars that we have to interpret this incident in the light of what S. Paul says about speaking with tongues in 1 Corinthians 14. This means that the traditional idea that the speakers were miraculously inspired to proclaim the Gospel in foreign languages, with which they were apparently previously unacquainted, must be abandoned.[1] What, then, was the glossolaly? One thing is reasonably clear. These utterances were the result of the breaking forth of pent-up emotion, a phenomenon with which all students of the psychology of religion are quite familiar. But we must beware of reducing this momentous event to the level of modern revivalism. That the experience was a strongly emotional one need not be doubted; but it must be remembered that emotion is wont to break forth in this way only when some barrier or inhibition is removed. In a modern revival, it is the breaking down of the barrier of sin and the newly-found sense of forgiveness which leads to the sense of emotional release. There is, however, no evidence that this was the case at Pentecost. Is it possible to discover what was the barrier that was broken down on this occasion? I suggest that it was the scandal of our Lord's Crucifixion. For almost the first words which S. Peter utters are: '*Him, being delivered up by the deliberate counsel and foreknowledge of God,* ye by the hands of lawless men did crucify and slay' (*Acts* 2. 23). We have to try to put ourselves in the place of the first disciples in this matter. The Cross to a devout Jew was an insuperable stumbling-block, for every one hung upon a tree was accursed (*Gal.* 3. 12). The

---

[1] Does the narrative really imply this?

horror with which they had viewed the Crucifixion can scarcely be imagined. It is true that the Resurrection made them realize that our Lord had triumphed over death; but the scandal of the Cross had still to be removed.[1] The disciples still had to see in all these events the hand of God. The barrier of the Cross, so to say, had to be broken down. If that took place on the Day of Pentecost, we should be able to account for the phenomenon of the glossolaly. This way of looking at the matter is confirmed by what we find in the second instance of speaking with tongues recorded in the Acts. In the case of Cornelius and his friends, a barrier was broken down; and there can be no doubt at all what it was. It was what S. Paul calls 'the middle wall of partition' (*Eph.* 2. 14) dividing Jew and Gentile. We are, therefore, not surprised to read that Jewish companions 'heard them speak with tongues, and magnify God' (*Acts* 10. 46). In the case of the Ephesian disciples, baptized only with S. John's baptism of repentance, the glossolaly may have been due to the removal of the barrier of the sense of sin, which S. John's preaching doubtless erected in many minds, but was powerless to remove. If this is so, we have in this third instance of glossolaly the forerunner of many subsequent examples.

The exact content of these utterances it is impossible to determine with certainty. If we are to judge by what S. Paul tells us, they were in themselves largely unintelligible, unless an interpreter was available. Unfortunately, the Apostle does not tell us how they were interpreted, nor, unfortunately, does he give us any instances. All that we are told is that 'the interpretation of tongues' is a gift of the Holy Spirit (1 *Cor.* 12. 10). From the available psychological evidence, it is probable that the content of those tongues would be repressed material suddenly coming into consciousness. There is some evidence to show that the mind can assimilate words of an unknown language and store them in the memory; and then produce them under stress of emotion. There is, for example, the well-known case of the servant girl who worked in the house of the Hebrew professor, producing from the subconscious 'chunks' of Hebrew. Indeed, it is possible that the utterances on the Day of Pentecost may have consisted of pieces of Hebrew prophecy which had been heard in

[1] Cf. 1 Cor. 1. 23.

the synagogue but had been only imperfectly understood by the Aramaic- and Greek-speaking Jews, who must have constituted the bulk of those present at the feast.[1] If so, we can understand something of what is meant by 'the interpretation of tongues.'

THE PAULINE DOCTRINE AND THE GIFT OF THE HOLY SPIRIT

In S. Paul's Epistles we see the beginnings of the development of what we may call a theology of the Holy Spirit. We shall have to consider this development; but first of all we must notice S. Paul's attitude to the tradition which is recorded in the Acts of the Apostles. We have seen that the claim that this tradition is inconsistent with itself is without foundation, as is the assertion that the primitive doctrine of baptism was that the washing rather than the subsequent laying on of hands conveyed the gift of the Holy Spirit. We must therefore consider whether there is any solid evidence to lead us to suppose that S. Paul held that water-baptism rather than the laying on of hands conferred the gift of the Spirit, or whether, on the other hand, the Pauline teaching on this subject is in accordance with what we have found in the Acts.

The evidence concerning this question falls into three categories. First, there are the passages in which S. Paul refers to the giving of the Holy Spirit at a definite moment in the past, without specifying what that moment was—i.e. whether it was on the occasion of water-baptism, or of the laying on of hands, or at some other time. Secondly, there are the passages in which there appear to be references or allusions to water-baptism followed later by the giving of the Spirit. Thirdly, there is a single passage in 2 Timothy 1. 6, when there appears to be a definite reference to the bestowal of the Holy Spirit through the laying on of hands. Although this passage occurs in the Pastoral Epistles, which, as letters, may well be post-Pauline, it is one ot the so-called 'Pauline fragments' which may be confidently accepted as going back to the Apostle himself. It will be convenient to consider this evidence in the reverse order.

We begin, then, with the passage, 2 Timothy 1. 3–7. It is as

---

[1] For a fuller discussion of this see my article 'The Problem of Pentecost' in *Theology*, vol. ix, pp. 249 ff.

follows: 'I thank God, whom I serve from my forefathers in a pure conscience, how unceasing is my remembrance of thee in my supplications, night and day longing to see thee, remembering thy tears, that I may be filled with joy; having been reminded of the unfeigned faith that is in thee; which dwelt first in my grandmother Lois, and thy mother Eunice; and, I am persuaded, in thee also. For the which cause I put thee in remembrance that thou stir up the gift of God, which is in thee through the laying on of my hands. For God gave us not a spirit of fearfulness; but of power and love (ἀγάπη) and discipline.'

This passage is commonly interpreted as referring to Timothy's ordination, which is certainly the case with the parallel passage in 1 Timothy 4. 14: 'Neglect not the gift that is in thee, which was given thee by prophecy, with the laying on of the hands of the presbytery.' But, apart from the very different phrasing in the two passages, the contexts are entirely different, and it may well be the case that in 2 Timothy 1 S. Paul is referring, not to Timothy's ordination, but to what we should call his confirmation. This would bring it into line with Acts 19 where, as we saw, it seems to be implied that what is described there is part of S. Paul's normal procedure. If this interpretation is correct, the passage is of decisive importance, and affords convincing proof that S. Paul held the same view as S. Luke with regard to the gift of the Holy Spirit through the laying on of hands.

Let us see, then, what there is to be said for this interpretation of the passage. In the first place, it certainly suits the context better. If S. Paul is referring to Timothy's ordination, the reference to the faith of his mother and his grandmother seems hardly relevant; but if he is referring to his confirmation it is entirely appropriate. In the second place, the contrast between the spirit of timidity and the spirit of power, of agapē and of discipline, is more in place if confirmation is in question. These gifts are the normal gifts of the Spirit to every Christian and not gifts specially linked with the work of the ministry. Thirdly, the difference between the ways in which the conferring of the gift here and the conferring of the gift of ordination in 1 Timothy 4. 4 is described suggests, if it does not require, the conferring of a different gift. Confirmation, at any rate, never was 'the gift of the elders,' and it may well be that the Apostle is choosing his language deliberately. The question cannot, unfortunately, be settled and must remain open. But at least we are entitled to claim the possibility of this interpretation, as against the prevalent assumption, without argument, that this passage refers to Timothy's ordination.

We pass next to the consideration of those passages in S. Paul's Epistles in which the Apostle seems to be referring to two rites,[1] or at least a twofold rite, in which water-baptism is the first part, and the conferring of the Spirit the second. If the evidence can be legitimately interpreted in this way, we have additional evidence that S. Paul adhered to the tradition which we have found in the Acts of the Apostles.

First, we take the passage in 1 Corinthians 6. 11: 'And such were some of you: but ye were washed, but ye were sanctified, but ye were justified in the name of the Lord Jesus Christ, and in the Spirit of our God.' The threefold repetition of the word 'but' suggests three stages—being washed, being sanctified, being justified. Washing clearly refers to water-baptism, sanctification refers to the gift of the Spirit,[2] justification refers to the third and final stage which supervenes. These three stages may have followed in quick succession: they probably did, and that is perhaps the reason why the Apostle is able to add at the end the phrases 'in the name of our Lord Jesus Christ' and 'in the Spirit of our God,' although, in strictness, the first refers to the washing, and the second to the sanctification in the Holy Spirit. We cannot say, of course, that the passage *demands* this interpretation; but we can say that this is the most natural interpretation.

We pass to another passage in 1 Corinthians: 'For in one Spirit were we all baptized into one body, whether Jews or Greeks, whether bond or free; and were all made to drink of one Spirit' (1 *Cor.* 12. 13). That there is an allusion here to two experiences and not one is surely on the face of it obvious. We do not drink the waters of baptism. How, then, do we drink of the Spirit? This passage has given a good deal of trouble to commentators, and yet there is a fairly obvious interpretation. The Apostle has previously spoken of drinking of the spiritual rock which is

---

[1] Not, of course, 'independent' rites, as some wrongly assert that supporters of the view we are maintaining claim—e.g. Lampe: *The Seal of the Spirit*, pp. 57, 89, 142.
[2] 2 Thess. 2. 13; Rom. 15. 16.

Christ; and according to S. John our Lord Himself had spoken of believers coming to Him to drink, the Evangelist explaining that this was a reference forward to the gift of the Spirit. If this was the apostolic teaching, S. Paul might be expected to be acquainted with it. Interpreted thus, this passage fits in exactly with the evidence which we found in the Acts. To say the least, therefore, it is a probable interpretation to understand the 'drinking of the Spirit' to be the gift bestowed by the laying on of hands.

We now come to the well-known passage in Titus 3. 4-7: 'But when the kindness of God our Saviour, and His love toward man, appeared, not by works done in righteousness, which we did ourselves, but according to His mercy He saved us, through the washing of regeneration and renewing of the Holy Ghost, whom He poured upon us richly, through Jesus Christ our Saviour; that, being justified by His grace, we might be made heirs according to the hope of eternal life.'

We notice, first, that we have here once more a threefold sequence: washing, renewing of the Holy Ghost, justification. It is, however, impossible to say with certainty whether we should interpret the phrase 'washing of regeneration and renewing of the Holy Ghost' as referring to one event or to two. Grammatically either is possible. But surely the probability is that we should understand the passage to indicate two experiences. For as a single expression, 'washing of regeneration and renewing of the Holy Spirit' is exceedingly awkward, and, in Pauline theology, there is no Spirit to 'renew' at the time of water-baptism. We should, therefore, probably accept the marginal rendering of the Revised Version, 'through the laver of regeneration and through renewing of the Holy Spirit.' If we do this, the passage is brought into line with the other evidence for a distinct (though, let it be reiterated, not independent) action of the Holy Spirit following upon water-baptism.

We come, finally, to those passages in S. Paul's Epistles in which the Apostle speaks of the bestowal of the Spirit at a definite moment in the past, without specifying further when it was. There are ten such passages. They are as follows, the three 'sealing' passages being, for convenience, put first:

'Now He that stablisheth us with you in Christ, and anointed us, is God; who also sealed us, and gave us the earnest of the Spirit (καὶ δοὺς τὸν ἀρραβῶνα τοῦ Πνεύματος) in our hearts' (2 Cor. 1. 21, 22).

'In whom, having also believed, ye were sealed with the Holy Spirit of promise, which is an earnest (ἀρραβῶν) of our inheritance' (Eph. 1. 13, 14).

'And grieve not the Holy Spirit of God, in whom ye were sealed unto the day of redemption' (Eph. 4. 30).

'But we received, not the spirit of the world, but the spirit who is of God; that we might know the things that are freely given to us by God' (1 Cor. 2. 12).

'Now He that wrought us for this very thing is God, who gave unto us the earnest (ἀρραβῶν) of the Spirit' (2 Cor. 5. 5).

'For if he that cometh preacheth another Jesus, whom we did not preach, or if ye receive a different spirit, which ye did not receive, or a different gospel, which ye did not accept, ye do well to bear with him' (2 Cor. 11. 4).

'This only would I learn from you, Received ye the Spirit by the works of the law, or by the hearing of faith?' (Gal. 3. 2).

'And because ye are sons, God sent forth the Spirit of His Son into our hearts, crying, Abba, Father' (Gal. 4. 6).

'The love of God hath been shed abroad in our hearts through the Holy Ghost who was given unto us' (Rom. 5. 5).

'For ye received not the spirit of bondage again unto fear; but ye received the spirit of adoption, whereby we cry, Abba, Father' (Rom. 8. 15).

These passages can clearly be interpreted in two different ways, according to the preconceptions of the interpreter. Those who hold that the gift of the indwelling Spirit accompanies water-baptism will naturally take all these passages as allusions to baptism. Those, on the other hand, who hold that the gift of the Spirit is bestowed subsequently will take these passages as allusions to confirmation. The passages per se prove nothing either way. The one mode of interpretation which is entirely illegitimate is to assume quietly one or other of these two presuppositions to be correct and then adduce these passages in support of it. There is certainly no direct evidence whatever that S. Paul associated the metaphor of 'sealing' with water-baptism. This is assumption, pure and simple.

The conclusion of the foregoing survey of S. Paul's teaching about the bestowal of the gift of the Holy Spirit is that there is no evidence to show that he held a different view of the subject from that which is to be found in S. Luke's writings. The burden of proof is on those who seek to drive a wedge between the two writers in this matter. So far they have not made out their case.

THE WORK OF THE HOLY SPIRIT IN MAN

We may now pass on to consider S. Paul's special contribution to the development of the doctrine of the Holy Spirit. We take first his teaching concerning the relation of the Holy Spirit to man, leaving until after that his teaching about the Holy Spirit in His own divine person.

In the Pauline doctrine of the operation of the Holy Spirit manwards we are faced by two contrasts: (a) between the 'natural' man (ψυχικὸς ἄνθρωπος) and the 'spiritual' man (ὁ πνευματικός); (b) between the 'flesh' and the Spirit. The former of these two contrasts is developed in 1 Corinthians 2, where he seems to draw a hard and fast line between the two. He tells us that the 'natural' or 'psychic' man cannot know the things of the Spirit of God (1 Cor. 2. 14). If this difference were innate, what the Apostle says would lead direct to Gnosticism; but, of course, he is not thinking of inborn differences. The Holy Spirit is offered freely to all believers, and the Corinthians were no exception. They were—to use S. Paul's famous expression—'in Christ,' even if he had to tell them that they were 'babes in Christ' (1 Cor. 3. 1). Their genus, so to speak, was pneumatikos. But they had fallen below their proper level: they were sarkikoi, or 'carnal.' S. Paul had to warn other Churches besides the Corinthians not to allow themselves to fall below their proper spiritual level. Thus he wrote to the Romans: 'Let not sin therefore reign in your mortal body, that ye should obey the lusts thereof: neither present your members unto sin as instruments of unrighteousness' (Rom. 6. 12, 13).[1] On the other hand, the psychic man is the non-Christian, i.e. the unbaptized and unconfirmed person.[2]

---

[1] Cf. Gal. 6. 1: 'Brethren, even if a man be overtaken in any trespass, ye which are spiritual, restore such a one in a spirit of meekness.'

[2] If our reading of the New Testament evidence is correct, a person who is baptized but not 'confirmed' is in an anomalous position, as is one who has received 'the gift of the Spirit' (like Cornelius) but not been baptized. As Christians, their initiation is incomplete in each case.

The other contrast—between the 'flesh' and the Spirit—is exactly parallel to this. Christians are 'in the Spirit' (ἐν πνεύματι), not in the flesh (ἐν σαρκί) (Rom. 8. 9). Therefore they must not live after the flesh (κατὰ σάρκα). Unfortunately, however, this is only too possible. And those Christians who do this are, in fact, the *pneumatikoi* who are living as *sarkikoi*. On the other hand, those who are 'in the flesh' (σαρκινοί) are identical with the *psychikoi*, or psychic persons. It is customary to translate ψυχικός as 'natural,' and to speak of the *psychic* man as the 'natural' man. But the rendering is not satisfactory. The 'natural' man is, in fact, most unnatural; for he is man in his fallen estate. It would be far less confusing if we could speak of the ψυχικὸς ἄνθρωπος as the unregenerate man.

In all this S. Paul seems to have little conception of any working of the Holy Spirit in the *psychic*, or unregenerate, man;[1] and it is surely a defect in his theology that here he lays too little stress on this. We have already seen that our Lord has a clear grasp of this in what He says about the sin against the Holy Spirit, and, indeed, in His constant appeal to the light of man's nature, especially in His parables. But S. Paul was a 'twice-born,' and, like other great 'twice-borns' after him, he was so much oppressed by the sense of his own weakness that he minimizes the gracious operations of the Holy Spirit in the 'natural' man. Yet, in fact, the 'twice-born' theology really demands this; for otherwise there is no solid ground of appeal for the supernatural solicitations of the Holy Spirit. Supernature requires the ground of nature on which to stand. Although it is true that S. Paul never in so many words states that human nature *per se* is utterly corrupt, as Calvin thought, yet at times he comes perilously near it (cf. Rom. 7. 18; 8. 3). If it is really true that the psychic man cannot receive the supernatural revelation of the Spirit, how is he ever to be enlightened? If he is *completely* blind *spiritually*, how can he ever be made to see? Surely the truth is rather that the power of spiritual vision is never totally destroyed in any human being, and that it is the supernatural work of the Spirit to unfilm the

---

[1] The Apostle may have been influenced—perhaps unconsciously—in this matter by Gnostic ideas which were prevalent, as Bultmann suggests. See R. Bultmann: *Theology of the New Testament* (E.T.), Vol. I, p. 174.

eye of the soul. 'The light that lighteneth every man' is an ever present reality even in the psychic man, in the *sarkinos*.[1]

This same failure to distinguish between the natural and the supernatural operations of the Holy Spirit is reflected in what S. Paul has to say about the 'gifts' (χαρίσματα) of the Spirit. In the list of these in 1 Corinthians 12 we find side by side natural 'gifts' which are inborn, and supernatural gifts which are available to all Christians. In the former category, obviously, we must place 'gifts of healings' and probably 'discerning of spirits' and perhaps 'working of miracles.' Thus, the 'gift of healing,' as we call it, is peculiar to certain persons and is a natural endowment, as, for example, the gift of bone-setting in the osteopath. It may be found in persons of any or no religion. Like other natural gifts—e.g. of music or painting—when they are consecrated they are greatly enriched; but *per se* they are not distinctively Christian. They are the manifestations of the Holy Spirit in the *psychic* man. On the other hand, other 'gifts' which S. Paul mentions are clearly supernatural gifts available to all Christian believers and in no way are they dependent upon natural talents. Such are the gifts of wisdom, spiritual knowledge, and faith which he mentions.

We are forced to conclude, therefore, that the Pauline doctrine of the Holy Spirit in His manward operations is here defective, and falls short of the teaching of his Master by failing to give due recognition to the work of the Holy Spirit in the unregenerate man. But in his account of the operations of the Spirit in redeemed mankind the Apostle reaches great heights. We must now examine further what he has to say about this.

The classical exposition here is the eighth chapter of the Epistle to the Romans. In this passage the Apostle uses a remarkable expression which has no parallel elsewhere in his writings. He speaks of 'the law of the Spirit of life in Christ Jesus,' and contrasts it with 'the law of sin and of death.' It is clear that the word 'law' here must be understood as meaning 'principle,' a usage which we find in the previous chapter where the Apostle speaks of 'the law of sin' (7. 23, 25). But what does he mean by 'the Spirit of life in Christ Jesus'? Grammatically, 'Spirit of life'

---

[1] S. Paul does clearly recognize, however, in Romans 1. 18 and 19, and 2. 14 and 15, that the light of the Holy Spirit shines in the mind of the unregenerate.

could be either a subjective or an objective genitive. In the former case, we should have the regular Hebrew idiom, and 'Spirit of life' would mean 'living, or life-giving Spirit.' But perhaps we should take the genitive objectively and understand the passage to mean 'the law of the Spirit who brings life in Christ Jesus.' There is not a great deal of difference in meaning between the two interpretations; but if the second is the right one we have an explicit statement which enables us to relate two phrases which frequently occur in the Pauline Epistles but which are elsewhere never brought into relation with one another, viz. the phrases ἐν Πνεύματι and ἐν Χριστῷ. The passage which we are considering will, therefore, make it clear that it is through the Spirit that we are regenerated and thus brought to the status of being 'in Christ,' and not that we are 'in the Spirit' because we are 'in Christ.'[1] The gift of the indwelling Spirit[2] brings to completion that state of vital union with our Lord, which is described by the significant phrase 'in Christ,' which S. Paul uses more than a hundred times to denote the supernatural life of the Christian.

To be 'in the Spirit,' then, is to be 'in Christ'; and to be 'in the Spirit' fully means to be possessed of the indwelling Spirit. S. Paul explicitly says this: 'But ye are not in the flesh, but in the Spirit, if so be that the Spirit of God dwelleth in you' (*Rom.* 8. 9; cf. 1 *Cor.* 3. 16). This new supernatural status which the Holy Spirit brings to Christians means deliverance from slavery and adoption into sonship of God. The Apostle emphatically states that only those who are directed by the Holy Spirit are entitled to be called sons of God (*Rom.* 8. 14). It is important to appreciate what this means. There is no trace in the Bible of the pagan idea that mankind are literally descended from God, and His sons in that sense. Men are, as our Lord expressed it, called to *become* the children of God (*S. John* 1. 12).[3] In the Old Testament Israel is called to be God's son—'Out of Egypt have I called my son'—but Israel was always backsliding from that call. It was the work of S. John the Baptist to arouse the conscience of the Israelites to realize this, and to remind them that this was not a physical relationship on which they could pride themselves. God

---

[1] As, for example, Lampe says, *op. cit.*, p. 92.
[2] Cf. 2 Tim. 1. 14.   [3] Cf. S. Matt. 5. 45.

could raise up children from the very stones, as he forcibly expressed it. Their only hope lay in repentance. All this was in very truth achieved by the coming of the Holy Spirit, who brought remission of sins at baptism and who indwelt the faithful, thus lifting them up to the level of sonship with God. As S. Paul says in another epistle: 'God sent forth the Spirit of His Son into our hearts, crying, Abba, Father' (*Gal.* 4. 6). That intimate, not-to-be-translated word *Abba*, so often on the lips of the Lord during His incarnate life, can also be taken upon the lips of all those whose life is 'in the Spirit.'

The most significant results of being 'in the Spirit,' however, are not prophecy, or speaking with tongues, or any such spectacular gifts: the most significant results are moral. The Apostle is very clear and firm about this. He has a special phrase to indicate the primacy of the ethical effects of the indwelling Spirit. He says it means 'walking by the Spirit' ($\sigma\tau o\iota\chi\epsilon\hat{\iota}\nu$ or $\pi\epsilon\rho\iota\pi\alpha\tau\epsilon\hat{\iota}\nu$ $\Pi\nu\epsilon\acute{\upsilon}\mu\alpha\tau\iota$). Thus he draws a distinction between living by the Spirit—all baptized and confirmed Christians do that—and walking by the Spirit, which means *behaving* as Christians should (*Gal.* 5. 25). This behaviour is compendiously described as 'walking in *agapē*' (*Eph.* 5. 2); for, as S. Paul says elsewhere, this is the most distinctive and characteristic of all the moral qualities of a Christian (1 *Cor.* 13). It may be called the hallmark of the Christian life. It is virtually a new word to denote a new quality of life. It is this virtue which stands at the head of the list of virtues which the Apostle describes as the harvest of the Spirit (*Gal.* 5. 22).

This is not the place for a detailed examination of the nature of *agapē*. It must suffice to say that it denotes the quality of life of our Lord Jesus Christ. What concerns us here is to notice the immense importance of the fact that S. Paul exerts all his great authority to teach that life in the Holy Spirit is a new life because of its *ethical* quality and not for any other reason whatsoever. This idea is, indeed, familiar enough to us who have been brought up in the age-long moral tradition of the Church; but we must never forget that it was far from obvious to the early Gentile Christians, who had not grown up in the moral tradition of the Hebrew prophets. Indeed, the New Testament abounds in evidence to show that, in fact, many of them apparently supposed that the status of a Christian was compatible with behaviour of a decidedly primitive kind. This was true even of the clergy of those early days. Whatever the failings of the modern clergy, no responsible authority to-day would think it needful to assert that a man who is given to brawling should not be admitted into holy orders (*Titus* 1. 7). It would have been easy for the early Church to have been led astray into thinking that the life of the Spirit ·was a very different kind of thing from that with which we have grown accustomed to associate it. That this was not the case was in no small measure due to the Spirit-guided influence of S. Paul. Since the ethical teaching of the great Apostle is sometimes questioned and criticized by modern writers, it is the more necessary to point this out.

In this great chapter in the Epistle to the Romans, the Apostle puts before us yet another aspect of the work of the indwelling Spirit, and it is perhaps the most profound of them all. It concerns the prayer life of the Christian. We must quote S. Paul's words in full: 'And in like manner the Spirit also helpeth our infirmity: for we know not how to pray as we ought; but the Spirit Himself maketh intercession for us with groanings which cannot be uttered; and he that searcheth the hearts knoweth what is the mind of the Spirit, because he maketh intercession for the saints according to the will of God' (*Rom.* 8. 26, 27). We notice, first, the strongly personal nature of the language used. The word 'helpeth' (συναντιλαμβάνεται, literally 'takes hold on the other side with') is the same as that used by Martha when she asks our Lord to bid her sister 'give her a hand' (*S. Luke* 10. 40). Next we observe that the Greek original, τί προσευξώμεθα, means 'what we should pray' rather than 'how we should pray.' The Apostle seems to be teaching that the Holy Spirit, indwelling the Christian, makes articulate the prayers which the latter cannot find words to express. Some scholars have seen in the phrase στεναγμοῖς ἀλαλήτοις an allusion to the speaking with tongues; but this can hardly be the case. For the word ἀλάλητος, a *hapax legomenon* in the New Testament, must mean 'which cannot be expressed,' and the 'tongues' were very much expressed. The Apostle's meaning seems to be different, as the context shows. For he goes on to say that he who searches the hearts knows what is the mind of the Spirit, the implication clearly being that the *inarticulate* longings in the mind of the believer are directed by the Holy Spirit, and understood by God. This is possible because the Holy Spirit indwells the faithful believer. There can be no question here of any blurring of the distinction between the human and the divine. The thought of the Apostle is not pantheistic in tendency, as the personal language which he employs of the Spirit clearly shows. He is, in fact, feeling his way to the doctrine of the *apex mentis*, the fine point of the soul, which is the meeting-place between man and God. Here in the hidden depths of his being the Christian has contact with the indwelling Spirit, who directs and controls and gives form to his prayer. We shall have to return to a further consideration of this doctrine at a later stage in our inquiry. It will suffice now to point out that it is doubtless the fact of this indwelling which leads the Apostle so frequently to use language in which it is difficult to say whether the word 'Spirit' refers directly to the Holy Spirit or to the spirit of man as influenced by the Holy Spirit.[1]

THE PERSONALITY OF THE SPIRIT

We must now consider the question of S. Paul's conception of the personality of the Holy Spirit. A careful examination of his epistles can leave us in no possible doubt that he thought of Him as fully personal—a 'he' and not an 'it.' It is unfortunate that in Greek πνεῦμα (spirit) is a neuter substantive for this has led—or rather misled—the English Authorized Version translators to render the expression τὸ Πνεῦμα αὐτὸ as 'the Spirit itself' (*Rom.* 8. 16) instead of 'the Spirit Himself,' as it is correctly rendered in the Revised Version. In that eighth chapter of Romans alone there is sufficient evidence to establish beyond doubt that the Apostle thought of the Holy Spirit as fully personal. We are told that 'the Spirit helpeth our infirmity: for we know not how to pray as we ought; but the Spirit Himself maketh intercession for us with groanings which cannot be uttered' (verse 26). The word rendered 'helpeth' (συναντιλαμβάνεται), as we have already noticed, is a strongly personal word. Furthermore, there is no evidence at all that S. Paul ever thought of Him, or spoke of

[1] Cf., for example, Rom. 8. 15; 13 Cor. 4. 21; 2 Cor. 4. 1; Eph. 1. 17.

Him, in impersonal terms. When he speaks of our being given the Spirit, or receiving the first instalment (ἀρραβῶν) of the Spirit, there is no need to interpret these expressions impersonally. A gift is not necessarily impersonal. Thus at the present time we often see a birth announced in the newspaper as 'the gift of a son' or 'the gift of a daughter.'

There can be little doubt, therefore, that S. Paul always thinks of the Holy Spirit in personal terms, judging by the language which he uses. Moreover, the impression which we receive from his writings is confirmed by what we read of his missionary journeys in the Acts of the Apostles. For example, we read of Paul and Silas that 'they assayed to go into Bithynia; and the Spirit of Jesus suffered them not' (*Acts* 16. 7). This experience of personal guidance by the Holy Spirit was evidently the normal experience of Christian prophets. So we read (for example) that Agabus bound himself with Paul's girdle, saying: 'Thus saith the Holy Ghost, So shall the Jews at Jerusalem bind the man that owneth this girdle' (*Acts* 21. 11). We must never forget that S. Paul was a prophet (1 *Cor.* 14. 18).

When we have established the conclusion that S. Paul definitely thinks of the Holy Spirit as a person, however, we have not thereby proved that he regards Him as a separate person; for he sometimes speaks of Him in such a way as to suggest that he identifies Him with the Risen Christ. There is one passage, in particular, which is held by some scholars to demonstrate this. It is 2 Corinthians 3. 15-17: 'But unto this day, whensoever Moses is read, a veil lieth upon their heart. But whensoever it shall turn to the Lord, the veil is taken away. Now the Lord is the Spirit: and where the Spirit of the Lord is, there is liberty.' In interpreting this passage, we may take it as reasonably certain that in verse 15 'the Lord' means Christ: the context clearly requires this. When, therefore, S. Paul goes on to say, 'The Lord is the Spirit,' it might at first appear to be convincing proof that he is identifying the two.

This conclusion does not follow, however; for he goes on immediately to say: 'And where the Spirit of the Lord is there is liberty.' This phrase 'the Spirit of the Lord' links up this passage with that other passage in which he speaks of the Holy Spirit as 'the Spirit of Christ' (*Rom.* 8. 9). It is quite clear, however, in that passage that he does *not* identify the two; for in the very next verse he goes on to speak of 'the Spirit of Him that raised up Jesus from the dead,' i.e. the Spirit of the Father. The argument would, therefore, prove too much, and show that S. Paul also identifies the Spirit with the Father. It would, then, follow that he by implication identifies Christ and the Father, which he obviously does not.

The true interpretation of this passage, therefore, must recognize that, while there is clearly in the Apostle's mind an intimate connection between the Spirit and our Lord and the Father, the three are carefully distinguished from one another. This is clinched by three other passages in which he mentions all the three persons together. First we have 1 Corinthians 12. 4–6: 'Now there are diversities of gifts, but the same Spirit. And there are diversities of ministrations, and the same Lord. And there are diversities of workings, but the same God, who worketh all things in all.' With this agrees Ephesians 4. 4–6: 'There is one body, and one Spirit, even as also ye were called in one hope of your calling; one Lord, one faith, one baptism, one God and Father of all, who is over all, and through all, and in all.' Finally, we have the well-known passage, commonly known as 'the Grace,' in 2 Corinthians 13. 14: 'The grace of the Lord Jesus Christ, and the love of God, and the communion of the Holy Ghost, be with you all.' This last passage is not without its difficulties of interpretation; but at least it makes it quite clear that the Apostle fully recognizes the distinction between what later came to be called the three persons of the Holy Trinity.

We may, therefore, conclude with some confidence that S. Paul thought of the Holy Spirit as a person distinct both from the Father and from the Son. It is true that in the majority of his letters he opens with a greeting which includes only the Father and the Son; but it is misleading to speak of S. Paul as being 'binitarian' in his theology at this stage in his thinking. If the argument were pressed, it would follow that by the time he wrote to the Colossians he had reverted to Jewish unitarianism; for in the opening salutation he refers to the Father alone. We cannot remind ourselves too often that S. Paul's letters are in no sense theological treatises. We can only arrive at the theology of the Apostle inferentially, and by asking what is the implication of all the pastoral language to be found in the epistles. If we do this, only one answer to the question is really possible. S. Paul is fundamentally Trinitarian in all his epistles, and thinks of the Holy Spirit in fully personal terms. For him, to be 'in the Spirit' was also to be 'in Christ.' In some mysterious way the believer shares in a mystic fellowship which is the creative work of the Holy Spirit, and by sharing in this fellowship he is brought into union with the Risen Christ, and with Him who raised Him from the dead.

THE 'KOINONIA' OF THE HOLY SPIRIT

The foregoing discussion has made it clear that there was from the first in the Christian Church a clear and definite belief in the personal Holy Spirit, who descended upon the disciples of our Lord at Pentecost, and thereby fashioned a new creation—or, to speak more accurately, completely refashioned and re-created the old Israel and turned it into the Catholic Church. The earliest name by which this creation seems to have been known was the *koinonia* or fellowship of the Holy Spirit; sometimes, just 'the fellowship' (*Acts* 2. 42). In this fellowship there was an experience of 'togetherness' which was unique, by reason of its relation to the Risen Lord; and it transcended all the deepest divisions of mankind, racial, economic, and social (1 *Cor.* 12. 18; *Gal.* 2. 28). This 'togetherness' is still the most distinctively Christian 'thing' in the world. It was, and is, symbolized by the one loaf in the breaking of the bread: and it was evidently this which led to the idea of the Church as the Body of Christ.[1] We to-day are quite familiar with the usage whereby a group of persons is described as a body: but we must not forget that this manner of speaking was unknown before the coming of Christianity.

In this experience the first Christians were conscious of an unseen personal presence, who mediated to them the presence of the Risen Christ. Consequently, to be 'in the Holy Spirit' and to be 'in Christ came to mean the same thing, as we have seen. No attempt seems to have been made to think out the metaphysical implications of this belief, but as to the reality of the belief itself there cannot reasonably be two opinions. The Church

[1] See page 46.

was the Spirit-bearing Body. To be a Christian was to share an intensely corporate experience.

There has been so much thinking of an entirely different order—thinking of which Calvin is the most thoroughgoing and logical exponent—that it is necessary to emphasize that the Church is not merely *coetus fidelium*, in the sense of being no more than the voluntary association of those who have individually experienced the redemption which is in Christ. On the contrary, it is the divinely created, Spirit-filled Body—the new Israel of God (*Gal.* 6. 16).

One of the most hopeful features of modern theological thought is the rediscovery of this truth by those who by tradition are Calvinistic and Protestant. For example, we may quote the following passage from Bishop Newbigin's book, *The Household of God*: 'That our Lord spent the days of His flesh primarily in choosing, training, and sending forth a fellowship which was to represent Him in the world; that this is in accordance with the whole pattern of the biblical record whose centre is the story of a people; that this is in turn congruous with the biblical teaching that God deals with men as social wholes and not only as individuals; that this in turn rests upon the whole biblical view of the natural world and of man as a psycho-somatic unity; that the central place given in the Gospel story to the sacraments of baptism and the Lord's Supper is congruous with this teaching; that Paul's use of the phrase "the body of Christ" involves a conception of our membership in Christ which is essentially membership in our undivided visible fellowship: these things at least are clear from the New Testament.'[1]

THE BODY OF CHRIST

We must, therefore, proceed to examine further this phrase 'the Body of Christ' if we are to understand the New Testament doctrine of the Holy Spirit. We must take this expression very seriously indeed; we must beware of watering down its meaning into a mere figure of speech. The New Testament writers intend it to be literally interpreted. From the invisible Head the Church receives never-failing light, life, and strength through 'the supply

[1] *Op. cit.*, p. 72. Cf. E. Best: *One Body in Christ* (S.P.C.K. 1955).

of the Spirit of Jesus Christ' (*Phil.* 1. 19; cf. *Gal.* 3. 5). It grows, as S. Paul says, 'through the growth of God' (*Col.* 2. 19).[1] This means that the Head is perceived in an entirely new and more intimate way, which was impossible in pre-Pentecostal times. This is the case even with those who closely associated with Him in the days of His flesh. 'Even though we have known Christ after the flesh, yet now we know Him so no more' (2 *Cor.* 5. 16). It was the very intimacy of this post-Pentecostal union between the Head and the other members of the Body which tended to obscure the metaphysical distinction between the Risen Lord and the Holy Spirit. The latter reveals the former with such immediacy that they may seem for practical purposes to be one, even as the light is one with the objects which it reveals to the bodily eye. The invisible Spirit is 'the master light of all our seeing' of the Risen Lord.

Such, then, is the mystical Body of Christ in its essential being. We naturally proceed to ask: What are the functions of the Body? Do we find in the New Testament any answer to this question? The most concise answer is to be found in a fine passage in one of the later New Testament books, the Epistle of Jude: 'But ye, beloved, building up yourselves in your most holy faith, praying in the Holy Spirit, keep yourselves in the *agapē* of God, looking for the mercy of our Lord Jesus Christ unto eternal life' (verses 20, 21).

'Building up yourselves in your most holy faith': the first task of the Body of Christ, as of the physical human body, is to *be* the Body. To use the New Testament figure of speech (which we also use) it is to 'build itself up.' The classical statement of what this means is to be found in Ephesians 4. 11 ff.: 'And He gave some to be apostles; and some, prophets; and some, evangelists; and some, pastors and teachers; for the perfecting of the saints, unto the work of ministering, unto the building up of the body of Christ: till we all attain unto the unity of the faith, and of the knowledge of the Son of God, unto a fullgrown man, unto the measure of the stature of the fullness of Christ: that we may be no longer children, tossed to and fro and carried about with every wind of doctrine, by the sleight of men, in craftiness, after the

---

[1] Moule: *Colossians and Philemon* (1957), p. 107, suggests: 'grows as God intends it to grow.'

wiles of error; but speaking truth in love, may grow up in all
things into Him, which is the head, even Christ; from whom all
the body fitly framed and knit together through that which every
joint supplieth, according to the working in due measure of each
several part, maketh the increase of the body unto the building up
of itself in *agapē*.' In other words, it is by the presence of *agapē*
within the Body that it becomes strong: it is, so to say, the
life-blood of the Body. As S. Paul says shortly in 1 Corinthians
8. 1: '*Agapē* builds up.' In another place he describes it as the
'cement' of perfection (*Col.* 3. 14). It is not a man-made quality.
Only the Holy Spirit can generate it within the Body, which
thereby becomes the *koinonia* of the Holy Spirit. To maintain
this is the primary task of each individual Christian. Every sin
is a sin against the *koinonia*, and therefore against the Holy Spirit.
This is vividly revealed in the story of Ananias and Sapphira.
'Thou hast not lied unto men but unto God,' says S. Peter to the
former (*Acts* 5. 4). Later on S. Paul was to warn his hearers not
to 'quench the spirit' (1 *Thess.* 5. 20), not even 'to grieve the
Holy Spirit of God' (*Eph.* 4. 30). We must be continually on
our guard against misinterpreting this language in the light of
the modern assumption that sin is a private matter 'between the
soul and God.' When a Christian sins, he sins not only against
a transcendent God, but also against One who is the indwelling
Spirit of the Body of Christ. To put the point in another way,
sin prevents the Body from fully being the Body, because it
weakens it. This is true of every sin. How heinous, therefore,
must be the sin of schism, which openly ruptures the Body. In
New Testament times this terrible sin is already beginning to
cast its shadow over the Church among the Corinthian Christians.
'Is Christ divided?' the Apostle exclaims with horror (1 *Cor.* 1.
13). When the Church forgot that its *primary* task is to *be* the
Church and not to do anything at all, the greatest disaster which
was possible overtook Christendom. Until that truth is clearly
apprehended by Christians the reunion of Christendom will not
come about; and it is a very long way from being generally
understood and accepted at the present time. A very large number of Christians and Christian 'bodies' cherish the illusion that
the primary task of the Church is to proclaim the Gospel,
apparently forgetting that it is possible that what we *are* may

speak so loudly to the world that it cannot hear what we *say*. That is largely the case with Christendom at the present time. We shall have to return to this matter again when we have to think about the later history of the Church.

'Praying in the Holy Spirit.' Next in order to the primary task of the Body to *be* the Body comes the activity of prayer. This activity includes worship, which is, as Evelyn Underhill pointed out, narrower in its scope, being prayer in the form of adoration. In the New Testament the two terms are not yet distinguished. Christian prayer is, as S. Jude says, 'in the Holy Spirit.' In other words, the Church is *per se* a praying body. Prayer is its fundamental activity, even as breathing is the primary function of the physical body. Here the primitive association between 'breath' and 'spirit' finds its fulfilment. We have already had occasion to consider the passage in which S. Paul elaborates this teaching (*Rom.* 8. 26, 27), but it is so important that something more must be said about it. 'And in like manner the Spirit also helpeth our infirmity: for we know not how to pray as we ought; but the Spirit Himself maketh intercession for us with groanings which cannot be uttered; and he that searcheth the hearts knoweth what is the mind of the Spirit, because he maketh intercession for the saints according to the will of God.' This statement of a crucial part of Christian doctrine is tantalizing in its brevity; but we may perhaps draw out its meaning as follows. As individual Christians, we know that our prayer is weak. We are unable to concentrate as we ought: our minds wander, as the phrase is. And even when they do not we cannot find words to express ourselves. But this does not matter because we are praying not as isolated individuals but as members of the Body of Christ; and in this Body is the indwelling Spirit who takes our shapeless prayers and gives them form, though we ourselves cannot find words to express what this form is.

We may perhaps go a stage further than this. We may think of Christian prayer as being in its essence the prayer of the Holy Spirit. When we pray, it is really His prayer on behalf of us, rather than our prayer. When we pray (as we say), what we are really doing is to enter into His prayer, which never ceases. This prayer of the Holy Spirit is possible because Christian prayer is the prayer of the Body of Christ. When on earth our Lord prayed *on behalf of* His disciples (*S. John* 17. 9). Now He prays *in* them, because to be 'in Christ' and to be 'in the Holy Spirit' are one condition.

We can think of this matter in a rather different way. The individual soul, as we know, exists at different levels—conscious, subconscious, unconscious. The deeper we go the closer do we seem to get to our fellow men; and if we are Christians it is clear that we get closer to our fellow Christians. At the deepest level—the *apex mentis* of the mystics—we are one in the Holy Spirit, without in any way losing our individuality. Indeed, the latter is enhanced, not diminished, by our fellowship in the Spirit.

There is an important but paradoxical truth here. The human personality is a strange combination of individuality and separateness on the one hand, and on the other, a capacity to enter into the lives of others. 'I am I' and not another. There is in each one of us an indestructible core of self-identity without which we could not be what we are—persons. At the same time, it is precisely true that 'whosoever loseth his soul shall find it.' It is the man or woman who in self-forgetfulness loses himself in the lives of others who finds himself and realizes himself. This power of sympathetic outgoing is enhanced and brought to fulfilment in the *koinonia* of the Body of Christ, where at the deepest level all the faithful are one in Him. In other words, it is only in the power of the Holy Spirit that the individual can so lose himself that he truly finds himself.

'Keep yourselves in the *agapē* of God.' We are now, it would seem, brought to the task of the individual Christian *qua* individual; hitherto we have been considering the activities of the Body as a Body. Here again the primary task is to *be* rather than to do something. 'Keep yourselves' or perhaps we should render 'observe yourselves' in the *agapē* of God. S. Jude's point seems to be that the primary task of the individual believer is to recognize and keep before his mind continually the truth that, as a Christian, he is in the *agapē* of God. In other words, first and foremost he has to remember his true status. He is informed by the indwelling Spirit, who is *fons amoris*. By holding that fact continually before his mind, the individual member of the Body will allow the gracious influence of the Holy Spirit to dominate his life. For him, as for the Body as a whole, to *be* must precede any particular form of Christian activity. 'Keep yourselves in the *agapē* of God.' Here, in intimate connection with the life of prayer, is brought before us the sacrificial aspect, and therefore the priestly aspect, of the Body. For the essence of sacrifice is *agapē*. We must at all costs rid our minds of the all-too-common idea that, the Old Testament Jewish sacrifices being done away, the whole conception of sacrifice—other than as a metaphor pure and simple—is rendered obsolete by Christianity. This is to look at the question the wrong way round. The Jewish sacrifices were the shadow; in the sacrifice of our Lord Jesus Christ we have the substance, the reality. Here is the full and free self-oblation of a sinless human being, prefigured in the involuntary offering of non-moral animals. And it was *agapē* which led to this sacrifice: therefore *agapē* is the heart of sacrifice. Consequently, the Church can only keep itself in the *agapē* of God by a continual self-offering to God in union with the perfect sacrifice of the Head. This is the action of the Holy Eucharist. It is this which makes the Church a priestly body, and the life of the Church *per se* sacrificial. This is only another way of saying that the life of the Body is the life of the Spirit who, as the New Testament teaches, is the *fons amoris*, the source of *agapē* (Rom. 5. 5).

We must be careful, furthermore, not to dissociate this priestly life of the Body from the pastoral or missionary aspect of the life of the Body. 'The good shepherd layeth down his life for the sheep.' In other words, the pastoral aspect of the life of the Body springs directly from the sacrificial aspect. And it is this which differentiates the Christian priest from all pagan priests. These had only to fulfil a liturgical ministry and their task was done. The Christian priest (acting as the instrument or organ of the priestly Body) is necessarily also a pastor, who gives his life for the sheep. Thus, by keeping itself in the *agapē* of God, the Church is necessarily and inevitably both sacrificial and pastoral—or to use the modern word, missionary. One of the great merits of the English Ordinal is that it emphasizes this vital connection. It is true that the technical and, by tradition, priestly language associated with the Christian ministry is too much cut down. Thus there is no reference to the duty of the Christian priest to offer, on behalf of the Body, the sacrificial action of the Eucharist to God; although the Prayer Book Catechism makes it clear enough that the primary purpose of the institution of the Sacrament was 'for the continual remembrance of the Sacrifice.' But in compensation—and it is no small compensation—the pastoral aspect of the priest's work is magnificently set forth in words which continually remind us of the charge which S. Paul gave to the presbyter-bishops at Ephesus: 'Take heed unto yourselves, and to all the flock, in the which the Holy Ghost hath made you bishops, to feed the Church of God which he purchased with his own blood' (*Acts* 20. 28). Only so can the priest, as the ministerial organ of the Body, keep himself in the *agapē* of God.[1]

'Looking for the mercy of our Lord Jesus Christ unto eternal life.' Finally we have the eschatological reference, which is the permanent background to all New Testament thought. The life of the Body, i.e. life in the Spirit, is here never lived at full stretch. That can only be when the limitations of earth have been fully transcended in the heavenly places.

CONCLUSION

We may sum up the results of our investigation into the teaching of the New Testament concerning the person and work of the Holy Spirit under the following nine headings:

1. The Jewish belief that the Old Testament Scriptures are inspired by God is taken over without question.

2. The Holy Spirit is fully personal and divine, being on an equality with the Father and the Son, but not to be confused with either. He speaks through the prophets. It is especially remarkable that the Old Testament phrase, impersonal in tone, about 'pouring out the Spirit' is nowhere used, after the reference to Joel's prophecy in Acts 2. 28 and 33, with the solitary exception of Titus 3. 6.

3. The Holy Spirit is at work in the world at two levels—the natural and the supernatural. Our Lord's teaching is explicit here (though it is not clearly apprehended in all parts of the New

---

[1] See R. C. Moberly: *Ministerial Priesthood*, chap. 7.

Testament) that the latter consists supremely in bringing Him back to them invisibly as 'another Paraclete.'

4. The coming of the Holy Spirit at Pentecost led to the creation, or rather the re-creation, of the supernatural *koinonai* or fellowship, in which the functions which our Lord had foretold of the Paraclete were fulfilled. Hence the intimate connection between the phrases 'in Christ' and 'in the Spirit.'

5. The Holy Spirit will progressively lead believers into all the truth.

6. The mode of entry into the *koinonia* is by water-baptism, followed as soon as possible by the laying on of hands and/or anointing and the gift of the indwelling Spirit.

7. The *koinonia* soon came to be called the *ekklesia*, or Church, which is described as the Body of Christ. There is no thought of the Church being a collocation of Spirit-filled individuals. It is a worshipping community and its meaning can be fully apprehended only in worship.

8. The Body of Christ is a praying Body. Christian prayer, therefore, is an essentially corporate action, which takes place 'in the Holy Spirit.'

9. The Spirit-bearing Body is a sacrificial Body, because the root of sacrifice is *agapē*, which comes from the Holy Spirit alone.

PART III

THE PATRISTIC AND LATER TEACHING

THE PATRISTIC AND LATER TEACHING

1. THE APOSTOLIC FATHERS

Clement of Rome (died c. A.D. 100)

The First Epistle of Clement

IN this lengthy epistle there is a decline in inspiration and in the apprehension of the meaning of the Dispensation of the Spirit. There are few references to the Holy Spirit—only ten in all—and more than half of these are conventional references to the fact that the Scriptures—i.e. the Old Testament Scriptures—are inspired by the Holy Spirit. It is, further, remarkable that there are two passages in which the Old Testament impersonal metaphor of 'pouring' the Holy Spirit is employed. In the first of these Clement says, at the opening of the epistle, that there was 'a full outpouring of the Holy Spirit'[1] on all his hearers. In the second he asks his hearers: 'Have we not one God and one Christ and one Spirit of Grace who was poured upon us?' It seems to be legitimate to translate the passage in this way, although, since *pneuma* is neuter in Greek, the participle which I have rendered 'who was poured' is necessarily also in the neuter. Thus it is possible that Clement may in fact be thinking of the Spirit as rather less than fully personal. The Trinitarian expression which he uses, it might be argued, really excludes this: but, on the other hand, this would be adopted as part of the *Rule of Faith*, and it does not at all follow that Clement had really assimilated its meaning.

Taking this epistle as a whole, therefore, it may fairly be said that it not only does not add anything to the New Testament doctrine of the Holy Spirit, or reveal any further insight; but, on the contrary, there is a most noticeable decline in inspiration—almost a falling back to the Old Testament level, but not quite.

The Second Epistle of Clement

This primitive and anonymous homily has little to our purpose, containing, as it does, only a single passage which refers to

[1] πλήρης Πνεύματος ἁγίου ἔκχυσις (chap. 2).

the Holy Spirit. The writer is here speaking of the Church as the Body of Christ, and he goes on to say that 'the male is Christ and the female, the Church,' which, as Lightfoot points out, is probably an allusion to the passage in the canonical Epistle to the Ephesians in which the writer, after quoting the passage from Genesis where it is said that a married man shall leave his father and mother and cleave unto his wife, adds, 'This mystery is great: I speak concerning Christ and the Church' (*Eph.* 5. 32). The author of 2 *Clement* proceeds to argue for purity in the members of the Church, since their flesh is the flesh of Christ, and by maintaining purity they 'shall receive her [*sc.* the spiritual Church] back again in the Holy Spirit' (2 *Clem.* xiv. 3). He then adds that he who has abused the flesh will not partake of the Spirit, who is Christ.

The passage is, to say the least, involved, and the author appears to be beset by the mistake into which many of the early Christian writers fell, in identifying our Lord and the Holy Spirit. He certainly lacks any clear understanding of the person and work of the Holy Spirit.

Before we leave 2 *Clement* we must pause to notice three passages in which the author refers to Christian initiation, because they are adduced by Professor Lampe to show that he believed that the Holy Spirit is given in water-baptism. The passages are as follows:

'With what confidence shall we enter into the kingdom of God, unless we keep baptism (τὸ βάπτισμα) pure and undefiled?' (vi. 9).

'How do you think? He who cheats in the contest for the incorruptible prize, what shall he suffer? For of those who have not kept the seal (ἡ σφράγις) he says: "Their worm shall not die, and their fire shall not be quenched, and they shall be a spectacle to all flesh"' (vii. 5, 6).

'Keep the flesh pure and the seal spotless, that we may obtain eternal life' (viii. 6).

On the strength of these passages Lampe commits himself to the following statement: 'That the Spirit is received in Baptism is made clearer by the author of 2 *Clement*. In this homily Baptism is directly equated with the "seal."' [1] Yet the facts are:

[1] G. W. H. Lampe: *The Seal of the Spirit*, p. 103.

(*a*) nothing whatever is said about the Holy Spirit in any of these three passages or in any other part of the epistle saving the passage in chapter xiv already quoted, and (*b*) the 'seal' is *not* directly equated with baptism: the two are never mentioned together. It might be argued that the two are *indirectly* equated, because in the first of the three passages the writer speaks of 'keeping baptism pure and undefiled' and in the third of 'keeping the seal spotless': but even this is to go beyond the evidence. It *may* be that the writer identifies baptism and the seal, but even if he does there is nothing whatever to show that he thinks of the former as water-baptism in isolation from what later came to be known as confirmation. In short, 2 *Clement* gives no indication at all as to his doctrine of Christian initiation or of the part played in it by the Holy Spirit.

Ignatius, Bishop of Antioch (martyred *c.* A.D. 110)

The Epistles of Ignatius

Apart from one passage where Ignatius uses the Trinitarian formula (it is noticeable that the order is Son, Father, and Spirit),[1] there is only one passage which has any bearing on our inquiry. It is the well-known passage in his Epistle to the Philadelphians where he speaks of his prophetic utterances: 'For if some wished to deceive me after the flesh (κατὰ σάρκα), yet the Spirit is not deceived, being from God (ἀπὸ θεοῦ ὄν). For He knows whence He comes and whither He goes, and reveals secrets (τὰ κρυπτὰ ἐλέγχει).[2] I cried out while I was with you, I spoke with a great voice, the voice of God: "Give heed to the Bishop, and to the presbytery and to the deacons." But some suspected me of saying this because I had previous knowledge of the schism (τὸν μερισμόν) of certain persons: but He is my witness, in whom I am bound, that I did not learn this from any human being. But the Spirit was preaching and saying this: "Apart from the bishop do nothing, keep your flesh as God's shrine, love unity, flee from schisms, be imitators of Jesus Christ, as He also was of His Father." '[3]

[1] *Ad. Mag.* xiii. 1.
[2] Evidently an allusion to S. John 16. 8 (ἐλέγξει τὸν κόσμον) as the first part of the sentence clearly is a quotation from S. John 3. 8.
[3] *Ep. ad Philadelph.* c. 7.

In this passage we have a continuation of an authentic New Testament tradition—the tradition of the Christian prophets. We should notice here the fully personal conception of the Holy Spirit. But the chief importance of what Ignatius says is that it shows very clearly that in his mind there was no kind of opposition between the ordered hierarchy of the Church and 'the liberty of prophesying.' On the contrary, the two are inseparably joined together. And here again we have a continuation of what we find in the New Testament. We are, for example, explicitly told there that it was through prophecy (διὰ προθητείας) that the gift of ordination came to Presbyters;[1] and S. Paul reminds the elders at Ephesus that it was the Holy Spirit who had made them bishops (ἐπίσκοποι) in the flock of Christ.[2] There is no sign here of the tension which later developed between the institutional and the prophetic aspects of Christianity in the outbreak of Montanism.

The Shepherd of Hermas (c. A.D. 130?)

Hermas has a good deal to say about the Holy Spirit, but he is such a muddled thinker that it is extremely difficult at times to be sure of his meaning. In particular he is involved in two serious confusions of thought.

In the first place, he is beset by a confusion which appears in so many other writers in the second and third centuries. He fails to distinguish between the Son and the Spirit. He writes: 'The Holy Spirit who goes forth, who created all creation, did God make to dwell in the flesh which He willed. Therefore this flesh, in which the Holy Spirit dwelled, served the Spirit well, walking in holiness and purity, and did not in any way defile the Spirit. When, therefore, it had lived nobly and purely, and had laboured with the Spirit, and worked with Him in every deed, behaving with power and bravery, He chose it as companion with the Holy Spirit: for the conduct of this flesh pleased Him, because it was not defiled while it was bearing the Holy Spirit on earth. Therefore He took the Son and the glorious angels as counsellors, that this flesh also, having served the Spirit blamelessly, should have some place of sojourn, and not seem to have lost the reward

[1] 1 Tim. 1. 14.   [2] Acts 20. 28.

of its service. For all flesh in which the Holy Spirit has dwelt shall receive a reward if it be found undefiled and spotless' (*Simil.* v. 6).

This passage is not free from ambiguity. Hermas appears to be identifying the second and the third Persons of the Holy Trinity, until he comes to the remark about God taking the Son and the angels as counsellors as to what should happen to the flesh which 'served the Spirit blamelessly.' His final remark about 'all flesh in which the Holy Spirit has dwelt' adds still further confusion to his thought; for it seems to imply that the Incarnation is not a unique event. We may, however, take it that Hermas does definitely identify the Son and the Holy Spirit, for later on we are explicitly told: 'That Spirit is the Son of God' (*Simil.* ix. 1. 1). It is not relevant to our purpose to discuss the strange Christology of this passage.

In the second place, Hermas fails to distinguish clearly between the Holy Spirit and the human spirit. In *Mandate* iii. 1 and 2 he writes: 'Love truth: and let all truth proceed from your mouth, that the spirit which God has made to dwell in this flesh may be found true by all men. . . . They therefore who lie set the Lord at naught, and become defrauders of the Lord, not restoring to Him the deposit which they received. For they received from Him a spirit free from lies. If they return this as a lying spirit, they have defiled the commandment of the Lord, and have robbed Him.' In a similar strain we read at the very end of the book that the shepherd (i.e. the Angel of Repentance who is his spiritual mentor) says to him: 'Give then back to Him your spirit whole as you received it' (*Simil.* ix. 31. 2). But in *Mandate* v. 1–3 we read: 'Be, said he, long suffering and prudent and you shall have power over all evil deeds and shall do all righteousness. For if you are courageous the Holy Spirit who dwells in you will be pure, not obscured by another [*sic*] evil spirit, but will dwell at large and rejoice and be glad in great cheerfulness, having well-being in Himself. But if any ill-temper enter, at once the Holy Spirit, who is delicate, is oppressed, finding the place impure, and seeks to depart out of the place, for He is choked by the evil spirit, having no room to serve the Lord as He will, but is contaminated (μιαινόμενον) by the bitterness.' A little later he says 'the delicate spirit (τὸ τρυφερὸν οὖν πνεῦμα) who is unaccustomed to dwell with an evil spirit, or with hardness, departs from such a man' (*Mandate* v. 2. 6).

It is impossible to extract a coherent doctrine from such statements as these. If the first extract stood alone, it might be possible to interpret it as referring solely to the human spirit of man, though the expression 'the Spirit which (or whom) God has made to dwell in this flesh' is strange in this connection, and is closely parallel to the phrase previously quoted in which he is apparently referring to the Incarnation. But in the second extract the Spirit is explicitly said to be 'the Holy Spirit who dwells in you' and yet it is said that He can be contaminated or defiled.

In these passages I have translated the relative pronouns, which are necessarily neuter in Greek, as masculines: but it may well be doubted if Hermas intends this or is really thinking of the Holy Spirit in personal terms at all. This doubt is reinforced by his strange doctrine of the virgins. It will be remembered that a large part of *The Shepherd* is taken up by a description of the building of the church in the form of a tower, which is based upon a rock, which is Christ. The stones which constitute this tower are said to be the different types of Christians. They all have to be carried in through the doorway, hewn in the rock, by the twelve virgins. These virgins 'are holy spirits (ἅγια πνεύματά εἰσι). And a man cannot be found in the kingdom of God in any other way, except they clothe him with their clothing. For if you receive the name alone but do not receive the clothing from them, you will benefit nothing, for these virgins are the powers of the Son of God' (*Simil.* ix. 12. 2). Later on the names of the virgins are given; they are the following virtues: faith, temperance, power, long-suffering, simplicity, guilelessness, holiness, joyfulness, truth, understanding, concord, love (*agapē*) (*Simil.* ix. 15. 2). Elsewhere Hermas speaks of 'the power of these virgins' (*Simil.* ix. 13. 7); 'the spirits of the virgins' (*Simil.* ix. 17. 4), and, in one passage, of 'the holy spirit of these virgins' (*Simil.* ix. 24. 2). From this it would appear that Hermas does not really distinguish the Holy Spirit from the Christian virtues.

One point, however, does emerge clearly and that is that however Hermas conceives of the Holy Spirit (i.e. whether as 'He' or 'It'), he clearly distinguishes in this passage between the sealing with the name of Christ in water-baptism, and the clothing with the Spirit.[1] Speaking of the seal, he says: 'Before a man bears the name of the Son of God, he is dead. But when he receives the seal he puts away mortality and receives life. The seal, then, is the water. They go down into the water dead, and come up alive' (*Simil.* ix. 16. 3, 4). This clearly shows that the clothing with the spirit of the virgins is distinct from 'receiving the name.' Hermas presupposes that it is possible to have the latter without the former,[2] though he does not explain how.

It must be admitted that Hermas's doctrine of the Spirit, so far from indicating any development of New Testament thought, falls far below it. This is apparent even when he is trying to follow New Testament teaching, as in the passage in which he adopts the Pauline expression, to 'grieve the Holy Spirit,' and attempts to expound its meaning. He says that when grief enters into a man it grieves the Holy Spirit and wears him (or it) out (ἐκτρίβει αὐτό). He concludes: 'Put therefore away from yourself grief and do not trouble (μὴ θλίβε) the Holy Spirit who dwells in you, lest He beseech God and He depart from you. For the Spirit of God who is given to this flesh endures neither grief nor oppression' (*Mandate* x. 2. 5). He goes on to say that grief hinders the power of intercession; 'for just as vinegar mixed with wine has not the same agreeableness, so also grief mixed with the Holy Spirit (ἡ λυπὴ μεμιγμένη μετὰ τοῦ Ἁγίου Πνεύματος) has not the same power of intercession' (*Mandate* x. 3. 3). We can only conclude from all this evidence that Hermas is not a theologian, but fortunately it does not also follow that the thoughts of the average Christian in his day were equally muddled.

In the rest of the Apostolic Fathers—the *Epistle of Barnabas*, the *Martyrdom of Polycarp*, and the *Didache* there is little that is relevant to our purpose. The author of Barnabas makes about a dozen references to the Spirit, but, apart from his reference at the beginning of his Epistle[3] to 'the outpouring' of the Spirit on his hearers, they all refer to the inspiration of the Spirit which he finds in his far-fetched allegorical interpretation of the Old

---

[1] So also *Simil.* ix. 13. 7 and cf. *Simil.* ix. 17. 4.

[2] In the light of this it is indeed strange that Lampe should say (*The Seal of the Spirit*, p. 105) that Hermas thinks of the robe of the righteous as 'the seal of the Spirit.' This is a phrase which Hermas never uses, and, as we have shown, it is foreign to his thought.

[3] *Ep. Barnabas* i. 3.

Testament. We have here fallen below the higher levels of
the Old Testament doctrine of the Spirit. *The Martyrdom of
Polycarp* contains only two references to the Holy Spirit: one is
the notable phrase 'the immortality of the Holy Spirit,'[1] and the
other is the Trinitarian formula. In the remaining book, *The
Didache*, we have, as is well known, the full Trinitarian formula
enjoined for use in water-baptism,[2] and there is also an interesting treatment of prophecy, which reveals very clearly the low
level to which it had fallen. The writer does not accept the
Biblical belief in the possibility of the discerning of spirits. He
says: 'Do not test or judge any prophet, for every sin shall be
forgiven, but this sin shall not be forgiven. But not every one
who speaks in a spirit is a prophet, except he have the behaviour
(τοὺς τρόπους) of the Lord. From his behaviour, then, the false
prophet and the true prophet shall be known. And no prophet
who orders a meal in a spirit shall eat of it: otherwise he is a false
prophet. And every prophet who teaches the truth, if he do not
what he teaches, is a false prophet. And no approved true
prophet, when acting with reference to an earthly mystery of
the church, but not teaching to do whatsoever things he himself
doeth, shall be judged by you: for he is judged by God and even
so did the ancient prophets. But whosoever shall say in a spirit,
Give me money or anything else, you shall not listen to him.
But if he shall tell you to give for others who are in need, let
nobody pass judgement on him.'[3]

Whatever obscurities there may be in this passage, one thing
is plain. Prophesying had sunk to a low level and had become
the instrument of cheats and humbugs. Before listening to the
prophet, therefore, he must be judged by his life. Hermas had
said the same (*Mandate* xi. 7). There is sanctified common sense
in this injunction: but it is a sad commentary on the times. Not
only was the theology of inspiration weak in the second-century
Church, but inspiration itself was languishing.

As we survey the results of our examination of what the
Apostolic Fathers had to say about the Holy Spirit, we cannot
but feel how disappointing they are. Perhaps this is not

[1] *Martyr. Polycarp* xiv. 2: ἐν ἀφθαρσίᾳ Πνεύματος ἁγίου.
[2] *Didache* vii. 1 (ed. J. Rendel Harris).   [3] Ibid., xi. 7–12.

surprising, for not one of these writers can be said to be other than a commonplace mind. We should, therefore, hardly expect any development in the theology of the Spirit. But we might not unreasonably have hoped that the many-sided teaching of the New Testament would at least have been preserved. In fact, this is far from being the case. We may conveniently summarize the position by relating the teaching of the Apostolic Fathers to our nine-point synopsis of the New Testament doctrine of the Spirit.

1. We find the belief in the inspiration of the Hebrew Scriptures everywhere taken for granted, though not always intelligently applied.

2. The doctrine of the full deity and personality of the Holy Spirit is by no means universally grasped. We seem almost to have fallen back to the Old Testament level. So far as the personality of the Spirit is recognized, it is confused with that of the *Logos*.

3. There is no trace anywhere of the vital distinction between the natural and the supernatural operations of the Holy Spirit.

4. There is nothing said directly about the *koinonia* of the Spirit, and the phrase never appears.

5. This seems to be entirely ignored.

6. Nothing is said explicitly as to the relation of water-baptism and the gift of the Spirit. But in some passages it seems to be implied that the gift of, or clothing with, the Spirit is subsequent to water-baptism. Certainly, nowhere is it said or clearly implied that the Spirit is given in water-baptism; still less is the latter ever spoken of as 'the seal of the Spirit.'

7. The word *ecclesia* appears to be in common use for the Christian society of believers. This *ecclesia* is a divine creation and very far from being constituted by the voluntary association of believers.

8. Nothing is said about prayer 'in the Spirit' apart from the utterances of the prophets. Apart from this there is no reference to prayer.

9. *Agapē* is mentioned more than once as the fruit of the Spirit, but the sacrificial implications of this are nowhere drawn out.

2. THE POST-APOSTOLIC FATHERS

Justin Martyr (*c.* A.D. 100–165)

In Justin, as in all the early Fathers, we find a definite adherence to the Trinitarian Rule of Faith. He takes this for granted. But he has barely begun to think out its full implications. He has no doubt as to the distinct personality of the second person of the Trinity, and he holds that it was the pre-existent *Logos* who 'appeared' in the Old Testament to men, whether as fire to Moses in the burning bush or as 'the Angel of the Lord.'[1] But he has not an equally clear understanding of the personality of the Holy Spirit. In one passage he identifies the Spirit with the *Logos*. He writes: 'But when you hear the utterances of the prophets spoken as it were personally, you must not suppose that they are spoken by the inspired themselves, but by the divine Logos who moves them. For sometimes he speaks prophetically, the things which are to come; sometimes as from the person of God the Lord and Father of all; sometimes as from the person of Christ; sometimes as from the person of the people answering the Lord or His Father, just as you can see even in your own writers, one man being the writer of the whole, but introducing the persons who converse.'[2] He thinks and speaks of the Holy Spirit continually as the prophetic Spirit (τὸ Πνεῦμα τὸ προφητικόν), but as to His distinct personality Justin is not clear.

Furthermore, there is a dangerous element of subordinationism in Justin's conception of the Spirit. He says: 'Our teacher . . . is Jesus Christ, who also was born for this purpose, and was crucified under Pontius Pilate, procurator of Judaea, in the times of Tiberius Caesar; and that we reasonably worship Him, having learned that He is the Son of the true God Himself, and holding Him in the second place, and the prophetic Spirit in the third (ἐν τρίτῃ τάξει), we will prove.'[3] And in one rather obscure passage he appears to put the Holy Spirit and the angels on an equality. 'But both Him [*sc.* the Father] and the Son who came forth from Him and taught us these things, and the host of the other good angels who follow and are made like to Him, and the prophetic Spirit we worship and adore.'[4]

The most that can be said for Justin's theology of the Holy

[1] *Apol.* i. c. 63.   [2] Ibid., i. c. 36.   [3] Ibid., c. i. 13.   [4] Ibid., i. c. 6.

Spirit is that, while adhering to the Trinitarian Rule of Faith, he has little appreciation of the richness of the New Testament pneumatology. Nowhere does he so much as hint at the *koinonia* of the Spirit, which is so fundamental in the New Testament. He seems to be solely concerned with the prophetic aspect of the work of the Holy Spirit 'who spake by the prophets,' i.e. the Old Testament prophets. The *Dialogue with Trypho* may be said to be one long exposition of that single theme. But there is no mention of the New Testament prophets. Nor is there any awareness of the work of the Holy Spirit in His natural operations.

With regard to the question of the bestowal of the Holy Spirit in Christian initiation, it is sometimes argued on the evidence of the *Apology* that Justin knows nothing of the appended rite of chrismation or of the laying on of hands whereby the gift of the Holy Spirit is conferred, because he makes no mention of it in describing how Christians are initiated.[1] The argument proves too much. If pressed, Justin's account implies that he knew nothing of *any* action of the Holy Spirit in the rite of Christian initiation, not even in water-baptism, which is absurd. The truth of the matter is surely, as Dix pointed out, that in the *Apology* Justin was concerned to defend Christianity from the charge of superstitious practices; and, if he had there made any reference to the gift of the Spirit following upon water-baptism, he would have laid himself open to the charge that Christians were in league with the demons. Consequently, all reference to the gift of the Holy Spirit is omitted in the account of the rite of initiation.

But in the *Dialogue with Trypho*, where Justin was not restricted in the same way, the evidence is clear that Justin held that Christ does bestow the gift of the Spirit on believers, since he quotes in this connection Psalm 68, in the same version as S. Paul had done, 'He ascended on high, He led captivity captive, and gave gifts unto men.'[2] It is quite true that he does not state at what moment our Lord imparts this gift 'to those who believe in Him.' But the suggestion undoubtedly is that this was *after* water-baptism. For Justin goes on to describe our Lord's baptism in Jordan, and the subsequent descent of the Spirit; and he is much concerned to point out that this was not at all because our Lord was in need

---

[1] *Apol.* i. 61.   [2] *Dialogue with Trypho*, c. 87.

of this, but to indicate that at the Incarnation all spiritual gifts and powers are vested in Him. It is in this way that he interprets the application to Him of the prophecy of Isaiah xi. 2: 'The Spirit of God shall rest upon him.' Justin argues that the baptism in Jordan was just as much for our sakes as the Crucifixion. The implication would seem to be that Christians receive the Holy Spirit *after* water-baptism, even as our Lord did. The burden of proof is, therefore, clearly on those who maintain that Justin's view of the bestowal of the Spirit in Christian initiation is entirely different from that of the slightly later writer, Tertullian, who, as we shall see shortly, explicitly states that the Holy Spirit is *not* given to Christians in water-baptism. The evidence, such as it is, points the other way. To adduce as evidence to the contrary, as is sometimes done, the words: 'What need have I of that other baptism who have been baptized with the Holy Spirit?'[1] is precisely to beg the questions as to whether baptism with the Holy Spirit here includes the subsequent chrismation (or laying on of hands) or, alternatively, refers simply to regeneration in water-baptism.

Origen (A.D. 184–255)

In Origen we have the first example, after New Testament times, of a first-rate theologian getting to work on the doctrine of the Holy Spirit; but it must be confessed that his treatment of it is distinctly disappointing.

The first passage in which he deals with the question is in his *Commentary on S. John's Gospel.*[2] He is considering the words in the Prologue when, in speaking of the *Logos*, the writer says: 'All things were made by Him.' Origen inquires whether this implies that the Holy Spirit is one of them. If the Holy Spirit is admitted to be 'made' (γενητόν), he concludes that this must be the case. The alternative is to say that he is ἀγεννητόν, i.e. unbegotten: or else to deny that He has any distinct existence at all (μηδέ οὐσία τις ἰδία) apart from the Father and the Son. This third possibility Origen holds is excluded by the tradition that there are three *hypostaseis* in God, and he adopts the view that since the Father only is ingenerate (ἀγέννητός), the Holy Spirit

---

[1] *Dialogue with Trypho*, c. 29.   [2] *In Evang. Joannis*, ii. 6.

must be in the category of things made (γενητά), though He is the most honourable of them all. Origen then considers certain Scripture passages in which the Holy Spirit appears to be regarded as more honourable than the Son, notably the passage concerning the sin against the Holy Spirit; but he gets out of the difficulty by arguing that this refers only to the Son in His state of humiliation during the Incarnation.

This is a very unsatisfactory kind of argument. It is strange that Origen does not appear to see that the alternative to saying that the Holy Spirit is made (γενητόν) is not to say that He is 'unbegotten' (ἀγέννητόν) but 'unmade' (ἀγένητόν); and this is surely the inference in accordance with later Catholic tradition.

In his later, and greater, work, On First Principles, Origen deals with the doctrine of the Holy Spirit more fully, and here he holds closer to the Catholic tradition: but unfortunately the Greek original of his work has for the most part perished and we are dependent upon the Latin translations of Rufinus and Jerome, which are far from being altogether reliable. At the very beginning of the book we are presented with a significant difference between the two versions. The passage in question, which occurs in the Preface, is as follows in the version of Rufinus: 'Then they [sc. the Apostles] handed down the tradition that the Holy Spirit was associated in honour and dignity with the Father and the Son. But in His case it is not clearly understood whether He is to be held as generate or ingenerate, or as actually the Son of God or not.'[1] It is clear that Rufinus read here γεννητόν and ἀγέννητόν, but Jerome renders the words 'factus aut infectus,' from which it is clear that he read γενητόν and ἀγένητόν. At all events, in this later work Origen rejects the possibility that the Holy Spirit might be γενητόν, for he remarks shortly afterwards: 'We have been able to find no statement in Holy Scripture in which the Holy Spirit could be said to be made or a creature.'[2] And he goes on to refer to the passage in Genesis i. i which speaks of the Spirit of God brooding upon the water, and this he takes to be none other than the Holy Spirit. He is, in fact, fully

[1] Tum deinde honore et dignitate Patri ac Filio sociatum tradiderunt Spiritum sanctum. In hoc non jam manifeste discernitur, utrum natus aut innatus vel Filius etiam Dei ipsi habendus sit, necne. (De Principiis, Preface 4.)
[2] Ibid., i. 3. 3.

Trinitarian, holding to the Rule of Faith, which requires initiation into the name of the Triune God.

In discussing the operations of the persons of the Holy Trinity in man, Origen says that all things derive their existence from the Father, their rational nature from the *Logos*, and their holiness from the Holy Spirit. He thus appears to conceive of creation as three concentric circles. The largest and outermost circle is the sphere of the Father's operations, the creator and sustainer of all things. Next comes the sphere of rational beings who derive their rationality from the Son. The innermost circle represents men who are striving after holiness by the power and inspiration of the Holy Spirit. But he is concerned to point out that this must not be taken to signify any division in the Trinity. In this connection he quotes 1 Corinthians 12. 4–7: 'There are diversities of gifts but the same Spirit; there are differences of administrations but the same Lord; and there are diversities of operations, but it is the same God who worketh all in all. But the manifestation of the Spirit is given to every man to profit withal.' Origen continues: 'From which it is clearly indicated that there is no difference in the Trinity, but that which is called the gift of the Spirit is manifested through the Son and operated through God the Father. "But all these worketh that one and the self-same Spirit, dividing to every one severally as he will." '[1]

This teaching is followed up in a later chapter where Origen states that it is the same Holy Spirit who spoke in the prophets and afterwards in the Apostles, nobody ever having asserted that there are two Holy Spirits, even if they have argued for two different Gods. According to Origen, 'Every rational creature, without any distinction, receives a share of Him in the same way as of the wisdom and the word of God.'[2]

This teaching cannot be regarded as entirely satisfactory, for it does not grasp firmly the purely natural operations of the Holy Spirit in the ordinary man and woman, His influence (according to Origen) being confined to the saints. The primitive confusion between the second and the third persons of the Trinity—or rather between their spheres of operation—which we found in Justin has not yet been wholly outgrown.

So far as Christian initiation is concerned, Origen consistently

[1] *De Principiis*, i. 3. 7.   [2] Ibid. ii. 7. 2.

holds that the bestowal of the gift of the Holy Spirit *follows* water-baptism. He says: 'The grace and revelation of the Holy Spirit was bestowed by the imposition of the Apostles' hands after baptism,'[1] though, of course, he knows only one rite of initiation in two parts.[2] Consequently he can say, without any inconsistency, 'By the imposition of the Apostles' hands the Holy Spirit was given in baptism.'[3] In the *Commentary on S. John* he draws out the distinction between John's baptism and the baptism of regeneration in a passage which is clearly reminiscent of Titus 3. 5. He writes: 'It is called the washing of regeneration being accompanied by the renewal of the Spirit (μετ᾽ ἀνακαινώσεως γενόμενον Πνεύματος) who still broods over the water, since He is from God.' He then adds somewhat obscurely, 'but He does not rest on all after the water.'[4] This might be taken to mean that the Holy Spirit is given in water-baptism, though He departs from some. But in view of the context which clearly alludes to the Epistle to Titus, and in view of the categorical statement in the *De Principiis* quoted above, to the effect that the Holy Spirit is given *after* water-baptism, the reference is most probably to those who, having received the gift of the Spirit *after* water-baptism, neglect it. It is clearly impossible to undo the new birth, but it *is* possible to neglect entirely the indwelling Spirit—only too easy, indeed.[5]

Irenaeus of Lyons (*c.* A.D. 133–203)

In dealing with Irenaeus, Bishop of Lyons from *c.* 178 to an uncertain date, we are at a disadvantage in that his book *Against Heresies*,[6] apart from some fragments of the original Greek, survives completely only in a Latin translation. His only other extant writing,[7] *The Demonstration of the Apostolic Preaching*, exists only in an Armenian version. The former of these two works is the earliest attempt made by a Christian writer to put forth a systematic exposition of the Faith. Irenaeus does this after first giving an exposition of the various heretical creeds now generally grouped together under the title of Gnosticism. It is,

[1] Ibid., i. 3. 7.
[2] *Selecta in Ezek.*, xvi. 9; *Hom. in Exod.* v. 5 ('in aqua et in Spiritu sancto').
[3] *De Principiis*, i. 3. 2.   [4] *In Evang. Joannis*, vi. 17.
[5] Cf. Origen's treatment of Simon Magus, *Hom. vi in Ezek.*
[6] Eusebius, *Eccles. Hist.* iii. 23.   [7] Ibid., v. 26.

therefore, a work of the greatest interest and importance; but it must be confessed that from the point of view of the doctrine of the Holy Spirit it is rather disappointing. Only on the first two of our nine points is Irenaeus explicit and clear.

First, we notice that Irenaeus, like all the early Fathers, assumes that the Holy Spirit is the prophetic Spirit, who inspired the Old Testament Scriptures. He writes: 'The Church, dispersed throughout the whole world, even to the ends of the earth, has received from the Apostles and their disciples that faith which is in one God, the Father Almighty, maker of heaven, and earth, and the sea, and all things that are in them; and in one Christ Jesus, the Son of God, who became incarnate for our salvation: and in the Holy Spirit, who proclaimed through the prophets the dispensations of God.'[1]

Secondly, we observe that he has a firm grasp of the personality of the Spirit, who is on full equality with the Son. In order to show this, it is sufficient to notice the doctrine, which Irenaeus was the first to put forward, that the Son and the Spirit are the two hands of God the Father. Thus he writes: 'Now man is a mixed organism of soul and flesh, who was formed after the likeness of God, and moulded by His hands, that is by the Son and the Holy Spirit, to whom also He said, "Let us make man." '[2] Again, in a later passage: 'For God did not stand in need of these [sc. angels] in order to perform what He had determined with Himself beforehand should be done, as if He did not possess His own hands. For with Him are always present the Word and the Wisdom, the Son and the Spirit, through whom and in whom He made all things fully and of His own will, to whom also He speaks, saying: "Let us make man after our image and likeness." '[3] Here we have a fully Trinitarian belief, and it is clear that Irenaeus was among the first Christian theologians to have a secure hold on the doctrine of the Trinity.

When we come to the third of our nine points, however, Irenaeus is disappointing, the more so in that he has a good deal to say about the Church. It must be admitted, however, that he fails entirely to grasp the distinction between the Holy Spirit as 'the Life-giver' and the Holy Spirit as the giver of supernatural

---

[1] *Adv. Haer.* i. 2. 1 (edn. Harvey); cf. i. 15.
[2] Ibid., *Praef. ad*, iv. 3.   [3] Ibid., iv. 34. 1.

grace. Thus, for example, he says that the *Logos* 'being made man for us sent the gift of the heavenly Spirit over all the earth.'[1] This might, of course, be interpreted to refer to the spread of the Church over the whole earth and to all nations, as in the case of the speech of S. Peter on the Day of Pentecost. But what Irenaeus says elsewhere forbids this interpretation of this passage. Thus he says, 'The breath of life, which also rendered man a living being, is one thing, and the quickening Spirit who made him spiritual is another.'[2] And this same teaching accords, in fact, with his celebrated dictum: 'Ubi ecclesia ibi Spiritus Dei, et ubi Spiritus Dei ibi ecclesia et omnis gratia.'[3] By inverting the proposition 'Where the Church is there is the Spirit of God' at one stroke of the pen he wipes out the doctrine of the Holy Spirit, the Life-giver.[4] Nor can this passage be interpreted safely as a merely rhetorical statement in view of what Irenaeus says elsewhere. It is true that at the close of the same chapter Irenaeus says: 'We should know that He who made and formed and breathed in them [*sc.* the gnostics] the breath of life, and nourishes us by means of the creation, establishing all things by His Word and by His Wisdom, this is He who is the only God.' In this passage by 'Wisdom' we must understand 'the Holy Spirit.' But, taken as a whole, Irenaeus' theology has little grasp, if any, of the doctrine of the working of the Holy Spirit at two levels.

With regard to the theology of initiation Irenaeus is likewise disappointing. He speaks of water-baptism as 'the power of regeneration unto God.' And he goes on to say with reference to the prophecy of God: 'This Spirit did David ask for the human race, saying, "And stablish me with Thine all-governing Spirit," who also, as S. Luke says, descended at Pentecost upon the disciples after the Lord's Ascension, having power to admit all nations to the entrance of life, and to the opening of the new Covenant . . . wherefore also the Lord promised that He would send the Paraclete, who should join us to God. For as a single lump cannot be formed of dry wheat without fluid matter, nor can a loaf possess unity, so in like manner neither could we, being many, be made one in Christ Jesus without the water from

---

[1] *Adv. Haer.* iii. 11. 11. [2] Ibid., v. 12. 2. See the whole passage.
[3] Ibid., iii. 38. 1. [4] Unless he has been misunderstood by his Latin translator.

heaven. . . . For our bodies have received unity by means of that laver which leads to incorruption, but our souls by means of the Spirit.'[1]

This passage throws little light upon the question as to the connection between the two parts of the rite of initiation as Irenaeus understood it; and the last sentence in which he says that our bodies are united by the water and our souls by means of the Spirit can only be interpreted as a piece of rhetoric, somewhat akin to the passage in the English Prayer Book where we pray that 'our sinful bodies may be made clean by His Body and our souls washed through His most precious Blood.' Irenaeus repeatedly speaks of our 'receiving the Spirit,' and in one passage[2] he specifically refers to the passage in Acts 8. 14–17 where the gift of the Spirit is said to be bestowed by the laying on of the Apostles' hands, but in no other place does he make it clear how he understands that the Spirit is received.

S. Cyril of Jerusalem (c. A.D. 315–386)

We must now direct our attention to the teaching of Cyril, Bishop of Jerusalem from 351 until his death. He was a pastor rather than a theologian. Nevertheless, his famous 'Catechetical Lectures,' delivered to catechumens on the eve of their baptism in the basilica of the Holy Cross, erected on Calvary by Helena, contain a good deal of teaching about the Holy Spirit. They are of considerable interest as revealing the place occupied by Him in Christian thought and doctrine at that time, and are worthy of our attention.

In the first place, we find that Cyril, like all the early Fathers, takes it for granted that the Scriptures of the Old Testament and the New Testament alike are inspired by the one Holy Spirit. He attacks the teaching of Marcion. He writes: 'Let nobody therefore separate the Old from the New Testament; let nobody say that the Spirit in the former is one, and in the latter another; since thus he offends against the Holy Spirit Himself, who with the Father and the Son together is honoured, and at the time of Holy Baptism is included with them in the Holy Trinity.' He then proceeds to quote the reference in S. Matthew 28. 19.[3] But,

---

[1] *Adv. Haer.* iii. 18. 1.   [2] Ibid., iv. 63. 1.   [3] *Cat. Lect.* xvi. 4.

like that of many other early Fathers, his use of the Old Testament to support the teaching of the New is fully allegorical and often fanciful in the extreme. What is important from the present point of view, however, is that Cyril has a firm grasp of the truth that the one Holy Spirit not only inspired the New Testament writers but also the Old Testament prophets.

Furthermore, as to the full personality of the Holy Spirit, Cyril is equally definite. He points out that the word 'spirit' is one of many meanings. It is, for example, applied to angels, both good and bad; it is applied to human beings; it is applied to virtues and to moods; and it is even applied to material things, such as the wind. But this diversity of usage must not mislead us (he says) into confusing the person of the Holy Spirit with any of these, any more than the unique nature of the Lord Christ is obscured by the fact that there have been many other anointed 'christs.'[1] Cyril, as so often in these lectures, rises to real heights of eloquence as he portrays the power and influence of the Holy Spirit. He writes: 'Thou hast seen His power, which is in all the world; tarry now no longer upon earth, but ascend on high. Ascend, I say, in thought even unto the first heaven, and behold there so many countless myriads of angels. Mount up in thy thoughts, if thou canst, yet higher; consider, I pray thee, the archangels, consider also the spirits; consider the virtues, consider the principalities, consider the powers, consider the thrones, consider the dominions—of all these the Comforter is the ruler from God, and the teacher and the sanctifier. Of Him Elijah has need, and Elisha, and Isaiah among men; of Him Michael and Gabriel have need among angels. Naught of things created is equal in honour to Him; for the families of the angels, and all their hosts assembled together, do not have equality with the Holy Spirit. All these the all-good power of the Comforter overshadows. And they indeed are sent forth to minister, but He searches the deep things of God, according as the Apostle says, For the Spirit searcheth all things, yea, the deep things of God.'[2]

Turning to the third of our nine points Cyril does not clearly distinguish between the natural and the supernatural operations of the Spirit. In a well-known passage[3] he asks why the grace of the Holy Spirit is likened to water; and he replies that it is

---

[1] *Cat. Lect.* xvi. 13.   [2] Ibid., xvi. 23.   [3] Ibid., xvi. 12.

because all things depend for their subsistence upon water. One and the same rain descends everywhere on the earth and yet it produces many different-coloured flowers; the white lily, the red rose, the purple violet, and the purple hyacinth. Even so does He impart various gifts to men, and these gifts Cyril proceeds to enumerate. But he makes no attempt to distinguish between the natural and the supernatural gifts.

With regard to the *koinonia* of the Spirit Cyril has nothing to say apart from two passages, in which he refers to the imparting of the *koinonia* of the Spirit by the laying on of hands. In the former, speaking of our Lord's Ascension, he says that Christ granted to His disciples 'so great enjoyment of the grace of the Holy Ghost as not only to have Him themselves but also, by the laying on of their hands, to impart the *koinonia* of Him to those who believe.'[1] In the latter passage he is speaking of the visit of S. Peter and S. John to Samaria, described in Acts 8, and he says that they 'with prayer and the laying on of hands imparted the *koinonia* of the Spirit.'[2]

It is clear and definite in both these passages that the *koinonia* of the Spirit is given by the laying on of hands. Before we inquire what Cyril understands by the latter, let us ask what he means in these passages by the *koinonia* of the Spirit. Since it is something which is imparted, it seems that we should interpret *koinonia* subjectively rather than objectively. Cyril appears to mean 'the sharing of the Spirit': in fact, much what we mean by the phrase 'the gift of the Spirit.' He does not seem to be thinking of that objective fellowship created at Pentecost. With regard to the second question, as to what he is thinking of when he speaks of the laying on of hands, we can refer to the other passage where he speaks of this. He says: 'And Joshua, the son of Nun, was filled with a spirit of wisdom; for Moses had laid his hands upon him. Thou seest the figure everywhere the same in the Old and New Testament; under Moses, the Spirit was given by the laying on of hands; and by laying on of hands Peter also gives the Spirit. And on thee also, who art about to be baptized, shall grace come; yet in what manner I say not, for I will not anticipate the proper season.'[3]

It is tantalizing that Cyril does not develop this last remark.

[1] *Cat. Lect.* xiv. 25.   [2] Ibid.   [3] Ibid., xvi. 26.

On the face of them, all these passages would appear to indicate that Cyril was speaking of what the Western Church later came to call confirmation, i.e. the bestowal of the gift of the Spirit by the laying on of hands after water-baptism. But elsewhere Cyril makes no contemporary reference to the laying on of hands after water-baptism but always speaks of chrism. Thus, speaking of the descent of the Spirit on our Lord after His baptism, he says: 'As the Holy Ghost in substance lighted on Him, like resting upon like, so, after you had come up from the pool of the sacred waters, there was given to you an unction, the antitype of that wherewith He was anointed, and this is the Holy Spirit.'[1] Elsewhere he speaks of the consecration of the oil, likening it to the invocation of the Holy Spirit on the Eucharistic bread. The passage is as follows: 'For as the bread of the Eucharist, after the invocation of the Holy Spirit, is mere bread no longer, but the body of Christ, so also this holy ointment is no more simple ointment, nor, as it were, common after the invocation, but it is the gift of Christ and of the Holy Spirit and by the presence of his deity has become effectual.'[2] The last phrase might grammatically refer either to the Son or to the Holy Spirit, but, in either case, according to a Trinitarian interpretation, the meaning is the same.

The most natural interpretation of these passages is to say that though both chrism and the laying on of hands were employed in the rite of initiation (as we know from other evidence), it so happens that, in fact, both are never mentioned together by Cyril. In any case, it is clear that Cyril regarded the bestowal of the gift of the Spirit as following upon water-baptism and not as synchronizing with it.[3]

Summing up, we see in the teaching of Cyril a pastor who is faithful to the rule of faith, but who is chary of theological speculation. He writes: 'The Father, through the Son, with the Holy Ghost, is the giver of all grace; the gifts of the Father are none other than those of the Son, and those of the Holy Ghost; for there is one Salvation, one Power, one Faith; one God, the Father; one Lord, His only-begotten Son; one Holy Ghost, the Paraclete. It is enough for us to know these things, but do not trouble yourselves concerning His nature or His substance. Had

---

[1] *Mystag.* iii. 1.   [2] Ibid., iii. 3; cf. v. 7.   [3] Cf. also *Cat. Lect.* iii. 4, iii. 16.

it been written, we should have spoken of it. What is not written, let us not venture upon. It is sufficient for our salvation to know that there is Father, Son, and Holy Spirit.'[1]

The 'De Spiritu Sancto' of S. Basil of Caesarea (A.D. 329–378)

This is the first complete treatise on the doctrine of the Holy Spirit written by a Greek Father. It illustrates very well the restricted range of thought which marks nearly all patristic discussions of the doctrine of the Spirit. No attempt seems to have been made to follow up and develop the many-sided New Testament teaching. Attention was largely concentrated on one point and one point only, viz. whether the Holy Spirit is on a full equality with the Father and the Son.

This is the case with the present work, which is a prolonged discussion of the significance of two alternative forms of doxology. One ascribes glory to the Father *with* the Son and *with* the Holy Spirit. The other ascribes glory to the Father *through* the Son and *in* the Holy Spirit. Basil was in the habit of using both forms, and he was attacked for his inconsistency since they were alleged to be contradictory in meaning. His opponents argued that the latter form ascribes a definitely inferior status to the Holy Spirit. Basil defends both formulae with abundance of scriptural quotations, and it may be said that he succeeds in showing that only by special pleading can a difference in meaning be forced upon them. But he is so much preoccupied with the task of defending the full Trinitarian position that he has no time to attend to other aspects of the doctrine. Indeed, there is only one other of the 'nine points' in which we summarized the New Testament teaching, to which he gives attention, and that is the part played by the Holy Spirit in the rites of initiation. He is referring to the passage in 1 Corinthians 10. 2 where S. Paul says that the Israelites were baptized into Moses in the cloud and in the sea. This, Basil says, is a type of Christian initiation, and we must not argue, as his opponents do, that because Moses was only a man, the Holy Spirit is not God. He continues: 'The sea which separated the Israelites from Pharaoh typifies baptism, since this laver also separates from the tyranny of the devil. The sea slew the enemy in itself; and here our enmity towards God dies also.

[1] *Cat. Lect.* xvi. 24.

The people emerged therefrom uninjured; we, too, ascend from the water alive as it were from the dead, saved by the grace of Him who called us. And the cloud is a shadow of the gift which is of the Spirit, who cools the flame of our passions through the mortification of our members.'[1]

It is specially to be observed that, in following out this symbolism of the sea and the cloud, S. Basil reverses the order of the symbols. S. Paul had written, 'Our fathers were baptized unto Moses in the cloud and in the sea.' S. Basil in developing the typology makes the cloud symbolize the bestowal of the gift of the Holy Spirit *following* upon water-baptism, which he says was prefigured by the passage through the Red Sea. In other words, he goes out of his way to transpose the symbols. It would be hard to find more convincing evidence that he did not associate the gift of the indwelling, or overshadowing, Spirit with water-baptism but with something which happened subsequently to it.[2]

S. Gregory Nazianzen (c. A.D. 325–390)

In S. Basil we had the first writer of a theological treatise on the Holy Spirit. In S. Gregory of Nazianzus, in Cappadocia, we have the first recorded instance of a Christian orator expounding the doctrine of the Holy Spirit. His *Fifth Theological Oration*, as it is called, was delivered on the eve of the Council of Constantinople in 381, when the heresy of Macedonius, explicitly denying the deity of the Holy Spirit, was condemned. In this eloquent discourse we not only have oratory of a high order but also some clear theological thinking. Again and again he emphasizes the truth of the deity of the Holy Spirit and also His personal being. He deals forcibly with the objections that if all things were made by the Son the Spirit must be one of these; and also with the objection that if the Spirit is God there must be two 'Sons' in the Godhead. But he never forgets that he is dealing with a mystery and points out the inadequacy of the familiar threefold analogies, spring, fountain and river; sun, ray and light. He perceives clearly the fact of a gradual revelation.

'The matter stands thus,' he writes. 'The Old Testament

---

[1] *De Spir. Sancto*, xiv. 31.
[2] As to the reason why S. Paul mentions 'the cloud' before 'the sea' see Gregory Dix: *Confirmation or the Laying On of Hands* (Theology Occasional Papers), p. 9.

proclaimed the Father openly, and the Son more obscurely. The New manifested the Son and suggested the deity of the Spirit. Now the Spirit Himself dwells among us, and supplies us with a clearer proof of Himself. For it was not safe, when the Godhead of the Father was not yet acknowledged, plainly to proclaim the Son; nor when that of the Son was not yet received to burden us further (if I may use so bold an expression) with the Holy Ghost; lest perhaps people might, like men surfeited with food beyond their strength, and presenting eyes as yet too weak to bear it to the sun's light, risk the loss even of that which was within their powers; but that by gradual additions, and, as David says, "ascents" and advances and stages from glory to glory the light of the Trinity might shine upon the more illuminated. . . . Indeed, it is by little and little that He is revealed by Jesus, as you will learn for yourself if you will read more carefully.'[1]

All this is helpful teaching, but probably the most important light which Gregory shed on the theology of the Spirit is his brief reference to Christian prayer 'in the Holy Spirit.' He is dealing with those who object to the doctrine of the deity of the Holy Spirit on the ground that it is not customary to address prayer directly to the Holy Spirit. He supposes an objector saying, 'Who ever prayed to Him? Where is it written that we ought to worship Him, or to pray to Him, and whence have you derived this tenet of yours?' Gregory replies that it is the Spirit *in* whom we worship and *through* whom we pray. 'For,' he writes, 'Scripture says, "God is a Spirit and they that worship Him must worship Him in Spirit and in truth." And again, "We know not what we should pray for as we ought; but the Spirit Himself maketh intercession for us with groanings which cannot be uttered," and "I will pray with the spirit and I will pray with the understanding also," that is, in the mind and in the Spirit. Therefore to adore or to pray to the Spirit seems to me to be simply Himself offering prayer in adoration to Himself. And what godly or learned man would disapprove of this, because, in fact, the adoration of One is the adoration of the Three, because of the equality of honour and deity between the Three?'[2]

This passage is tantalizing in its brevity. Gregory here men-

---

[1] *Fifth Theological Oration*, § 26.   [2] Ibid., § 12.

tions two points of considerable importance in connection with
the doctrine of the Holy Spirit without developing either of them.
First, he states the objection to the deity of the Holy Spirit based
on the ground that it was not customary to pray directly to the
Holy Spirit. Gregory does not question this, so that we must
assume that it is a true account of current practice. Secondly, he
meets the objection by pointing out that, according to the
Scriptures, Christian prayer is 'in the Holy Spirit.' We should
have expected him to argue that, from the point of view of
Trinitarian theology, this amounts to the same thing, and that
this is a substitute for prayer to the Holy Spirit. Instead of that
he argues that this means that the Holy Spirit is addressing prayer
to Himself and that there is no objection to this, for, being one
with the Father and the Son, they also are praying with Him.
The argument appears to be circular. He assumes what has to
be proved in order to get out of the difficulty raised by the fact
of the Holy Spirit's addressing prayer to God, while Himself
being God. Yet the difficulty is one which Gregory created for
himself by interpreting 'prayer in the Holy Spirit' as meaning
that the Holy Spirit is offering adoration. Surely it need not mean
that at all, and the relevant New Testament passages do not
suggest that. Christian prayer is said to be 'in the Holy Spirit'
because, as S. Paul says, the Spirit is 'helping our infirmities.' In
other words, the Holy Spirit makes good the deficiencies of our
human prayer. When we pray as Christians, therefore, there is
a sense in which we do not need to pray to Him: for He is 'there'
before we begin to pray. In other words, Gregory has given a
forced explanation, when a simple one was ready to hand.
Nevertheless, the matter-of-fact way in which he refers to
Christian prayer as being in the Holy Spirit perhaps entitles us
to conclude that this was something which was generally recognized in his day.

    Gregory devoted another oration to the doctrine of the Holy
Spirit, viz. No. 41, on Pentecost. Although we do not find here
what we might have hoped to find, a full exposition of the meaning of the koinonia of the Spirit, we have a magnificent account
of the supernatural operations of the Holy Spirit, leading up to
the climax of Pentecost. Part of this great discourse must be
quoted: 'This Spirit shares with the Son in working both the

Creation and the Resurrection, as you may be shown by this Scripture, "By the word of the Lord were the heavens made, and all the hosts of them by the breath of his mouth," and this, "The Spirit of God that made me, and the breath of the Almighty that teacheth me," and again, "Thou shalt send forth Thy Spirit and they shall be created, and Thou shalt renew the face of the earth." And He is the author of spiritual regeneration. Here is your proof: "None can see or enter into the kingdom except he be born again of the Spirit," and be cleansed from the first birth, which is a mystery of the night, by a remoulding of the day and of the light, by which every one singly is created anew. This Spirit, for He is most wise and most loving, if He takes possession of a shepherd makes him a psalmist, subduing evil spirits by his song, and proclaims him king. If He possesses a goatherd and scraper of sycamore fruit, He makes him a prophet. Call to mind David and Amos. If He possesses a goodly youth, He makes him a judge of elders, even beyond his years, as Daniel testifies, who conquered the lions in their den. If He takes possession of fishermen, He makes them catch the whole world in the nets of Christ, taking them up in the meshes of the Word. Look at Peter and Andrew and the sons of thunder, thundering the things of the Spirit. If of publicans, He makes gain of them for discipleship, and makes them merchants of souls; witness Matthew, yesterday a publican, to-day an evangelist. If of zealous persecutors, He changes the current of their zeal and makes them Pauls instead of Sauls, and as full of piety as He had found them of wickedness.... But as the old confusion of tongues was laudable, when men who were of one language in wickedness and impiety, even as now some venture to be, were building the tower—for by the confusion of their language the unity of their intention was broken up, and their undertaking destroyed—so much more worthy of praise is the present miraculous one. For, being poured from one Spirit upon many men, it brings them again into harmony."[1]

Tertullian (c. A.D. 155–c. 225)

We turn now from the Greek to the Latin Fathers, and, in the earliest of the latter, Quintus Septimius Florens Tertullianus,

[1] *Oration on Pentecost*, §§ 14–16.

we find a good deal that is relevant to our inquiry. In later middle life Tertullian became a member of the sect called Montanists. Unfortunately, we have no first-hand evidence of their teaching and practice except from their opponents. We have, therefore, here to be cautious in our judgements. There is no doubt that Montanus, the originator of this sect, and his disciples were, or claimed to be, Christian prophets. There is nothing wrong in this. But it is clear from what Eusebius tells us[1] that these people roused the most intense antagonism in the minds of their fellow Christians, who recognized indeed their supernatural inspiration, but ascribed it to Satan. It must be confessed that the brief sayings of theirs which have survived seem sufficiently harmless in themselves: but, of course, a great deal depends upon the way in which things are said and done, and it is likely that these simple people, who were probably possessors of a real prophetic gift, were led away by their own simplicity to behave arrogantly, and to look down upon those who did not share their opinions. Tertullian's writings afford clear evidence of this. In his Montanist works he speaks most disparagingly of those whom, following Pauline terminology, he calls 'psychics.'

These are historical questions which do not really concern us now. Our immediate purpose is to discover how far this movement was instrumental in developing the doctrine of the Holy Spirit. There is a passage in the opening chapter of Tertullian's work, *On the Veiling of Virgins*, which is useful in this connection. We may remind ourselves that this was probably the first book which he wrote after espousing the Montanist cause: he writes as follows:

'This law [i.e. the Rule] of faith abiding, the other matters of discipline and conduct admit the novelty of correction, the grace of God, that is to say, operating and advancing even to the end. How should it be that while the devil is always at work and adding daily to the ingenuities of iniquity, the work of God should either cease or stand still? Whereas the Lord sent the Paraclete, in order that since human mediocrity could not take in everything at the same time, discipline might be gradually directed, and led on to perfection by that Vicar of the Lord, the

[1] *H.E.* v. 16 and 17.

Holy Spirit. He said: "I have still many things to say unto you, but ye are not yet able to bear them; but when He, the Spirit of Truth, shall have come, He will lead you into all truth and will report to you the things which are supervening." But above all He made a declaration concerning this His work. What, therefore, is the administrative work of the Paraclete but this, the direction of discipline, the revelation of the Scriptures, the reformation of the intellect, the advancement towards the better things.'[1]

It is clear from this passage that there is nothing *necessarily* heretical in this teaching. But, of course, everything depends upon a strict regard to the Rule of Faith. Otherwise we have here the seeds of Papalism, on the one side, or individualistic Protestantism and sectarianism on the other. Alas, it was a case of coming events casting their shadows before. But, at any rate, it remains true that this movement did serve a valuable purpose in preventing the early Church from losing sight of the fact that it was living in the dispensation of the Spirit. It reminded them that the Church is a living organism, the Spirit-bearing Body of Christ. It is also true that the movement helped to preserve the New Testament belief in the fully personal nature of the Holy Spirit. Unfortunately, however, from the very nature of the case, it failed to grasp and to emphasize the vital New Testament belief in the *koinonia* of the Spirit, as supremely manifested in the worship of the holy Eucharist. Tertullian, so far as I am aware, makes no reference to this point. Montanistic practice very easily led to the false supposition that the Church is an aggregation of Spirit-filled individuals.

In his late, perhaps his latest, work, directed against the Unitarian teacher, Praxeas, Tertullian has a good deal to say about the person of the Holy Spirit. We find here for the first time a fully Trinitarian theology, which he ascribes especially to those whom he calls 'followers of the Paraclete.'[2] He deals faithfully and ably with the three main 'proof-texts' of Praxeas: 'I am the Lord, there is none else; beside Me there is no God' (*Isa.* 45. 5): 'I and the Father are one' (*S. John* 10. 30): 'He that hath seen Me hath seen the Father' (*S. John* 14. 10). But, never a philosopher, Tertullian is betrayed into some crude and indefensible expressions, notably when he speaks of the Son and the Holy Spirit

---

[1] *On the Veiling of Virgins*, c. i (ed. Rigalt.).   [2] *Against Praxeas*, c. 13.

being a part (*portio*) of the Godhead.[1] But these crudities may be overlooked in one who was a pioneer in Trinitarian theology; and we owe to him the illustrations which later established themselves widely, viz. the analogies of the root, the tree, and the fruit; the fountain, the river, and the stream; the sun, the ray, and the apex of the ray.[2]

There is one other aspect of the doctrine of the Holy Spirit in which the evidence of Tertullian is important. This is what he has to say about the part played by the Holy Spirit in baptism. The relevant passage is well known, but is not always quoted in its entirety. It will be convenient for us to have it before us.

Tertullian is speaking of the angel at the pool of Bethesda, pointing to this physical healing in the waters as a figure of the healing of the soul which was to take place in Christian water-baptism. He continues: 'And so when the grace of God had further advanced among men, an increase of it was granted to the waters and to the angel. Those who were wont to remedy bodily defects now heal the spirit: those who brought about temporal health, now renew eternal health: those who used to set free once a year now save the people daily, death being destroyed by the washing away of sin. The guilt being removed, the penalty is also taken away. So man is restored to God in His likeness, who previously was in the image of God. (The image is thought to be in the likeness, the likeness in eternity.) For he receives that Spirit of God, whom he had originally received from his afflatus, but afterwards had lost through sin. Not that in the waters we receive the Holy Spirit, but cleansed in water, and under the angel, we are prepared for the Holy Spirit.'[3]

Later on he reverts to the same subject and adds: 'Then that most Holy Spirit descends being poured out by the Father upon bodies cleansed and blessed. Upon the waters of baptism He reposes, recognizing as it were His pristine seat, who fell upon the Lord in the form of a dove. . . . Just as after the waters of the flood by which the ancient sin was purged—after the baptism of

---

[1] *Against Praxeas*, c. 9 and c. 26. The passages are as follows:

'Pater enim tota substantia est, filius vero derivatio totius et portio, sicut ipse profitetur, Quia Pater major me est.' (c. 9.)

' "Deus superveniet, et Altissimus obumbravit te." Dicens autem spiritus Dei, et si Spiritus Dei Deus, tamen non directo Deum nominans, portionem totius intelligi voluit, quae cessura erat in Filii nomen.' (c. 26.)

[2] Ibid., c. 8.   [3] *On Baptism*, cc. iv and v.

the world, so to say—a dove announced to the world the appeasing of the wrath of heaven.'[1]

This passage is important for several reasons. The first is that, if we were to stop short at the end of line 13 of the quotation, we should almost be compelled to infer that Tertullian must have believed that we receive the gift of the Spirit in water-baptism. In fact, he proceeds forthwith to say explicitly that we do nothing of the kind. This goes to show how careful we must be not to assume that the gift of the indwelling Spirit is bestowed by water-baptism merely because we are told that the Holy Spirit is active in water-baptism. Moreover, this caution should be intensified when we remember that the word 'baptism' may be used by the early Fathers to denote the rite of initiation as a whole, and therefore cannot be assumed to denote water-baptism, as is the case to-day.[2]

The second reason for the importance of this passage is that we have here the first book ever written on the doctrine of Christian baptism; and in this book we have the most explicit statement possible to the effect that the gift of the Holy Spirit is bestowed in the rite following upon water-baptism and not in the water-baptism itself. The way in which Tertullian expresses himself lends some support to the supposition that he is correcting the false belief that the Holy Spirit *is* given in water-baptism; but it is impossible to be certain of this. Certainly there is no evidence from Tertullian's writings (so far as I am aware) that he himself ever held such an opinion.[3]

S. Ambrose (c. A.D. 340–397)

S. Ambrose, in response to a request from the Emperor Gratian, wrote a work, *On the Holy Spirit*, in three books. This work is entirely devoted to showing the full equality of the Holy Spirit with the Father and the Son. There is a certain amount of allegorizing, as might be expected, but on the whole this is a full and clear exposition of the scriptural evidence for holding

---

[1] *On Baptism*, c. 8.

[2] See, e.g., Ignatius, *Ep. ad Smyr.* 8: Irenaeus, *Haer.* iii. 17. 182: Origen, *De Princ.* v. 3. 2, *Comm. in Ep. ad Rom.* viii, *Comm. in Joann.* xvii: Eusebius, *H.E.* vii. 2: Tertullian, *De Bap.* 3 (*in baptismo aquae* not *aquae baptismi*), *Adv. Marc.* i. 28: Cyril Hier., *Cat.* iv. 16, xvi. 26, xviii. 21.

[3] I find no evidence at all for Lampe's statement that there is 'a real confusion in Tertullian's theology,' on this point (Lampe: *op. cit.*, p. 161). See additional note.

the full Godhead of the Holy Spirit. Here, as in so many other early writers, we see the influence of the Rule of Faith in the Baptismal formula in safeguarding Trinitarian doctrine. Ambrose in the main follows four lines of argument to defend his thesis. He says that there are four undisputed marks of Godhead, and he seeks to produce scriptural authority for ascribing all of them to the Holy Spirit. First, God is without sin. So is the Holy Spirit said by the author of Wisdom to be 'undefiled' (*Wisd.* 7. 22). Second, God has alone the right to forgive sins. But when our Lord breathed on the disciples and said 'Receive ye the Holy Spirit' He added immediately, 'Whose soever sins ye forgive they are forgiven,' thereby clearly showing that forgiveness is the work of the Holy Spirit. And Ambrose points out that sin is forgiven in baptism which is in the Spirit. Third, God is the Creator. So, according to the Psalmist (Ambrose argues), is the Holy Spirit: 'Thou sendest forth Thy Spirit, and they are created' (*Ps.* 104. 30). Finally, God does not give but receive worship. Ambrose deals with this by means of prophecy. Prophecy is acknowledged to be 'in the Spirit'; but plainly He who is in the prophets is worshipped. Therefore the Spirit is worshipped.

Since Ambrose is solely concerned to prove the deity of the Holy Spirit, not much light is shed by this book on any other of our 'nine points.' Indeed, it has little to our purpose. Ambrose does not even explicitly deal with the question of the personality of the Spirit, though indirectly again and again he makes it clear that he never thinks of the Holy Spirit save in personal terms.

In reading this book of Ambrose we are driven once more to regret the fact that the Church was so greatly preoccupied first with the establishing of the doctrine of the Incarnation, and, as soon as that was done, with the safeguarding of the deity of the Holy Spirit that the many-sided New Testament doctrine of the Spirit was to a large extent ignored and neglected.

Augustine of Hippo (A.D. 354–430)

When the powerful mind of Augustine was brought to bear on the doctrine of the Holy Spirit we find, as we should expect to find, a real advance in theological understanding. Practically every one of our 'nine points' has light shed upon it.

We may begin by considering the question as to the relation of the natural to the supernatural operations of the Spirit. This exercised the mind of Augustine at an early stage in his thought when in his *Liber de Diversis Questionibus*[1] he discusses the meaning of the passage in S. John 7. 39: 'The Spirit was not yet given, because Jesus was not yet glorified.' Augustine argues that the Holy Spirit must have been active in the world prior to the Resurrection of Christ, for only in this way can the words of the penitent thief, spoken to our Lord on the Cross, be understood. He quotes S. Paul: 'No man can say that Jesus is Lord but by the Holy Spirit.' Had Augustine known the true text of S. Luke 23. 42 where 'Jesus, remember me' is read for 'Lord, remember me,' his argument would have fallen to the ground. But this would not perhaps have mattered much, since he goes on to refer to Zacharias and Anna and Simeon, all of whom are said to have been illumined by the Holy Spirit prior to the Pentecostal gift.

What, then, according to Augustine, is the precise difference between the pre-Pentecostal and the post-Pentecostal operations of the Spirit? He replies that it is the difference between the hidden and the manifest, the secret and the open. At Pentecost there was an outward and visible bestowal of the Holy Spirit who had previously come only invisibly. Augustine argues that the same holds good of the second person of the Holy Trinity who came down from heaven in visible form on Christmas Day but who as the *Logos* had invisibly inspired prophets and wise men in Old Testament days.

It cannot be said that this attempt to deal with the problem is satisfactory. The difference between the New Testament dispensation and the Old is far more than the difference between the hidden and the manifest, and this Augustine himself sees when in his later and much more mature *Tractatus* on S. John's Gospel he reverts to the same theme. Here we have a far more profound treatment of the same subject. He realizes that the distinctive mark of the Pentecostal gift is that it is a *corporate* manifestation. After again referring to Zacharias, Simeon, and Anna, he adds: 'We therefore have many indications of the Holy Spirit before the Lord was glorified by the resurrection of His flesh; for the

---

[1] Question 62 (ed. Tertia Veneta).

prophets who foretold Christ's coming were not possessed of a different Spirit.' But he goes on to say that we never, before Pentecost, hear of a *group of persons*, having received the Holy Spirit, speaking in all languages. And this is exactly what the Church does, and every member of the Church may be said to do the same, since the Church is Christ's Body and every member of that Body may be said to participate in this speaking with many tongues, as he participates in the other activities of the Body.

'Thus it is that we may receive the Holy Spirit, if we love the Church, if we are united in love (*caritas*), if we rejoice in the Catholic name and faith. We are entitled to believe, Brethren, that in so far as anybody loves the Church of Christ he has the Holy Spirit.' He then goes on to enumerate the manifestations of the Spirit as found in 1 Corinthians 12. He continues: 'For there are many manifestations but you perhaps have none of all those which I have mentioned. If you love, you do not have none: for if you love the unity, you also have anything which anybody in it has. Take away hatred, and what I have is yours: take away hatred, and what you have is mine. Disease separates; health unites. The eye is the only member of the body which sees: but does the eye see only for its own benefit? It sees also for the hand, and for the foot, and for the other members. . . . Therefore we have the Holy Spirit, if we love the Church: and we love if we stand fast in its fellowship and charity. For the Apostle himself when he had said that different gifts were given to different individuals, just like the offices of the various members, adds, "Nevertheless I show you a more excellent way," and he proceeds to speak of love. . . . Have that and you will have everything, because without it nothing is profitable, whatsoever you have. For indeed to the Holy Spirit appertains the love of which we speak. . . . Hear the Apostle saying, "the love of God is poured into our hearts by the Holy Spirit who is given to us" [1] (*Rom.* 5. 5).

This is an elaboration of the position which Augustine had taken up in his controversy with the Donatists. Their sacraments were valid: that he admitted. But they were devoid of the power of the Holy Spirit and therefore profitless. They had a

---

[1] *Tractatus xxxii in Johannis Evang.*

name that they lived, but in fact they were dead. The reason is that by breaking away from the unity of the Church they had broken away from love (*caritas*). For they have not the love of God who do not love the unity of the Church: and for this reason it is true to say that the Holy Spirit is received only in the Catholic Church.'[1] He proceeds to quote, as usual, Romans 5. 5: 'The love of God is poured out in our hearts by the Holy Spirit who is given to us.'

Thus it is that the idea of the Church as an aggregate of Spirit-filled individuals is entirely foreign to Augustine's thought. He brings out more clearly than any Christian writer before him the organic unity of the Church. Thus he says: 'But what the soul is to the body of a young man, this the Holy Spirit is to the Body of Christ, which is the Church. What the soul does in the several members of a single body, that the Holy Spirit does in the Church as a whole. But see what you must beware of, see what you must give heed to, see what you must fear. It happens in the case of a human body that one of the members is severed— a hand, a finger, a foot. Does the soul follow the severed member? While it was in the body, it was alive; when it is cut off it becomes lifeless. Even so a Christian man is a Catholic while he lives in the Body; when he is cut off, he becomes a heretic; the Spirit does not follow the severed limb. If therefore you wish to live by the Holy Spirit, hold fast charity, love truth, desire unity, that you may attain to eternal life.'[2]

In view of language like this, it is perhaps surprising—and disappointing—to find very little, if anything, in Augustine's works about the Spirit-filled Body being a praying Body, nor any elaboration of the teaching embodied in the phrase 'praying in the Holy Spirit.' In his commentary on Psalm 119. 45 (our notation), however, referring to the giving of the Holy Spirit by God to those who persevere in prayer, Augustine writes: 'Here is that Spirit by whom love (*caritas*) is poured out in our hearts that by loving God and our neighbour we may keep the divine commandments. Here is that Spirit in whom we cry, *Abba*, Father. And thereby He Himself makes us to seek whom we desire to find; He Himself makes us to knock at what we strive to reach. This is what the Apostle means when he says

[1] *De Baptismo*, iii. 21.   [2] Sermo 267.

that the Holy Spirit cries, *Abba*, Father. Again, in another place
he says: "God sent the Spirit of His Son into our hearts, crying,
Abba, Father." How can we be said to cry, if He Himself cries
in us, unless it is that He makes us to cry, when He begins to
dwell in us?"[1]

As to the fully personal nature of the Holy Spirit, this is
expounded in his great work on the Trinity. In this book
Augustine makes use of a conception which is deeply embedded
in his thinking, and that is that all created things reflect in some
measure the goodness of the Creator. Even the devil does this.
Consequently he finds reflections of the Holy Trinity in the
nature of man, though he warns us of their inadequacy. Thus
there is the trinity of memory and understanding and will.
These activities are distinct yet inseparable. Augustine argues
that they are one mind, one substance.[2] The Trinity is also
reflected in the mechanism of the senses—the object seen, the
vision, and the spectator. But it is supremely in love (*amor*) that
Augustine finds the Trinity reflected. 'Love is the property of
some one who loves, and something is loved by love. Behold
the three, the lover, the object, and love.'[3]

Augustine goes on to say that the Holy Spirit is specially called
love (*amor*), even as the second person of the Holy Trinity is
called wisdom. He infers this from a careful examination of
1 S. John 4. 10 ff. Here S. John says, 'Love is of God.' This
phrase 'of God' must refer either to the Son or to the Holy
Spirit. It is clear that it refers to the Holy Spirit because S. John
says, 'Hereby we know that we dwell in Him and He in us,
because He hath given us of His Spirit.' Since it is 'love' which
causes us to do this, it follows that the Holy Spirit is 'love' (*amor*).
Augustine then quotes the saying of S. Paul, which he is continually quoting, 'The love of God is poured out in our hearts
by the Holy Spirit who is given to us.' Moreover, if among the
gifts of God there is none greater than love, it again follows that
the Holy Spirit is love, since He is the greatest gift of God.
Again, if the love by which the Father loves the Son and the Son
loves the Father ineffably demonstrates the communion of both,
what is more appropriate than that He should be specially called

---

[1] *Enarrationes in Psalmos cxviii.* sermo 14. Cf. Sermo 382.
[2] *De Trinitate*, x. 11. 18.   [3] Ibid., viii. 10. 14.

'love' who is the Spirit common to both.[1] Even as He is called 'holy' and 'Spirit,' although both the Father and the Son are holy and Spirit, so may He be rightly called 'love,' although this is true of both the Father and the Son.[2] Augustine adds that the Holy Spirit may be specially called the will of God, 'for what is love except will?'[3]

This theology of Augustine has been criticized on the ground that the love which unites the lover and the loved cannot be a person in the same way as the subject and the object. But it is a misunderstanding of Augustine's meaning to say that 'he tries unsuccessfully to make love suggest a third person.'[4] Augustine was far too great a thinker to make such a crude error. We have to remember that in Latin theology *persona* did not mean exactly what we mean by the word 'person' to-day. It meant 'subsistence,' and we must not attribute to the term the limitations of human personality as we know it. Augustine repeatedly says that he uses the word *persona* because he can find no better term. His main point is that the Holy Spirit, as the *vinculum amoris*, is consubstantial with the Father and the Son. 'Therefore the Holy Spirit, whatever He is, is something common both to the Father and the Son. But that communion itself is consubstantial and co-eternal; and if it may fitly be called *amicitia*, let it be so called; but it is more aptly called *amor*. And this also is a "substance," since God is a "substance," for "God is love," as it is written.'[5]

Doubtless, objection can logically be raised to this doctrine on the ground that if the relation between the Father and the Son is thus hypostatized, then two new relations would be constituted, viz. between the Spirit and the Father, and between the Spirit and the Son, and a fresh *vinculum* would have to be postulated between these respectively; and so on *ad infinitum*. But we must bear in mind that this doctrine is not primarily a matter of abstract logic, but arises from within the living experience of the Church. In this connection, as Kirk said, we mean by 'personal' 'the terminus of a distinct and recognizable relationship with man.' It was through the Holy Spirit that *agapē* was realized in humanity. This is the unequivocal teaching of the New Testa-

---

[1] *De Trinitate*, xv. 19. 37.   [2] Ibid.   [3] Ibid., 20. 28.
[4] Gore: *Belief in Christ*, p. 246.   [5] *De Trinitate*, vi. 5. 7.

ment and it is this which is the basis of Augustine's theology of the Holy Spirit.

Turning to the question of the connection between water-baptism and the gift of the Holy Spirit, there are certain passages in which Augustine clearly uses the word 'baptize' to indicate water-baptism only, and where he makes it quite plain that the gift of the Spirit follows afterwards. Such a passage, for example, is the following in the well-known Sermon 272, in which he is commenting on S. Paul's words, 'We being many are one bread, one body': 'Understand and rejoice: unity, truth, piety, charity. "One bread": who is that one bread? "Many are one body." Remember that bread is not made from a single grain, but from many. When you were exorcized, you were, so to speak, ground. When you were baptized, you were, so to speak, watered. When you received the fire of the Holy Spirit, you were, so to speak, baked.'[1] Nothing could show more clearly that the giving of the Spirit is quite a distinct process from the rebirth of baptism. Identical teaching is given in another sermon,[2] where he puts the matter in a nutshell, 'post aquam ignis.'

In another sermon Augustine argues that the evidence of the New Testament clearly shows that we have to distinguish between 'baptism' and the gift of the Holy Spirit. For in some cases the Holy Spirit came quite independently of water-baptism. It was so on the Day of Pentecost. It was so in the case of Cornelius and his friends. On the other hand, the incident at Samaria shows the matter the other way round, those who had received water-baptism not yet having had the bestowal of the Spirit. He concludes: 'And so this distinction between the reception of baptism and the reception of the Holy Spirit shows us clearly enough that we should not think that those whom we do not deny to have received baptism forthwith have the Holy Spirit.'[3]

This teaching is entirely consonant with the position which Augustine adopts concerning schism—teaching which was developed as a result of the Donatist controversy, but which he held before that arose. So he says in another sermon[4] that those who are outside the unity of the Church do not possess the Spirit, and he quotes in support of this Jude 1. 19, 'these are sensual, not having the Spirit'; and he draws a careful distinction between

[1] Sermo 273.   [2] Sermo 227.   [3] Sermo 269.   [4] Sermo 71.

such persons and those within the Church who are 'spiritual babes.' Defective as they are, they are in quite a different category from schismatics, who 'have not the Spirit.'

In the anti-Donatist writing, *De Baptismo*, Augustine develops this teaching by arguing that those who are outside the unity of the Church are lacking in the virtue of charity (*caritas*), which is essentially the gift of the Holy Spirit. 'That the Holy Spirit is said to be given by the imposition of the hand in the Catholic Church alone without doubt our fathers wished it to be understood, because the Apostle says, For the love (*caritas*) of God is poured out in our hearts by the Holy Spirit who was given to us. That is the love which those who are severed from the communion of the Catholic Church do not possess.'[1]

ADDITIONAL NOTE ON TERTULLIAN'S DOCTRINE OF INITIATION

Professor Lampe asserts that 'there is a real confusion in Tertullian's theology' of initiation (*The Seal of the Spirit*, p. 161) because (he claims) the latter sometimes says that the Holy Spirit is given, not in water-baptism, but subsequently by the imposition of the hand, whereas in other passages he implies that the gift of the Spirit is conveyed through the water. This, however, is not the case. There is, I believe, not a single passage in Tertullian's writings in which he asserts, or implies, that the Holy Spirit is given in water-baptism. Tertullian, indeed, usually seems to use the term *baptismus* to denote the act of submersion. Nor is this surprising, since it must be so used in connection with John's baptism, and it is a natural term to use in order to describe the act of immersion. But there are not a few passages in which he seems to use the word to cover the whole rite of initiation (e.g. *De Baptismo*, cc. 3. 8). But the point is that whenever he speaks specifically of the gift of the laver he consistently states that it is regeneration, and never once says that it conveys the gift of the indwelling Spirit. Yet Lampe again and again reads this idea into Tertullian's language, and then accuses him of inconsistency. A good example of his exegesis is to be found in his handling of Tertullian's application of the Parable of the Prodigal Son to the sin of apostasy (*De Pudicitia*, c. 8). Tertullian is arguing that if this parable is applied to those who have been initiated and is interpreted in such a way as to sanction apostasy the results will be most unfortunate. He continues: 'Quis enim timebit prodigere, quod habebit postea recuperare? Quis curabit perpetuo conservare quod non perpetuo poterit amittere? Securitas delicti etiam libido est ejus. Recuperabit igitur et apostata vestem priorem, indumentum Spiritus Sancti, et annulum denuo signaculum lavacri, et rursus illi mactabitur Christus.' On this passage

---

[1] *De Baptismo*, iii. 20.

Lampe (*op. cit.*, p. 158) comments as follows: 'He [*sc.* Tertullian] can, however, also speak of the laver of Baptism as the "seal" which is typified by the ring given to the prodigal son. The ring at the same time signifies the "vestem priorem, indumentum Spiritus Sancti" which was lost at the Fall, but has been restored to man by the gift of the Spirit in Baptism. The clear implication of this passage is that the seal of the Spirit is given in the "laver," that is, water-baptism.' Yet what are the facts of the case? I submit that they are as follows: (*a*) Tertullian clearly distinguishes the symbolism of the ring from that of the robe. The former he identifies with baptism (i.e. water-baptism), the latter, with the subsequent clothing with the Holy Spirit (see *De Praescriptione*, c. 33). (*b*) There is no allusion to the Fall. The context makes it crystal clear that the allusion is to the act of apostasy and to the condition prior to that. (*c*) The phrase 'the seal of the Spirit' does not occur, still less the expression 'the gift of the Spirit in Baptism.' Lampe is reading his own theology into Tertullian's words and not out of them. Other instances of a similar subjectivist exegesis could be quoted from Lampe's book.

ADDITIONAL NOTE ON THE EPICLESIS

It is doubtless rash for one who is no expert in the liturgical field to say anything upon the difficult and disputed question of the epiclesis in the Holy Eucharist; and yet it is hardly possible to omit all reference to the subject in a book dealing with the theology of the Holy Spirit. As I understand the matter, liturgists are much divided on this question. Some of them claim that the earliest epiclesis of the Holy Spirit in the Holy Eucharist was upon the oblations. Thus, for example, Mr. Cuthbert Atchley wrote in 1935: 'So far as documentary evidence goes, the object of the invocation from the first was the hallowing of the oblation,'[1] and with this agrees the Latin text of the *Apostolic Tradition* of Hippolytus: 'And we pray Thee that Thou wouldest send Thy Holy Spirit upon the oblation of Thy holy Church: do Thou gather into one and grant to all Thy saints who partake that they may be filled with the Holy Spirit for the confirmation of faith in truth.' On the other hand, Dom Benedict Steuart writes in a recent book: 'But in its earlier forms this prayer calls upon the Holy Spirit to come down—not upon the offerings, but *upon those who have offered them* [italics in the original], upon the people present and about to communicate—in order to sanctify them and make them worthy of the Holy Food.'[2]

The question is further complicated by the fact that in the Syrian tradition there is, as we have previously noticed, a theological confusion of thought whereby the second and the third persons of the Holy Trinity are not clearly distinguished. It is, moreover, more than possible that in the earliest times those who used rites which contained any kind of epiclesis (and, of course, many

[1] C. Atchley: *On the Epiclesis of the Eucharistic Liturgy and in the Consecration of the Font* (1935), p. 54.
[2] Dom Benedict Steuart: *The Development of Christian Worship* (Longmans 1953), p. 152.

did not) could hardly have themselves given a clear answer to the question: 'Is your *epiclesis* on the elements or on the worshippers?' Their theology was not sufficiently developed. But what they *ought* to have said—according to the argument of the present book—is that the Holy Spirit cannot rightly be invoked on material objects and on initiated worshippers *in the same sense*. For He already supernaturally indwells the latter, as 'the Spirit of Christ,' whereas prior to the Eucharistic epiclesis He indwells the former only at the natural level, as the Lifegiver and sustainer of all creation. And, indeed, it would appear that a specific invocation on the elements and on the worshippers—in such a form as that found in the Liturgy of S. James (for example): 'Send forth upon us and upon these gifts'—is, in fact, a later development. In this form of epiclesis and in the similar forms found in the liturgies of S. Basil and S. Chrysostom, Gregory Dix[1] was of the opinion that the words 'upon us' are clearly a later intruder into the rites, which elsewhere take no cognizance of them.

Whatever may be the truth on this obscure and difficult question, it would seem that the practice of invoking the Holy Spirit upon the worshippers in the Eucharist led to the rise of the custom of invoking the Spirit upon the faithful at other times also. This had evidently become a firmly established custom before the ninth century, when the famous *Veni, Creator Spiritus* appears to have been written.[2]

This practice of invoking the Holy Spirit directly on the faithful (i.e. those fully initiated by baptism-confirmation) has become deeply embedded in our English worship by reason of the popularity of Cosin's splendid rendering of the *Veni, Creator Spiritus*. Nevertheless, this great hymn may only too easily lead us to forget that when He is invoked on the faithful this is an entirely different prayer from that which invokes Him upon the 'unconfirmed' person or the inanimate eucharistic elements. And this naturally prompts the question how this practice of asking the Holy Spirit to 'come' upon the faithful originated. It might perhaps be said that it arose as a parallel to the *maranatha* prayer to our Lord to come, despite the fact that the faithful knew full well that He was always present. But this explanation is not really adequate for, after all, the coming of the Holy Spirit upon the faithful at Pentecost and in the Christian rites of initiation was understood to be the fulfilment of the *maranatha* prayer, although, of course, there was always in the background the looking for the Last Advent. Moreover, it arose several centuries later than the *maranatha* prayer.

Perhaps the truth of the matter is that by the time that the *Veni, Creator Spiritus* was composed—and before that—the life of the Church had begun to wane and the strong awareness of the presence of the Holy Spirit in the Church which characterized the early days had disappeared. Consequently it became natural to invoke the Holy Spirit to come upon the worshippers as well as upon the elements—and even *in that order*. This clearly presupposes a completely different theological outlook from that which underlies what

---

[1] G. Dix: *The Shape of the Liturgy*, p. 296.
[2] See Julian's *Dictionary of Hymnology*, pp. 1207 and 1208.

may well be the more primitive type of epiclesis where the Holy Spirit was invoked directly on the elements, and only indirectly on the worshippers that they might as a result of the reception of the Blessed Sacrament be filled with the Spirit.

However this may be, we certainly need to be on our guard against allowing the established practice of asking the Holy Spirit to 'come'—as, for instance, in the *Veni, Creator Spiritus*—to give even the suspicion of a suggestion that we are calling upon One to 'come' who is in any sense absent from us as members of Christ's Body, the Church. This prayer to the Holy Spirit 'to come' is a prayer of the kind, 'Be, for Thou art' (*Ps.* 31. 3, 4). It means, 'Come, for Thou art already present.'

3. THE REFORMATION AND POST-REFORMATION DOCTRINE

Martin Luther (1483–1546)

The vast political and religious explosion which we know as the Reformation was 'touched off' by the hand of Luther. If he had not done this, however, doubtless it would have been brought about by some other hand; and it is much to be wished that this had been the case. For despite the stature of his personality and his versatility, Luther was essentially a man of one idea; and that idea was Justification by Faith. He said of himself: 'One can preach of nothing else but Jesus Christ and faith.'[1] The difference between this remark and a similar one made by the Apostle Paul should be carefully noted. It is this 'one-track-mindedness' which makes Luther so unsatisfactory as a Biblical commentator, despite his phenomenal knowledge of the text of the Scriptures. And it is this which gave the Reformation at the outset such an unfortunate theological bias. Certainly it fatally obscured Luther's insight into the Biblical doctrine of the Holy Spirit. Sanday and Headlam, in speaking of Luther as a commentator, do not exaggerate when they say: 'Exegesis was not Luther's strong point, and his commentaries bristle with faults. They are defective and prolix; full of bitter controversy and one-sided.'[2]

We may take as the starting-point of our examination of Luther's doctrine of the Holy Spirit what he has to say in commenting on Galatians 4. 6: 'And because ye are sons, God sent forth the Spirit of His Son into our hearts, crying Abba, Father.'

---

[1] Sermon for Whit-Monday 1532 (Vol. 36, Weimar Edition).
[2] Sanday and Headlam: *Romans* (I.C.C.), p. ciii.

Luther writes: 'But the Holy Spirit is sent in two different ways. In the early Church He was sent in manifest and visible form. In this way He came down to Jordan upon Christ in the form of a dove; upon the Apostles and other believers in the form of fire. That was the first sending of the Holy Spirit, necessary for the early Church. On account of the unbelievers it was necessary that He should be poured out with open signs, as S. Paul testifies. . . .

'There is another way by which the Holy Spirit is sent, by the word, into the hearts of believers, as is here said: "God sent the Spirit of His Son, etc." That happens without any visible sign when, that is to say, we conceive by the spoken word zeal and light by which we become new and different persons; by which a new judgement, new senses and motives arise in us. That change and new judgement is not the work of human reason or virtue but the gift and working of the Holy Spirit, who comes when the word is preached; who cleanses by faith our hearts and brings forth spiritual motives in us.

'Accordingly there is the greatest difference between us and the enemies and debasers of the word. We, by the grace of God, are certainly free to resolve and pass judgement by the word concerning God's will for us. Contrariwise, the Papists and fanatical spirits can judge certainly of nothing. For the latter deprave and pervert it; but we are persecuted and they blaspheme the word. But without the word no certain judgement can be passed on anything. It may, indeed, not be obvious that we are renewed in mind and have the Holy Spirit. Nevertheless, the fact of judging, our speech and our confession sufficiently show that the Holy Spirit with His gifts is in us.'[1]

Luther is obsessed by the dilemma: Either we receive the Holy Spirit by the hearing of faith or by the Law. Since it is clearly not by the latter, it must be by the former. There is, however, a fatal flaw in the argument, which is based on an over-pressing of Galatians 3. 2: 'Received ye the Spirit by the works of the law or by the hearing of faith?' The flaw is that this is not a true disjunction, as Luther explicitly claims. There are other ways in which the Spirit may be given. The first is that He may be given

[1] *Commentary on Galatians, ad loc.* (Weimar Edition, Vol. 40 (i)).

by the natural law. Secondly, He may be given through the sacraments of the Church.

Luther, indeed, is forced to consider the former of these ways because his opponents continually cited the case of Cornelius, who is said to have been a 'righteous man and one that feared God.' If Luther had rightly appreciated the significance of the Natural Law and the operation of the Holy Spirit at the natural level, there would have been no difficulty here. But Luther does not admit that the natural man can perform a single good work. Accordingly he seeks to get out of the difficulty by saying that Cornelius and the Old Testament Fathers were justified by faith in Christ who was to come (*propter fidem in venturum Christum*). But now that Christ *has* come, this is no longer possible. We must have faith in Christ who has come, and so go 'from faith to faith' (*Rom.* 1. 17).

But this is not exegesis. If Luther had not been blinded by his dominant idea, he would have been compelled to see this even in his favourite Epistle to the Romans, in what S. Paul says in 2. 14 to the effect that 'when the Gentiles which have no law do by nature the things of the law, these, having no law, are a law unto themselves.' But Luther is unable to see the plain meaning of this passage. He comments on it as follows: 'To be just before God and to be justified, i.e. to be held just, are the same thing. For it is not because one is just that one is held to be just by God, but because one is held to be just by God one is just, as is said below (chapter 4). But nobody is held to be just unless he fulfils the law. And nobody fulfils it unless he believes in Christ. And so the Apostle intends this conclusion: Apart from Christ nobody fulfils the law, nobody is just, as we see from the following chapter.'

We turn to the second point, viz. that the Holy Spirit may be given through the sacraments of the Church. Once more Luther is blinded by his own teaching to such an extent that he can actually write in the preface to the Acts of the Apostles: 'You will find this book is a splendid mirror which reflects the truth, *sola fides justificat.*' All grace, according to Luther's interpretation of the Acts, is given in this way. He entirely ignores what is said there about the grace of baptism and the gift of the Holy Spirit through the laying on of the Apostles' hands. Once more, this is not exegesis. Luther is reading his own opinions into the book and not out of it.

The same applies to what he has to say about the Johannine teaching. He did not write a complete commentary on the Fourth Gospel, but judging by the teaching of those sermons which deal with the Last Discourses of our Lord in chapters 14 to 16, it is not difficult to see what lines it would have followed. S. John's Gospel, indeed, has nothing to say about justification by faith and a good deal about sacramental grace. Luther, however, manages to turn the Johannine teaching about the Holy Spirit to support his thesis. The following remarks are characteristic: 'What is the Church? The Communion of Saints, not of the dead but of the living. How does holiness come to the Church? By cowls and bald pates? No: for even a profane person can possess these. That holiness comes from the remission of sins, by the renewing of the man through faith, knowledge, and fear, and not from the cowl. So you see that the Holy Spirit does not make us holy by laws, but by the word of promise, by remission of sins. In sum, what Christ teaches by word to His friends, this the Holy Spirit promotes by actions. Consider whether there is any need for the Holy Spirit to seek justification by external phenomena. From this we can conclude what Councils, either future or past, are worth, which have taken place apart from the Spirit (*extra Spiritum*). The Council of the Apostles (Acts 15) is sound. In this one Council I see nothing wrong. All succeeding Councils have turned aside to tradition; they have neglected grace and the preaching of the word, they have initiated laws and ceremonies. This is the punishment for our ingratitude, to take a lie for the truth. Therefore we conclude that the Holy Spirit is the gift of God by which we attain to that knowledge.' Such is Luther's way of commenting on the words, 'But the Comforter, even the Holy Spirit, whom the Father will send in My name, He shall teach you all things, and bring to your remembrance all that I said unto you.'[1] It is, I think, fair to say that nobody could have guessed the text from the sermon. Luther, in fact, is hardly doing more than using his text as a peg,

[1] Sermon for Whit-Monday 1529 on S. John 14. 23–26 (Weimar Edition, Vol. 29, p. 364).

on which to hang his own ideas. And there is a great deal more in the same strain in other sermons.

Professor Troeltsch has clearly pointed out the significance of this new doctrine of grace. 'Grace is no longer a mystical miraculous substance, to be imparted through the sacraments, but a Divine temper of faith, conviction, spirit, knowledge, and trust which is to be appropriated; in the Gospel and in the Love and Spirit of Christ towards mankind it can be discerned as the loving will of God which brings with it the forgiveness of sins. Religion thus steps out of the material substantial sphere, which was merely accompanied by thought and feeling, and enters into the intellectual psychological, spiritual sphere. This does not mean that it ceases to be a miracle. But the miracle now consists in the fact that man in his weakness, rebellion, despair, and impurity can grasp such an idea from the Gospel; it is so entirely beyond the reach of his natural powers, and the religious idea of redemption is so far removed from the natural intellectual sphere, that only through the miracle of predestination can it come to pass. It is an inner miracle of faith in the Gospel and in Christ, not an interior-external miracle of the hierarchical sacramental impartation of grace, which produces the power to do good works and to acquire merit. Moreover, it is not an idea which can be altered and changed at will, but a knowledge which is offered with the absolute certainty of revelation, which starts from a picture of the incarnate, suffering, risen Son of God, even though, in detail, the Bible is not free from all kinds of human imperfections. In Protestantism, therefore, the heart of religion consists in the spirit of faith which is thus effected by the "Word," just as for Catholicism it consists in priesthood and sacrament, in obedience and mysticism. Religion is now a matter of faith and conviction, instead of one which is bound up with a hierarchical-sacramental system. The two Protestant sacraments which are retained are special methods of representing the Gospel; their spiritual influence does not exceed that of the influence of the Word of God in the Scripture; hence, in the Catholic sense, they are no longer sacraments.'[1] Although Professor Troeltsch completely misrepresents the traditional doctrine of sacramental grace, at least he indicates the novelty of Luther's teaching in this matter.

[1] E. Troeltsch: *The Social Teaching of the Christian Churches II*, 468, 469.

If, however, Luther had taken his own doctrine of hearing the word by faith more seriously, he would at least have seen that it must guard the rational element in Christianity. Sacramental grace might indeed be regarded as a non-rational mysterious power, but surely it is of the essence of a word that it should appeal to the understanding. Disastrously, however, Luther turned his new teaching into an irrational channel by his doctrine of predestination. The Holy Spirit ceases to be the Holy Spirit of truth enlightening the mind rationally, and becomes the spirit of unreason. So he can write: 'This is the highest degree of faith, to believe that He is merciful, who saves so few, and condemns so many; to believe Him just, who, of His own will, makes us necessary objects of damnation; thus seeming, according to Erasmus's account, to be delighted with the torments of the wretched, and to deserve hatred rather than love. If, then, I could by any means comprehend how this God is pitiful and just, who shows so great wrath and injustice, there would be no need of faith; but now since this cannot be comprehended, space is given for the exercise of faith, whilst these things are preached and published.'[1] The fact of the matter is that, according to Luther, faith is every bit as much an unethical irrational power as is sacramental grace most crudely understood. We have moved a long way from the Spirit of truth.

'Faith,' writes Luther, 'killeth reason, and slayeth that beast which the whole world and all creatures cannot kill. So Abraham killed it by faith in the Word of God, whereby seed was promised to him of Sarah, who was barren, and now past childbearing. Unto this Word, reason yielded not straightway in Abraham, but it fought against faith in him, judging it an absurd and impossible thing that Sarah, now ninety years of age, should bear a son. Thus faith wrestled with reason in Abraham, but herein faith got the victory, killed and crucified reason, that most cruel and pestilential enemy of God.'[2]

Not only is Luther's way of regarding the work of the Holy Spirit irrational, but it is also completely individualistic. He appears to have no understanding of the *koinonia* or Fellowship of the Spirit, and, so far as I am aware, in his various Whitsuntide

<hr />

[1] *De Servo Arbitrio*, I. 23 (Vaughan's translation).
[2] *Commentary on Galatians* 3. 6 (J. P. Fallowes' translation).

sermons, in which he constantly refers to the account of the Coming of the Holy Spirit in the second chapter of the Acts of the Apostles, there is no reference at all to the creation of the *koinonia*.

How completely individualistic is Luther's treatment of the indwelling of the Holy Spirit the following passage will suffice to show: 'We ought not, therefore, to doubt whether the Holy Ghost dwelleth in us or not; but to be assuredly persuaded that we "are the temples of the Holy Ghost" (1 *Cor.* 3. 16). For if any man feel in himself a love toward the Word of God, and willingly heareth, talketh, writeth, and thinketh of Christ, let that man know, that this is not the work of man's will or reason, but the gift of the Holy Ghost: for it is impossible that these things should be done without the Holy Ghost. . . .

'This I have said concerning the inward testimony, whereby a Christian man's heart ought to be fully persuaded that he is under grace, and hath the Holy Ghost. . . . When we are conscious of the terrors of the Law, the thundering of sin, the assaults of death, the roarings of the devil, the Holy Ghost, saith Paul, crieth in our hearts, "Abba, Father." This cry pierceth the clouds and the heaven, and ascendeth up into the ears of God.'[1]

There is little doubt that the stark individualism of this doctrine of the Holy Spirit was the result of the scrupulosity from which Luther suffered. The scrupulous person is always, at root, an individualist. *His* conscience means more to him than anything else. He is right in his judgement: nobody can argue him out of that position. If Luther's conscience had not been a diseased conscience the whole history of the Reformation would probably have been different; and certainly the Lutheran doctrine of the Holy Spirit would have been entirely different.

John Calvin (1509–1564)

Calvin is by far the greatest of all the Reformation theologians, and he has had a decisive influence upon the post-Reformation doctrine of the Holy Spirit. Although his writings are voluminous, it is true that Calvin is a compendious writer. As he says in one of his letters (to Simon Gryney), he has a love of com-

[1] *Commentary on Galatians* 4. 6 (Fallowes).

pendiousness. This makes it easier to obtain a conspectus of his teaching—especially his teaching on any particular aspect of theology—than is possible in the case of many writers. There has indeed grown up a vast literature dealing with Calvin and his teaching, and much disputation has taken place as to the interpretation of his writings. This is what usually happens in the case of a great thinker. But if we allow Calvin to speak for himself, and do not try to explain away those points of his teaching which are distasteful to us, as the manner of some is, we shall find him, on the whole, a remarkably clear and consistent writer.

We have seen that most of the early Fathers—and the same is true of the Schoolmen—did little to develop the doctrine of the Holy Spirit. It might have been expected, however, that it would have been different with the Reformers, since the Reformation was, or claimed to be, a return to the New Testament. In point of fact, however, it was not different. Calvin, who unfortunately followed Luther's teaching in this matter to a considerable degree, really throws little fresh light on the doctrine of the Holy Spirit. Indeed, his understanding of the subject is markedly inferior to that of S. Augustine, to whom, among the Fathers, he pays the greatest deference.

At the outset we notice that there is no question as to the orthodox Trinitarianism of Calvin's teaching. His controversy with Servetus is sufficient guarantee of that. He bases his belief in the deity of the Holy Spirit partly upon Holy Scripture and partly upon experience. The former he uses rather uncritically, making use (for example) of the passage in Genesis about the Spirit of God brooding over the abyss, to establish the position which he is defending. With regard to the latter, he says: 'The best proof to us is our familiar experience. For nothing can be more alien from a creature than the office which the Scriptures ascribe to him, and which the pious actually feel him discharging—his being diffused over all space, sustaining, invigorating, and quickening all things, both in the heaven and on earth. The mere fact of his not being circumscribed by any limits raises him above the rank of creatures, while his transfusing vigour into all things, breathing into them being, life and motion, is plainly divine. Again, if regeneration to incorruptible life is higher, and much more excellent than any present quickening, what must be thought of him by whose energy it is produced?'[1]

In this passage is adumbrated the distinction between the natural and the supernatural operations of the Holy Spirit. Calvin fully recognized this; but unfortunately his doctrine of the fall of man caused him to take away with one hand what he had given with the other, as we shall see. 'In reading profane authors,' Calvin says, 'the admirable light of truth displayed in them should remind us that the human mind, however much fallen and perverted from its original integrity, is still adorned and invested with admirable gifts from its creator. If we reflect that the Spirit of God is the only fountain of truth, we shall be careful, as we would avoid offering insult to Him, not to reject or contemn truth wherever it appears. In despising the gifts, we insult the Giver.'[2] Calvin continues a little farther on: 'Nor is there any ground for asking what concourse the Spirit can have with the ungodly, who are altogether alienated from God? For what is said as to the Spirit dwelling in believers only, is to be understood of the Spirit of holiness, by which we are consecrated to God as temples. Notwithstanding this, He fills, moves, and invigorates all things by the virtue of the Spirit, and that according to the peculiar nature which each class of beings has received by the law of creation. But if the Lord has been pleased to assist us by the work and ministry of the ungodly in physics, dialectics, mathematics, and other similar sciences, let us avail ourselves of it, lest by neglecting the gifts of God spontaneously offered to us, we be justly punished for our sloth.'[3]

But all this natural enlightenment, according to Calvin, avails nothing for the knowledge of God. Unregenerate men are 'blinder than moles.' God, indeed, has given them 'some slight perception of His Godhead'—thus he interprets S. Paul's famous statement about the natural law (Rom. 2. 14–16)—so that they may not plead ignorance as an excuse for their sin, yet it remains true that seeing they see not. 'Their discernment was not such as to direct them to the truth, far less to enable them to attain it, but resembled that of the bewildered traveller, who sees the flash of lightning glance far and wide for a moment, and then vanish into the darkness of the night, before he can advance a single

[1] *Instit.* 1. 13. 14.   [2] Ibid., 2. 2. 15.   [3] Ibid., 2. 2. 16.

step. . . . To the great truths, what God is in Himself, and what He is in relation to us, human reason makes not the least approach.'[1] Again: 'In vain for us, therefore, does creation exhibit so many bright lamps lighted up to show forth the glory of its Author. Though they beam upon us from every quarter, they are altogether insufficient of themselves to lead us into the right path. Some sparks, undoubtedly, they do throw out; but these are quenched before they can give forth a brighter effulgence. . . . But though God is not left without a witness, while with numberless varied acts of kindness, He woos men to the knowledge of Himself, yet they cease not to follow their own ways, in other words, deadly errors.'[2] Hence the dreadfulness of the sin of ingratitude, to which Calvin rightly points as being basic to fallen mankind, rooted as it is in sinful human pride. 'Though they have in their own persons a factory where innumerable operations of God are carried on, and a magazine stored with treasures of inestimable value—instead of bursting forth in His praise, as they are bound to do, they, on the contrary, are the more inflated and swelled with pride.'[3]

Man, therefore, is helpless until the Holy Spirit shines forth supernaturally upon him through the word of God. 'It is by faith alone we know it was God who created the world.'[4] 'It is,' he says, 'the faithful to whom He has given eyes, who see the sparks of His glory, glittering in every created thing.'[5] 'For the soul, when illumined by Him, receives as it were a new eye, enabling it to contemplate heavenly mysteries, by the splendour of which it was previously dazzled. And thus, indeed, it is only when the human intellect is irradiated by the light of the Holy Spirit that it begins to have a taste of those things which pertain to the kingdom of God; previously it was too stupid and senseless to have any relish for them. Hence our Saviour, when clearly declaring the mysteries of the kingdom to the two disciples, makes no impression until He opens their minds to understand the scriptures (S. Luke 24. 27, 45). Hence also, though He had taught the Apostles with His own divine lips, it was still necessary to send the Spirit of truth to instil into their minds the same doctrine which they had heard with their ears. The word is, in

---

[1] Instit., 2. 2. 18.   [2] Ibid., 1. 5. 1 .   [3] Ibid., 1. 5. 4.
[4] Commentary on Hebrews 11. 3.   [5] Ibid.

regard to them to whom it is preached, like the sun which shines upon all, but is of no use to the blind; hence the word cannot penetrate the mind unless the Spirit, that internal teacher, by His enlightening power make an entrance for it.'[1]

Thus we see that Calvin wrongly rejects the traditional doctrine of the operation of the Holy Spirit in the natural law as providing *praeambula fidei*.[2] The natural light has been turned to darkness. Calvin interprets the sin of blasphemy against the Holy Spirit not as rebellion against the natural light of conscience which is in every man, but as referring to believers. He says: 'The reason why blasphemy against the Spirit exceeds other sins is not that the Spirit is higher than Christ, but that those who rebel, after that the power of God has been revealed, cannot be excused on the plea of ignorance. Besides, it must be observed that what is here said about blasphemy does not refer merely to the essence of the Spirit but to the grace which He has bestowed upon us. Those who are destitute of the light of the Spirit, however much they may detract from the glory of the Spirit, will not be held guilty of this crime.'[3] Here is an implicit rejection of the doctrine of natural law, for, according to the latter, there can be nobody 'destitute of the light of the Spirit.'

Once more, Calvin fails to see in our Lord's teaching by parables, appealing as He did to the moral judgement of the ordinary man, an appeal to the light of the natural law. Rather he takes it that our Lord taught thus in order to obscure His teaching. Commenting on the words: 'Therefore speak I to them in parables; because seeing they see not, and hearing they hear not, neither do they understand,' Calvin says: 'He says that He speaks to the multitude in an obscure manner because they are not partakers of the true light. And yet, while He declares that a veil is spread over the blind, that they may remain in their darkness, He does not ascribe the blame of this to themselves but takes occasion to commend more highly the grace bestowed on the Apostles, because it is not equally communicated to all. He assigns no cause for it, except the secret purpose of God.'[4] Again, 'The Lord conceals its mysteries, so that the perception of them may not reach the reprobate. There are two ways in which He

---

[1] *Instit.* 3. 2. 34.　　[2] See the sermon on Deuteronomy 19. 14, 15.
[3] *Commentary on S. Mark* 3. 30.　　[4] *Commentary on S. Matthew* 13. 13.

deprives them of the light of His doctrine. Sometimes He states in a dark manner what might have been more clearly expressed; and sometimes He explains His mind fully, without ambiguity and without metaphor, but strikes their sense with dullness and their minds with stupidity, so that they are blind amidst bright sunshine.'[1]

This teaching accords entirely with Calvin's predestinarianism, and with the face meaning of S. Mark 4. 11, 12: 'And He said unto them, Unto you is given the mystery of the kingdom of God: but unto them that are without, all things are done in parables: that seeing they may see, and not perceive; and hearing they may hear, and not understand; lest haply they should turn again, and it should be forgiven them.' Commenting on this latter passage, Calvin says: 'Here it may suffice to state briefly what has been already fully explained, that the doctrine is not, strictly speaking, or by itself or in its own nature, but by accident, the cause of blindness. When persons of a weak sight come out into the sunshine, their eyes become dimmer than before, and that defect is in no way attributed to the sun but to their eyes. In like manner, when the word of God blinds and hardens the reprobate, as this takes place through their own depravity it belongs truly and naturally to themselves, but is accidental in respect of the word.'[2]

Such a doctrine as this, however, is irreconcilable with belief in a God who loves the world; and when Calvin comments on the famous passage declaring this (S. John 3. 16), he does not at all succeed in explaining how God who (as he says) 'loves the human race' can, in the secret purpose of His will, allow most of it to perish. 'In all cases, I admit,' Calvin says, 'those whom God blinds will be found to deserve this condemnation; but as the immediate cause is not always obvious in the persons of men, let it be held as a fixed principle, that God enlightens to salvation, and that by a peculiar gift, those whom He has freely chosen; and that all the reprobate are deprived of the light of life, whether God withholds His word from them, or keeps their eyes and ears closed, that they do not hear or see.'[3]

There is, however, another grave objection to Calvin's treat-

[1] *Commentary on S. Matthew* 13. 11.   [2] *Commentary, ad loc.*
[3] *Commentary on S. Matthew* 13. 14.

ment of the connection between the natural and the supernatural (Christian) operations of the Holy Spirit, and that is the individualistic way in which he regards the latter. This will be clear from a careful consideration of the passages which have been quoted. Calvin never seems to have appreciated what the New Testament means by the *koinonia* of the Holy Spirit. So far as I am aware, he makes only two references in the *Institutes* to the famous Trinitarian formula of 2 Corinthians 13. 14: 'The grace of our Lord Jesus Christ, the love of God, and the *koinonia* of the Holy Spirit.' In the first of these (2. 17. 2) he is concerned entirely with the first of the three expressions; in the second (3. 1. 2) he speaks of the *koinonia* of the Holy Spirit as that 'without which no man shall even taste the paternal favour of God, or the benefits of Christ,' thus missing the essential meaning of the phrase by giving it a subjectivist interpretation, as perhaps he does in his commentary on 2 Corinthians 13. 14. He seems to have no appreciation of the meaning of the phrase 'the *koinonia*' as it occurs in Acts 2. 42: 'And they continued steadfastly in the Apostles' doctrine and fellowship, and the breaking of bread, and in prayers.' In expounding this last passage, Calvin takes 'fellowship' to mean 'mutual society and fellowship, unto alms, and unto other duties of brotherly fellowship,'[1] i.e. something subjective and not something objective.

The fact is that, despite apparent evidence to the contrary, Calvin's doctrine of the supernatural operation of the Spirit of Christ is individualistically conceived, and consequently does not adequately represent the teaching of the New Testament, where the doctrine of the *objective* fellowship, or *koinonia*, of the Spirit is fundamental. The essentially individual nature of Calvin's doctrine of the Spirit is most clearly seen (*a*) in his doctrine of inspiration and (*b*) in his doctrine of justification by faith.

We turn, therefore, to his doctrine of inspiration. This, as is well known, has been and still is the subject of much controversy. To some extent this has been due to the unwillingness of some of Calvin's commentators to accept his own plain statements, because they are unpalatable to the modern mind. Let us take as our starting-point the following passage: 'Let it therefore be held as fixed, that those who are inwardly taught by the Holy

[1] *Commentary on Acts* 2. 42.

Spirit acquiesce implicitly in Scripture; that Scripture, carrying its own evidence along with it, deigns not to submit to proofs and arguments, but owes the full conviction with which we ought to receive it to the testimony of the Spirit. For though in its own majesty it has enough to command reverence, nevertheless, it then begins truly to touch us when it is sealed in our hearts by the Holy Spirit. Enlightened by Him, we no longer believe, either on our own judgement or that of others, that the Scriptures are from God; but, in a way superior to human judgement, feel perfectly assured—as much so as if we beheld the divine image impressed on it—that it came to us, by the instrumentality of men, from the very mouth of God. We ask not for proofs or probabilities on which to rest our judgement, but we subject our intellect and judgement to it as too transcendent for us to estimate. . . . Because we feel a divine energy living and breathing in it—an energy by which we are drawn and animated to obey it, willingly indeed, and knowingly, but more vividly and effectually than could be done by human will and knowledge. . . . I say nothing more than every believer experiences in himself, though my words fall far short of the reality.'[1]

Leaving on one side the various other theological problems which are raised by this passage—which may fairly be said to be typical of many others in Calvin's writings—I would draw attention to the essentially individual nature of the experience to which Calvin refers. It is, as he says, 'what every believer experiences in himself.' The same Spirit who spoke by the prophets must speak in our hearts in order to assure us that they rightly delivered the message of the word.

There seem to have been two main reasons for this individualistic, and non-New Testament, approach to the doctrine of

[1] *Instit.* 1. 7. 5. '*Maneat ergo hoc fixum, quos spiritus sanctus intus docuit, solide acquiescere in scriptura, et hanc quidem esse neque demonstrationi et rationibus subici eam fas est; quam tamen meretur apud nos certitudinem, spiritus testimonio consequi. Etsi enim reverentiam sua sibi ultro majestate conciliat, tunc tamen demum serio nos afficit quum per spiritum obsignata est cordibus nostris. Illius ergo virtute illuminati, iam non aut nostro, aut aliorum iudicio credimus, a Deo esse scriptam; sed supra humanum iudicium, certo certius constituimus (non secus ac si ipsius Dei numen illic intueremur) hominum ministerio, ab ipsissimo Dei ore ad nos fluxisse. Non argumenta, non verisimilitudines quaerimus quibus iudicium nostrum incumbat; sed, ut rei extra aestimandi aleam positae, iudicium ingeniumque nostrum subiicimus . . . quia non dubiam vim numinis illic sentimus vigere ac spirare, qua ad parendum, scientie quidem ac volentes, vividius tamen et efficacius quam pro humana aut voluntate aut scientia, trahimur et accendimur. . . . Non aliud loquor quam quod apud se experitur fidelium unusquisque, nisi quod longe infra iustam rei explicationem verba subsidunt.*'

the Spirit. The first was the fact that Calvin wished to by-pass the alleged authority of the Church over Scripture. He says: 'As to the question, How shall we be persuaded that it came from God without recurring to a decree of the Church? it is just the same as if it were asked, How shall we learn to distinguish light from darkness, white from black, sweet from bitter? Scripture bears upon the face of it as clear evidence of its truth as white and black do of their colour, sweet and bitter of their taste.'[1]

In this appeal to the self-evident truth of the Scriptures the real ground is the wonderful sense of illumination which came to the ordinary believer at the Reformation when he first began to read the Bible for himself. It was as a light from heaven. As Calvin says, 'The word is the instrument by which the illumination of the Spirit is dispensed.'[2] This was what Luther had said before him. But Calvin went a step further than Luther. The testimony of the Spirit (he claims) assures the individual believer that God is the author of Scripture. As Professor Hendry has written, 'The position is not that men, finding the *message* of Scripture confirmed in their hearts by the testimony of Scripture, are led to a conviction of its divine origin; but first they receive by the Spirit certification of the authority of Scripture, and then they experience the power of the message.'[3]

Calvin is led into this false doctrine because he is anxious to dispose of the idea that the authority of the Scriptures is in any way dependent on the authority of the Church. And it is just here that Calvin's failure to appreciate the doctrine of the *koinonia* of the Spirit is so disastrous. He says, 'With great insult to the Holy Spirit, it is asked, Who can assure us that the Scriptures proceeded from God?; who guarantee that they have come down safe and unimpaired to our times; who persuade us that *this* book is to be received with reverence, and *that one* expunged from the list, did not the Church regulate all these things with certainty? On the determination of the Church therefore, it is said, depend both the reverence which is due to Scripture and the books which are to be admitted into the Canon. . . . But what is to become of miserable consciences in quest of some solid assurance of eternal life, if all the promises with regard to it have no better support than man's judgement?'[4]

---

[1] Ibid., 1. 7. 2.   [2] Ibid., 1. 9. 3.   [3] G. S. Hendry: *op. cit.*, p. 76.   [4] *Instit.* 1. 7. 1.

Calvin does not face the question why the Holy Spirit may not illuminate and inspire a corporate body of persons just as much as a collection of individuals; and this is strange in view of the fact that the history of the canon clearly indicates that this in fact is what He has done. At this point, indeed, Calvin was embarrassed by the well-known saying of his master, S. Augustine: 'I should not indeed believe the Gospel, if the authority of the Catholic Church did not move me.'[1] Calvin tries to explain this away by arguing that Augustine merely means that those who are unenlightened by the Gospel are assisted by the witness of the Church so that they become teachable. But, as it has more than once been pointed out, if Augustine had meant to say this, he would have written: 'I should not *have believed* the Gospel if the authority of the Catholic Church *had not moved me*.' Calvin would not have been driven to such a forced explanation if he had followed Augustine's insight into the corporate aspect of inspiration.

There is, of course, a fatal objection to this version of the doctrine of the inspiration of the Holy Spirit, and that is that it is flatly inconsistent with the facts. If it were true, an illuminated Christian would be able to know whether or not a passage is canonical by looking at it, and there could be and would have been no dispute about the matter among the enlightened. In fact, there were such disputes, or at any rate differences of opinion, among the faithful during the early centuries when the canon was coming into existence; and these differences were resolved not by 'a decree of the Church' but by the silent consensus of opinion in the mind of the Church, the Spirit-bearing Body. Calvin seems to have no inkling of this. It is significant that when he is commenting on S. Paul's words, 'We have the mind of Christ' (1 *Cor.* 2. 16), he asks whether this refers to all believers or to ministers only. He inclines to the latter view, but it does not even occur to him to ask whether it might not refer to the faithful in their corporate capacity. For it is this corporate or common mind which is one of the most distinctive marks of the Holy Spirit. It was this which Luther was blindly feeling after in his reaction against the repressive hand of the Papacy. For during the Middle Ages the Pope has accumulated more and

[1] *Contra Manichaeos* 8. 6.

more power. The Bishop of Rome came to be regarded as the vicar of Christ, whereas in the second century Tertullian had spoken of the Holy Spirit as the vicar of Christ.[1] The contrast between the primitive conception and the Papal conception is complete. The latter fatally obscures the true doctrine of the *koinonia* of the Spirit, which was expressed in the aims of the Conciliar Movement. The mind of the Spirit is expressed by an invisible Head in and through the whole body of the faithful, and not through a visible Head, the authority of whom over the other members is absolute.

Unfortunately, the attempt of Luther and Calvin to counter the ultra-authoritarianism of the Papacy by subordinating the Church to the Word speaking to the heart of each individual believer opened the door wide to individualism and sectarianism, as subsequent history has clearly shown. It was unfortunate in the extreme that Calvin, acute thinker as he was, failed to appreciate the primitive doctrine of the *koinonia* of the Spirit as providing the true means whereby the Church is subordinate to the Word. 'Hear what the Spirit saith unto the churches' (*Rev.* 2. 7).

There is a further difficulty in Calvin's doctrine here, and that is the question of the authority of Scripture in the minds of the reprobate. Since, *ex hypothesi*, only God knows who are the elect and who are the reprobate, how are we to distinguish between the authority of the Holy Spirit in the minds of those members of the visible Church who are elect and those who are reprobate? Calvin recognizes this difficulty, which is a very serious one for his doctrine of inspiration. All he can say in reply is to argue rather lamely that 'there is nothing to prevent an inferior operation of the Holy Spirit from taking its course in the reprobate,'[2] which means in plain English that, though they think they are being illuminated, in fact they are not, the light in them being only a 'glimmer.' In this case, however, what becomes of Calvin's claim that the testimony of the Spirit exists precisely to give clear light and guidance to the individual who is fogged and bemused by the fallible guidance of the Church? It is difficult to see what has become of the internal authority of

---

[1] Tertullian: *On the Veiling of Virgins*, c. 1.
[2] *Instit.* 3. 2. 10. 'Sed hoc minime obstat quia illa inferior Spiritus operatio cursum suum habeat etiam in reprobis.'

the Holy Spirit; for none of us can compare our individual spiritual illumination with that of another believer; consequently, we may delude ourselves that we have the light of the Spirit when in fact we have only a confused glimmer. We are back where we started.

The extremely vulnerable nature of this doctrine of the inspiration of the Holy Spirit was doubtless responsible for Calvin's utterances on the inerrancy of the Scriptures which have been so great an embarrassment to some of his followers, and which led in Calvin's successors to a more rigorous fundamentalism. So Professor Hendry is surely right when he says: 'The refusal to accept the historical testimony of the Church's faith as the external correlate or counterpart of the inner witness of the Holy Spirit left the latter vulnerable to the charge of subjectivism, and it was to escape this charge that the appeal was made to the quality of Scripture itself, which was considered to furnish objective evidence of its having been divinely inspired. But the equation of inspiration with inerrancy reflects a conception of spirit that belongs to the mantic cults of ancient Greece rather than to the faith of the New Testament.'[1]

Thus Calvin is led to commit himself to such a passage as the following: 'Let this then be a sure axiom—that there is no word of God to which place should be given in the Church save that which is contained, first, in the Law and the Prophets; and secondly, in the writings of the Apostles, and that the only due method of teaching in the Church is according to the prescription and rule of His word. Hence also we infer that nothing else was permitted to the Apostles than was formerly permitted to the prophets—namely to expound the ancient Scriptures, and show that the things delivered there are fulfilled in Christ: this, however, they could not do, unless from the Lord; that is, unless the Spirit of Christ went before, and in a manner dictated words to them.'[2] Shortly afterwards there follows the following celebrated passage which has caused such a fluttering in the more enlightened Protestant dovecots: 'There is this difference between the Apostles and their successors, they were sure and authentic amanuenses of the Holy Spirit; and, therefore, their writings are to be regarded as the oracles of God, whereas

[1] *Op. cit.*, p. 87.   [2] *Instit.* 4. 8. 8.

others have no other office than to teach what is sealed and delivered in the Holy Scriptures.'[1]

Statements of this kind, however, have not only embarrassed Calvin's disciples: they also embarrassed him. As Mr. Mitchell Hunter has written: 'The commentaries afford abundant evidence of the embarrassments into which he was driven by his theory. One may say that never did the idea of the verbal inspiration of the Scriptures receive such emphatic refutation as at the hands of this vehement champion, whose frequent transparent evasions, jugglings, and violences are in themselves a confession of its futility.'[2]

We now turn to Calvin's doctrine of justification by faith in order to see how it reveals further the individualistic nature of his doctrine of the Holy Spirit. This doctrine of justification, according to Calvin, is 'the principal ground on which religion must be supported' (*praecipuum esse sustinendae religionis cardinem*) so that we may reasonably expect to find a good deal of light thrown on the doctrine of the Holy Spirit by it. Faith, Calvin says, 'is a firm and sure knowledge of the divine favour toward us, founded on the truth of a free promise in Christ, and revealed to our minds, and sealed in our hearts, by the Holy Spirit.'[3] Apart from the Holy Spirit the word has no power on a person's mind and heart. 'Faith is the special gift of God in both ways— in purifying the mind so as to give it a relish for divine truth, and afterwards in establishing it therein. For the Spirit does not merely originate faith, but gradually increases it, until by its means he conducts us into the heavenly kingdom.'[4] Again: 'The word is, in regard to those to whom it is preached, like the sun which shines upon all, but is of no use to the blind. In this matter we are all naturally blind; and hence the word cannot penetrate the mind unless the Spirit, that internal teacher, by His enlightening power make an entrance for it.'[5] Again: 'So long as your mind (*animus tuus*) entertains any misgivings as to the

---

[1] *Instit.* 4. 8. 9. '*Quanquam inter apostolos et eorum successores hoc, ut dixi, interest, quod illi fuerunt certi et authentici Spiritus Sancti amanuenses, et ideo eorum scripta pro Dei oraculis habenda sunt.*'

[2] A. Mitchell Hunter: *The Teaching of Calvin* (James Clark, 1950), p. 76.

[3] *Instit.* 3. 2. 7. '*Esse divinae erga nos benevolentiae firmam certamque cognitionem, quae gratuitae in Christo promissiones veritate fundata per Spiritum Sanctum et revelatur mentibus nostris et cordibus obsignatur.*'

[4] Ibid., 3. 2. 33. [5] Ibid., 3. 2. 34.

certainty of the word, its authority will be weak and dubious, or rather it will have no authority at all.'[1]

Again, in his commentary on the Epistle to the Romans, in expounding the famous passage, 'Being therefore justified by faith we have peace with God' (*Rom.* 5. 1), he writes: 'We have peace with God, and this is the peculiar fruit of the righteousness of faith. When any one strives to seek tranquillity of conscience by works (which is the case with profane and ignorant men) he labours for it in vain; for either the heart is asleep through his disregard or forgetfulness of God's judgement, or else it is full of trembling and dread, until it reposes on Christ.'

I think that the foregoing quotations give a fair representation of the way in which Calvin understands the work of the Holy Spirit in justifying faith. It is clear that it is regarded as being an essentially individual experience. Either a person has it or he has not, although, of course, he may, as we say, grow in grace. And this necessarily leads to an essentially individualistic conception of the Church. Consequently, despite all appearances to the contrary—and they are many[2]—Calvin's Church is not the organic fellowship or *koinonia* of the Spirit but a collocation of saved individuals.

This is obviously true of the invisible Church, which is the Church of the elect; for this is the sum total of the elect who are, Calvin says, 'a small and despised number, concealed in an immense crowd, like a few grains of wheat buried among a heap of chaff.'[3] Clearly this invisible Church can have no corporate life, for nobody but God knows who are the members of it. As for the visible Church, despite all that Calvin has to say about its importance, it is not regarded as a divinely constituted organic society continuous throughout its life, but as the collocation of those who by faith have embraced the promises. So Calvin writes in the preface to his commentary on Genesis: 'The perpetual succession of the Church has flowed from this fountain, that the holy Fathers, one after another, having by faith embraced the offered promise, were collected together into the family of

---

[1] *Instit.* 3. 2. 6.
[2] So, e.g., F. Heiler can write: 'Calvin's religious thinking is corporate throughout. He looks never at individuals but always at the host of the elect, the Church, the fellowship of Christ' (*Der Katholizismus*, p. 584). A superficial judgement this, but frequently encountered.   [3] *Instit.* 4. 1. 2.

God, in order that they might have a common life in Christ.'
Though Calvin often speaks of the Church as our mother, we
must not be misled by this figure. She is rather our foster-mother
'into whose bosom God is pleased to collect His children.'[1] This,
Calvin says, is the meaning of the clause in the Creed—'the
communion of saints.' 'It admirably expresses the quality of the
Church; just as if it had been said, that saints are united in the
fellowship of Christ on this condition, that all the blessings which
God bestows upon them are mutually communicated to each
other. . . . For if they are truly persuaded that God is the common
Father of them all, and Christ their common head, they cannot
but be united together in brotherly love, and mutually impart
their blessings to one another.'[2]

That Calvin's visible Church is a very different conception from
the Spirit-filled Body of the New Testament and the early
Fathers is clearly shown by Calvin's doctrine of baptism and the
Lord's Supper, and the way in which he understands the operation
of the Holy Spirit in them. Baptism, according to Calvin, is 'a
kind of sealed instrument'[3] by which we are assured that we
have been forgiven and regenerated in Christ. But we are not
regenerated in baptism. Commenting on S. Peter's words,
'Baptism also doth now save us' (1 S. Pet. 3. 21), Calvin says: 'For
he did not mean to intimate that our ablution and salvation are
perfected by water, or that water possesses in itself the virtue of
purifying, regenerating, and renewing, but only that the knowledge and certainty of such gifts are perceived in this sacrament.'[4]
Hence, according to Calvin, there is no essential difference
between the baptism of S. John and Christian baptism. In both
cases the baptism was for the remission of sins. In other words,
we are not by baptism incorporated by the regenerating power
of the Holy Spirit into the Body of Christ; but, having been
regenerated by the Holy Spirit through faith, baptism enables
each individual to perceive more clearly the fact of these benefits.
'Wherefore, there can be no doubt that all the godly may, during
the whole course of their lives, whenever they are vexed by the
consciousness of their sins, recall the remembrance of their
baptism, that they may thereby assure themselves of that sole
and perpetual ablution which we have in the Blood of Christ.'[5]

[1] Ibid., 4. 1. 1.   [2] Ibid., 4. 1. 3.   [3] Ibid., 4. 15. 1.   [4] Ibid., 4. 15. 2.   [5] Ibid., 4. 15. 4.

Such a doctrine as this naturally presents some difficulties for those who would defend infant baptism, for clearly infants cannot have the saving experience of which baptism is the pledge and sign. Nevertheless, Calvin defends it, relying in the main on the parallel between baptism and circumcision. Yet this analogy really holds only if baptism is understood as regeneration into the organic Body of Christ. This, however, as we have seen, Calvin will not accept. Consequently, he is driven to some rather lame arguments on behalf of paedobaptism. For example, he says there must have been infants in some of the families whose baptism is recorded in the New Testament. He argues also that this practice strengthens the faith of the parents (how the parish priest in England wishes that it did!) and makes the child 'an object of greater interest to the other lay members.'[1]

In like manner, Calvin's doctrine of justification by faith gives an individualistic twist to his doctrine of the Lord's Supper. 'We now, therefore, understand the end which this mystical benediction has in view—viz. to assure us that the Body of Christ was once sacrificed for us, so that we may now eat it, and, eating, *feel within ourselves* the efficacy of that one sacrifice—that His blood was once shed for us, so as to be our perpetual drink.'[2] Again: 'As we cannot at all doubt that it [*sc.* the Body of Christ] is bounded according to the invariable rule in the human body, and is contained in heaven, where it was once received, and will remain until it return to judgement, so we deem it altogether unlawful to bring it back under these corruptible elements, or to imagine it everywhere present. And, indeed, there is no need for this, in order to our partaking of it, since the Lord by His Spirit bestows upon us the blessing of being one with Him in soul, body, and spirit. The bond of that connection, therefore, is the Spirit of Christ, who unites us to Him, and is a kind of channel by which everything that Christ has and is is derived to us. For if we see that the sun, in sending forth its rays upon the earth, to generate, cherish, and invigorate its offspring, in a manner transfuses its substance into it, why should the radiance of the Spirit be less in conveying to us the communion of His flesh and blood? Wherefore the Scripture when it speaks of our participation in Christ, refers its whole efficacy to the Spirit.

[1] *Instit.* 4. 16. 9.   [2] Ibid., 4. 17. 1.

Instead of many, one passage will suffice. Paul in the Epistle to
the Romans (*Rom.* 8. 9–11) shows that the only way in which
Christ dwells in us is by His Spirit. By this, however, he does
not take away that communion of flesh and blood of which we
now speak, but shows that it is owing to the Spirit alone that
we possess Christ wholly and have Him abiding in us.'[1] Again:
'Moreover, since He has only one Body of which He makes us
all to be partakers, *we must necessarily by this participation all become
one body.* This unity is represented by the bread which is exhi-
bited in the sacrament. As it is composed of many grains mingled
together so that one cannot be distinguished from another, *so
ought our minds to be cordially united.*'[2]

The words which I have italicized in the foregoing passages
indicate that the working of the Holy Spirit is not otherwise that
individualistically conceived. This individualistic bias was, of
course, not the creation of Calvin. It was, in fact, an unfortunate
legacy of the Middle Ages, when the truly corporate nature of
the Holy Eucharist had degenerated into a service which was
carried out by the officiant, the members of the congregation as
individuals joining in as and when they felt inclined. The tragedy
of the situation is that the Reformers, in going back to the New
Testament, should have devoted so much energy to arguing
about the mystery of the Sacramental Presence instead of concen-
trating on the essentially corporate nature of the rite as indicated
by the New Testament. Had it not been for the individualistic
nature of the doctrine of justification by faith, this might have
happened. But if the essence of the Christian religion consists in
a state of mind which cannot be otherwise than intensely individual and personal, that which is organic and corporate must be
entirely secondary. Gregory Dix wrote: 'The real eucharistic
action is for Calvin individual and internal, not corporate. It is
one more example of the intractability of the scriptural sacraments to the protestant theory, and the impossibility of adapting
to "a religion of the spirit" and pure individualism the institutions
of a "religion of incarnation" which presupposes the organic
community of the renewed Israel.'[3]

The fact of the matter is that Calvin never really appreciated

[1] Ibid., 4. 17. 12.   [2] Ibid., 4. 17. 38.
[3] G. Dix: *The Shape of the Liturgy* (1944), p. 633.

the meaning of the saying of S. Paul: 'There is one Body and one Spirit' (*Eph.* 4. 4), and that the Church is the Spirit-bearing Body. This is clear from his commentary on this passage: 'He [S. Paul] proceeds to show more fully in how complete a manner Christians ought to be united. The union ought to be such that we shall form one body and one soul. These words denote the whole man. We ought to be united not in part only, but in body and soul.' But S. Paul says nothing of the kind. He is not talking about what ought to be but about what is. He says: 'There *is* one Body and one Spirit.' This is something which Calvin, for all his emphasis on corporateness, never grasped.[1] It is, perhaps, not without significance in this connection that for Calvin's thought the physical body is an embarrassment. He constantly speaks of the human body as an encumbrance. It is a prison[2] from which we seek deliverance. He talks about 'this weight of flesh'[3] and about being freed from this mortal frame.[4]

Richard Hooker (1553–1600)

We turn from Calvin to his most formidable rival among what we may call the Reformation theologians. Unfortunately, we do not, however, find that Hooker directly addressed himself to correct the errors in Calvin's pneumatology, though, of course, he does not fall into them. The fact is that Hooker pays surprisingly little attention to the doctrine of the Holy Spirit, and probably this constitutes the chief blemish in his great work, *The Ecclesiastical Polity*.

We notice first that Hooker has not clearly grasped the fact that the Holy Spirit works at two levels, the natural and the supernatural. Hence in his famous exposition of the doctrine of Natural Law in Book I of the *Ecclesiastical Polity* there is no direct reference to the Holy Spirit. Furthermore, when Hooker passes on in Book II to examine and refute the Puritan claim that the Holy Scriptures *alone* are the basis of right conduct, he fails to refer to the natural operations of the Holy Spirit. Instead of this he refers only to wisdom. He says: 'The bounds of wisdom are large, and within them much is contained. Wisdom was Adam's instructor in Paradise; wisdom endued the fathers who

[1] Cf. Calvin's sermon on Ephesians 4. 1–5.   [2] *Instit.* 4. 1. 1; 4. 15. 11; 4. 16. 19.
[3] Ibid., 3. 2. 3.   [4] Ibid., 3. 3. 10.

lived before the Law with the knowledge of holy things...
Whatsoever either men on earth or the angels of heaven do know,
it is as a drop of that unemptiable fountain of wisdom; which
wisdom hath diversely imparted her treasures unto the world.
As the ways are of sundry kinds, so her manner of teaching is
not merely one and the same—some things she openeth by the
sacred books of Scripture; some things by the glorious works of
Nature; some things she inspireth them from above by spiritual
influence; in some things she leadeth and traineth them only by
worldly experience and practice. We may not so in any one
special kind inspire her, that we disgrace her in any other; but
let all her ways be unto according their place and degree adored.'[1]

It is hardly too much to say that this passage cries aloud for the
identification of wisdom with the Holy Spirit working at the
natural level. Doubtless if Hooker had been questioned he might
have agreed that this was his meaning, though elsewhere he
equates wisdom with the *Logos*; but the fact that the identification is not made *explicitly* is of great significance. For nothing
less than such an identification can provide the right understanding
of the specifically *Christian* operations of the Holy Spirit.

In the third book, Hooker appears to identify human reason
with the Holy Spirit in contrast with what he calls 'the special
grace of the Holy Ghost.' The passage is as follows: 'Whereupon
if I believe the Gospel, yet is reason of singular use, for that it
confirmeth me in this my belief the more: if I do not as yet
believe, nevertheless to bring me to the number of believers
except reason did somewhat help, and were an instrument which
God doth use unto such purposes, what should it boot to dispute
with infidels or godless persons for their conversion and per-
suasion in that point?'

'... wherefore albeit the Spirit lead us into all truth and direct
us in all goodness, yet because these workings of the Spirit in us
are so privy and secret, we therefore stand on a plainer ground,
when we gather by reason from the quality of things believed
or done that the Spirit of God hath directed us in both, than if
we settle ourselves to believe or to do any certain particular
thing, as being moved thereto by the Spirit.'[2]   Unfortunately,

---

[1] *Eccles. Polity*, II, 1. 4.   [2] *Op. cit.*, Book III, 8. 14, 15.

however, Hooker breaks off his argument abruptly at this point and does not follow it up.

This failure to grasp the essential distinction between the natural and the supernatural operations of the Holy Spirit is reflected in the unsatisfactory treatment of the doctrine of the Holy Spirit and the Church. Following upon his famous exposition of the doctrine of the Incarnation, there follows a chapter on 'the Union of Christ with His Church.' Here we find no doctrine of the Holy Spirit in any way comparable to his Christology. Hooker accepts, indeed, a fully Trinitarian theology, but he nowhere shows any appreciation of the distinctively Christian doctrine of the *koinonia* of the Spirit, still less of the relation of that to the natural operations of the Holy Spirit. In fact, in his treatment of the subject he makes no reference to the account of the coming of the Spirit at Pentecost. He quotes S. Paul's first Trinitarian formula from 2 Corinthians 13. 10, but he equates this with the expression in 2 S. Peter 1. 4, 'The participation of divine nature,' and interprets it as meaning that 'the Church is in Christ as Eve was in Adam.'[1] As to the nature of this indwelling he throws little light. He goes on to say: 'Seeing therefore that Christ is in us as a quickening Spirit, the first degree of communion with Christ must needs consist in the participation of his Spirit'[2]—a statement which he supports not by a reference to the New Testament but to S. Cyprian.

There can be little doubt that Hooker is hindered here from developing the New Testament doctrine of the Spirit by the influences of mediaeval theology. He explicitly quotes with approval the unscriptural statement of Eusebius of Emesa: 'The Holy Ghost which descendeth with saving influence upon the waters of baptism doth then give that fullness which sufficeth for innocency, and afterwards exhibiteth in Confirmation an augmentation of further grace.'[3] This mediaeval doctrine of Confirmation as an *augmentum* is nowhere to be found in the New Testament. If Hooker had stood fast by the New Testament doctrine that the effect of water-baptism is regenerative—a doctrine which he explicitly defends—he would have been in a better position to appreciate the significance of the further doctrine to be found in the New Testament that the gift of the indwelling Spirit is to be

---

[1] *Op. cit.*, V, 56. 7.   [2] V, 56. 8.   [3] VI, 66. 4.

attached to the second part of the rite of initiation—viz. the laying on of hands and/or anointing.

This gift of the indwelling Spirit in the New Testament is closely associated with the doctrine of the *koinonia* of the Holy Spirit: indeed, the two ideas are really inseparable aspects of a single experience. It is *the* distinctively Christian form of experience. There is, as S. Paul says, One Body and One Spirit: the Church is the Spirit-bearing body, and the Christian life can be lived only in that holy fellowship. All distinctively Christian actions and graces must be understood in that context: for the Church is the Body of Christ manifesting His Spirit (i.e. the Holy Spirit as His interpreter and revealer) or, to change the figure of speech, the vine producing the fruit of the Spirit.

Unfortunately, there is little, if any, of this teaching to be found in Hooker's great work: and that was because of the *damnosa haereditas* of the age in which he lived. Whereas the Catholic Church traditionally stood for precisely this theology, in practice it was almost entirely ignored. That was the dreadful tragedy of the Reformation. And when the doctrine of the Holy Spirit was rediscovered, it was fatally perverted by the largely individualistic approach of the Reformers.

Hooker's failure to appreciate the New Testament doctrine of the *koinonia* of the Spirit comes out very clearly in the eighth book of his *Ecclesiastical Polity* when he has to deal with the legislative power of the Church and the place which the laity have in this. He gets into great difficulties because he fails to distinguish between the authority of the Church over its members, which springs from the authority of the Holy Spirit, and that authority of the civil state over its members which results from the acceptance of the principles of democracy.

Thus Hooker argues against the authority of the bishops and clergy to legislate for the laity in matters of doctrine on the ground that 'against all equity it were that a man should suffer detriment at the hands of men, for not observing that which he never did either by himself or by others, mediately or immediately, agree unto' (*E.P.* VIII, 6. 7). But he had previously found himself much embarrassed in maintaining this thesis in the face of the evidence of the Council of Jerusalem (*Acts* 15. 6 ff.). In dealing with this evidence he says: 'It will be therefore perhaps alleged that a part of the verity of the Christian religion is to hold the power of making ecclesiastical laws a thing appropriated unto the clergy in their synods; and that whatsoever is only by their voices agreed upon, it needeth no further approbation to give unto it the strength of law: as may plainly appear by the canons of that first most venerable assembly, where those things which the Apostles and James had concluded, were afterwards published and imposed upon the churches of the Gentiles abroad as laws, the records thereof remaining still in the book of God for a testimony, that the power of making ecclesiastical laws belongeth to the successors of the Apostles, the bishops and prelates of the Church of God.

'To this we answer, that the Council of Jerusalem is no argument for the power of the clergy alone to make laws. For, first there hath not been sithence any council of like authority to that in Jerusalem: secondly, the cause why that was of such authority came by a special accident: thirdly, the reason why other councils being not like unto that in nature, the clergy in them should have no power to make laws by themselves alone, is in truth so forcible, that except some commandment of God to the contrary can be showed it ought notwithstanding the aforesaid example to prevail.

'The decrees of the Council of Jerusalem were not as the canons of other ecclesiastical assemblies, human, but very divine ordinances for which cause the churches were far and wide commanded everywhere to see them kept, no otherwise than if Christ Himself had personally on earth been the author of them.

'The cause why that council was of so great authority and credit above all others which have been sithence, is expressed in those words of principal observation, "Unto the Holy Ghost and to us it hath seemed good": which form of speech, though other councils have likewise used, yet neither could they themselves mean, nor may we understand them, as if both were in equal sort assisted with the power of the Holy Ghost; but the latter had the favour of that general assistance and presence which Christ doth promise unto all His, according to the quality of their several estates and callings; the former, that grace of special, miraculous, rare, and extraordinary illumination, in relation whereunto the Apostle, comparing the Old Testament and the

New together, termeth the one a Testament of the letter, for that God delivered it written in stone, the other a Testament of the Spirit, because God imprinted it in the hearts and declared it by the tongues of His chosen Apostles through the power of the Holy Ghost, framing both their conceits and speeches in most divine and incomprehensible manner' (*E.P.* VIII, 6. 7).

All this is special pleading, and Hooker would not have been driven to it if he had not previously confused the issue by introducing the democratic principle into his argument when he wrote: 'The natural power civil all men confess to be the body of the commonwealth: the good or evil estate whereof dependeth so much upon the power of making laws, that in all well settled states, yea though they be monarchies, yet diligent care is evermore had that the commonwealth do not clean resign up herself and make over this power wholly into the hands of any one. . . . So we affirm that in like congruity the true original subject of power also to make Church laws is the whole entire body of that Church for which they are made. Equals cannot impose laws and statutes upon their equals' (*E.P.* VIII, 6. 1).[1]

The real solution of Hooker's problem is to be found in a right understanding of what the New Testament means by the *koinonia* of the Spirit, whereby the decrees of the Apostles and elders at the Council of Jerusalem found recognition by the whole body of the faithful. In those days the body of Christians was small and therefore it was possible for the process of recognition to be rapid. As time went on, and the body became large, this process of recognition took a long time; but the process was essentially the same. It was the expression of a silent consensus of opinion through the *koinonia* of the Spirit. It was in this way that the canon of the New Testament was determined. It was also in this way that (for example) the heresy of Arianism was overcome. The bishops put forward their judgement, and it was subsequently ratified by the silent consensus of the opinion of the faithful in the *koinonia*. But this is something entirely different from democracy. If at the time of Nicaea a referendum of the faithful had been taken, Arianism would undoubtedly have won the day.

---

[1] Hooker is here under the influence of Marsilius of Padua (cf. VII, 11. 8). Soon afterwards he quotes with approval the dictum: '*Quod omnes tangit ab omnibus tructari et approbari debet.*' He has wandered a long way from the New Testament.

This fatal confusion between the authority derived from the *koinonia* of the Spirit and the authority derived from the consent of the governed bedevils the whole of Hooker's argument concerning the place of the bishops and clergy in the formulation of doctrine and the ordering of worship. He admits that 'the most natural and religious course in making of laws is, that the matter of them be taken from the judgement of the wisest in those things which they are to concern. In matters of God, to set down a form of public prayer, a solemn confession of the articles of the Christian faith, rites and ceremonies meet for the exercise of religion; it were unnatural not to think the pastors and bishops of our souls a great deal more fit, than men of secular trades and callings' (*E.P.* VIII, 6. 11). But when he concludes, 'Howbeit, when all which the wisdom of all sorts can do is done for the devising of laws in the Church, it is the general consent of all that giveth them the form and vigour of laws" his appeal is not to the fact that the mind of the Spirit is ultimately expressed in and through the whole Body, but to the democratic principle that nobody is bound by a law to which he has not given his consent. If Hooker had rightly appreciated the doctrine of the *koinonia* of the Spirit, his argument would have been very different, and he would not have been driven to defend the authority of the Council of Jerusalem by appealing to a sub-Christian idea of inspiration which has more affinity with the teaching of Philo than with that of the New Testament.

George Fox (1624–1691)

At first sight it may seem unfitting to speak of such a man as George Fox in the same breath with such giant intellects as Calvin and Hooker; for he was, in fact, an entirely illiterate person, as the extraordinary spelling which occurs in his famous *Journal* clearly shows. Nevertheless, he was a genius, and he has undoubtedly had a considerable influence upon many persons, including a large number who are not Quakers or his professed followers. Moreover, in his *Journal*, whatever its theological and literary limitations, there are frequent references to the Holy Spirit. As we shall see, these references show all too clearly how completely muddled and confused was Fox's theology of the

Holy Spirit; and to this fact must be attributed not a little of the
confusion which still exists. It is, therefore, worth while to devote
a little space to the theology of the Holy Spirit, as it appears in
the *Journal*.

The following passage is characteristic and contains the whole
substance of Fox's teaching about the Holy Spirit: 'Soe I declared
Gods everlastinge truth and worde of life for about 3 houres to
ye people & all was quiett and brought ym all to ye spiritt of
God in ymselves by which they might knowe God & Christ and
ye Scriptures & to have heavenly fellowshippe in ye spiritt: &
showed ym howe every one yt comes Into ye worlde was
Inlightened by Christ ye life with which light they might see
there sinns & Christ there saviour whoe was come to save ym
from there sin with which light they might see there preist yt
dyed for ym there shepheard to feede ym & there great prophett
to open to ym; soe with ye light of Christ they might see Christ
always present with ym whoe was ye author of there faith & ye
finisher shereof.

'Soe opninge ye first covenant & sheweinge ym ye types & ye
substans & bringeinge ym to Christ ye 2d covenant & howe they
had beene in ye night of Apostacy since ye Apostles days; but
now ye everlastinge Gospell was preacht againe yt brought life
and immortality to light & ye day of ye Lords was come &
Christ was come to teach his people himselfe by his light Grace
power and spiritt And many 100s was convinct yt day.'[1]

We notice first in this passage a fundamental error which
occurs again and again in Fox's *Journal*, and that is the confusion
between the working of the Holy Spirit in the natural man, and
His supernatural operation through Christ. Fox constantly
appeals to the light which lighteneth every man—a light which
he often states to be the light of conscience—but he appears to
be totally unaware that there is any essential difference between
the natural light of conscience and the light which is brought to
Christians by the Paraclete. Indeed, he makes no reference to
the Comforter in the *Journal*, nor does he refer to the Pauline
distinction between the natural, or psychic man, and the spiritual
man. Although he talks a great deal about the Scriptures, and
does not hesitate to say roundly that the whole Church has been

[1] *Journal* (edited by N. Penney), Vol. I, p. 112.

in a state of apostasy from the days of the Apostles until he, George Fox, arrived on the scene, he makes no attempt to study the New Testament teaching as a whole. It is this failure which vitiates the whole of Fox's theology, if that is not too large a term to apply to his teaching. Although he rightly grasps the fact that the Church consists not of bricks and mortar but of people, nowhere in the *Journal* does he attempt to show in terms of the doctrine of the Holy Spirit how the members of the Church differ from those who have not been made members of Christ.

This leads to a second criticism, and that is Fox's apparent incapacity to appreciate the personality of the Holy Spirit. He constantly refers to Him as 'it' and 'which.' The following passage is typical in this respect: 'For with ye power of ye Lord God I was manifest & seekt to be manifest to ye spirit of God (in all) which they vext and quenched & grieved yt with it they might bee turned to God.'[1]

The truth of the matter is that George Fox has no doctrine of the Church. It is significant that in the doctrinal statement which he made for the Governor and the Assembly at Barbadoes in 1671 there is no mention of the Church.[2] Fox does, indeed, speak about the unity of the Spirit, but he appears to be entirely oblivious of the fact that his teaching about the Spirit necessarily splits that unity. Indeed, his entire ministry involved a negation of the unity of the Spirit in one Body; for he would take no part at all in the ordered worship of the Church. He was, therefore, schismatic to the core. It never seems to have entered Fox's head that he may have been mistaken.

It is hardly enough to say with Penney, the editor of Fox's *Journal*: 'His words must not be taken as an accurate intelligible symbol of his thought, but rather as flashes revealing imperfectly depths that the theologian may describe but cannot fathom.'[3] This is, I suppose, another way of saying that Fox was a prophet and exercised a prophetic ministry; but this by no means exonerates him if he makes theological statements which cannot stand the test of fair criticism. And this is what Fox frequently does. If he had been content to make prophetic affirmations which were luminously clear to him, it would have been different. He would

---

[1] *Journal*, Vol. I, p. 184. [2] Ibid., Vol. II, pp. 197 ff.
[3] Ibid., Introduction, p. xxv.

not then have been guilty of the theological ineptitude (not to say the arrogance) of asserting that there had been a complete spiritual apostasy from the Apostles' day until his own appearance.

What, then, was the positive truth after which Fox was feeling, and trying to express? Perhaps it cannot be more accurately expressed than by saying that it was the doctrine of 'praying in the Holy Spirit.'[1] This doctrine and belief came like a refreshing breeze on a sultry day. The Church in England had been grievously smitten by Puritan dissension and the formalism which is never far away from any religious community. Fierce disputes had taken place as to the merits and demerits of a fixed liturgical worship; and doubtless many of the clergy then, as in all ages, were not the spiritual men they might have been. The prophetic voice of Fox telling the people that they had the internal witness of the Holy Spirit and the inner light not unnaturally awakened a strong echo in the minds of many sincere believers and seekers after truth. Like all heretical or schismatical teachers, Fox was, in fact, drawing attention to an aspect of Christian doctrine which had been largely forgotten. If he had been content with doing that, as John Wesley and the Evangelicals at a later date were to do, all would have been well.[2] But the dangerously one-sided theology of the Holy Spirit which is all that can be ascribed to Fox issued in most harmful results, and undoubtedly did much to strengthen the schismatic temper even among those who were far from acknowledging themselves to be his disciples. If only this remarkable man of indomitable spirit had been gifted with something of the grace of humility—and, what goes with it, a sense of humour—how much more fruitful his teaching might have been in the Church.

[1] S. Jude 21. [2] See Appendix.

PART IV

THE PSYCHOLOGICAL INTERPRETATION

THE PSYCHOLOGICAL INTERPRETATION

I. THE NATURAL OPERATIONS OF THE HOLY SPIRIT

WE begin our consideration of this part of our subject by asking what light (if any) modern thought throws on the distinction between the natural and the supernatural operations of the Holy Spirit, which we have seen to be of such great importance for clear thinking on the doctrine. First of all, let us consider the bearing of what are technically known as *psi* phenomena. A *psi* phenomenon possesses two characteristics: (1) it is personal, in the sense that it cannot be attributed to any impersonal agency known to us; and (2) it is inexplicable in terms of orthodox science, because it appears to transcend or to deny the accepted limiting principles of science. In other words, *psi* phenomena are occurrences which 'are downright impossible if the standard text-book ideas about the world and men are correct.'[1]

Psi phenomena fall into two groups, known respectively as extra-sensory perception or ESP, and psychokinesis or PK. These are respectively defined as follows: ESP is 'a partial or complete correspondence (*a*) between the mental patterns of two persons A and B which is not to be accounted for by normal sense perception or by inferences drawn from sense perception or by chance coincidence *or* (*b*) between a mental pattern of a person A and an object or event in the physical world which is not to be accounted for by normal sense perception or by inferences drawn from sense perception or by chance coincidence. In neither (*a*) nor (*b*) need the correspondence be between contemporaneous patterns or between a mental pattern and a physical object which are contemporaneous.'[2] Experience (*a*) in the foregoing definition is what is generally known as telepathy; experience (*b*) is called clairvoyance.

PK, or psychokinesis, is 'an alleged direct influence exerted on a physical system by a person without the use of any known

---

[1] J. B. Rhine: *The New World of the Mind* (Faber & Faber 1954), p. 5.
[2] S. G. Soal and F. Bateman: *Modern Experiments in Telepathy* (Faber & Faber 1954), p. 359.

physical instruments or intermediating forms of physical energy. The term is usually employed to cover experiments in which certain persons are alleged to have influenced the fall of a die by means unknown to science.'[1]

Clearly, if the foregoing phenomena can be shown by experiment to be genuine, they open up many questions and afford a scientific disproof of the claims of materialistic science, which excludes all but physical forms of causation. It is obviously impossible to argue this large question fully here. What I propose to do instead is to state briefly how the problem stands in the minds of psychologists and others who have concerned themselves with it; and then, having done this, I shall proceed to examine its implications for the doctrine of the Holy Spirit, on the assumption that ESP and PK will one day be generally accepted by all students of science.

At the outset it must be frankly admitted that the majority of professional psychologists have not accepted the findings of those who claim to have scientifically established the existence of *psi* phenomena. Those who make this claim have relied upon an elaborate series of card-guessing experiments, in which (they hold) the percipient cannot conceivably have known which card was being turned up by the experimenter by any means other than clairvoyance, or have known which card was being thought of by the experimenter by any means other than telepathy. A detailed examination of these experiments is to be found in Soal and Bateman's book, already mentioned; the latter also deals with the experiments in dice-throwing. These issued in results far in excess of any which could reasonably be ascribed to chance.[2]

Why, then, it will be asked, have they not been accepted more widely? The answer is that the prejudice against their acceptance is so great that a questionnaire carried out in the United States of America in 1952 revealed the fact that as many as two-thirds of those questioned admitted that they had not even troubled to read a report of any of the experiments, much less study the evidence carefully for themselves. There is, unfortunately, nothing new in this reaction. Nearly every fresh scientific dis-

---

[1] Ibid.

[2] If the results of an experiment exceed the odds of 200 to 1 against chance, it is usually held by statisticians that they are 'significant'—i.e. they warrant careful investigation.

covery has met with a similar reception from the world of science. William James once remarked that the story of every new discovery or invention is the same. First it is ignored by men of science, then it is pooh-poohed, and, finally, being forced to accept it, they try to maintain that this, in fact, is what they have always believed.

If we may judge by past history, therefore, *psi* phenomena one day will receive universal scientific recognition. Any impartial person who will take the trouble to study the evidence carefully—a tedious and troublesome matter—will, I venture to think, find that it is compelling. At any rate, it is sufficiently strong to justify the attempt which I propose to make to ascertain what light, if any, it throws on the doctrine of the Holy Spirit.

We may take as our point of departure the statement in 1 Samuel 9. 9: 'He that is now called a prophet was beforetime called a seer.' This makes it clear that prophecy, as understood in the Old Testament, is rooted in clairvoyance; and the stories of Samuel, Elijah, and (especially) Elisha afford many instances of this fact. The story which gave rise to the historical note which has just been quoted provides as good an instance as any. It relates that Saul in looking for the asses which had disappeared went (as a matter of course, it would seem) first of all to the nearest prophet for information as to where they might be, because all prophets were believed to be clairvoyant. Moreover, the Old Testament makes it clear that this gift of clairvoyance is not confined to the prophets of Israel as, for example, the instance of Balaam shows (*Num.* 22–24). It was evidently a natural endowment, as we should say, but peculiar to certain individuals.

This is entirely in accordance with the evidence provided by the *psi* experiments. They were more successful with some individuals than with others. This is exactly what we should have expected from the various relevant Old Testament stories of prophecy. Only the few were gifted with this power of clairvoyance; at any rate, to any marked degree. But the Old Testament writers do not hesitate to suggest that this gift comes from the Spirit of God, i.e. from God who is Spirit. This fact is not affected if the individual concerned fails to recognize the source of this gift.

In the first instance, the gift may be used for all kinds of purposes, both good and bad. Some of the purposes for which Elisha (for example) used it were not above suspicion. But as time went on, prophecy became increasingly elevated, and the natural gift of clairvoyance in Isaiah became higher—i.e. ethically higher—than it had been in Elisha. Does this mean that we can say that in Isaiah (for instance) it has been raised to the level of the supernatural? In other words, does the Holy Spirit in speaking through Isaiah descend, so to say, *ab extra* upon him, or have we here nothing more than the consecration of a natural gift?

Making allowance for the fact that we must not be misled by the inevitable use of spatial metaphors in this connection, it seems to be legitimate to distinguish in the greater prophets between natural and supernatural levels of insight. At any rate, recent *psi* experiments render fully credible the claims made for prophecy as based on a natural endowment or gift. It is plainly not within the province of scientific psychology to distinguish between what is natural and what is supernatural. That must remain a theological judgement.

Turning to the consideration of PK, we may perhaps say that, just as ESP vindicates the ancient belief in clairvoyance and prophecy, so does PK, if genuine, vindicate the ancient belief in the power of spells and of blessing and cursing. In the former case, as we saw, the gift was associated with personal endowments. They might, indeed, run in a family, so that 'the son of a prophet' might be a periphrasis for a prophet—as, for example, was the case with Amos[1]—but for all that they remained personal endowments. The power of casting spells, or of blessing and cursing, however, was more commonly associated with the occupying of some official position. Thus, in the Old Testament the blessing of the priest was efficacious, or the blessing of the father of a family, because of their respective positions. The well-known story of Isaac's blessing of Jacob clearly illustrates how the whole procedure was understood. It was firmly believed that the course of events could be influenced in this way. There is, indeed, a big difference between this and PK in that the latter is concerned only with the present, whereas the casting of spells seems to have been

[1] See Amos 7. 14. 'Thus answered Amos and said to Amaziah, I was no prophet, neither was I a prophet's son.'

mainly concerned with the future. But we have to bear in mind that in the case of ESP the patterns involved do not have to be contemporaneous, so that the same might well be the case here; and, in any case, the principle that the course of physical events can be influenced by purely mental causes is vindicated.

Once again, the process involved appears to be a purely natural one. Nor is it necessarily to be associated with the Holy Spirit. On the other hand, when the action of blessing is involved, we do seem to be within the sphere of His working. Since the power to give a blessing is not regarded as being derived from the individual personality of the blesser but from the position which he occupies, we must regard this as an appeal to a divine and supernatural intervention. The Holy Spirit, in other words, is *invoked* to come down upon the recipient of the blessing in such a way as to influence favourably his future actions and the future course of events in which he is going to play a part.

But PK does much more than throw light on the casting of spells. Clearly it also has an important bearing upon the theory of intercessory and petitionary prayer. If PK is a genuine pheno-menon, we can begin to understand 'how prayer works.' But here, of course, we have definitely passed from the realm of the natural to the supernatural. In the case of spells, we have a phenomenon which is essentially magical in nature. I have tried to show elsewhere[1] that magic is a natural phenomenon, being nothing more than a species of hypnotic influence. As contrasted with this, prayer is dependent, not primarily upon the personality of the petitioner or intercessor, but upon the power of God. It is religious, not magical, in its nature.

The Teleological Nature of Unconscious Processes

We pass to the consideration of the question of the essential nature of unconscious mental processes. Freud thought of the unconscious mind of the individual as a kind of cage in which were imprisoned the thoughts and wishes which were unaccept-able to his conscious mind. In his view it was a closed system, to be likened, let us say, to the Dead Sea, which supports no life—an 'id' or 'it,' to use Freud's word; and if this is a true

[1] *Magic and Grace* (S.P.C.K. 1929).

account of the matter, it is obvious that we cannot look for the influence of the Holy Spirit in this quarter. Jung, on the other hand, regards the unconscious as being more like an ever-springing fountain of clear water; and more than that. For he thinks of it as perpetually leading towards what he calls an internal goal. In other words, it seeks an objective which cannot be accounted for by any interplay of external factors. If this is the case, we may expect to find in unconscious mental processes a good deal which is relevant to the understanding of the doctrine of the Holy Spirit. We must, however, hear the matter in Jung's own words:

'There is in the analytical process,' he writes, '. . . a development or an advance towards some goal or end the perplexing nature of which has engaged my attention for many years. Psychological treatment may come to an *end* at any stage in the development without one's always or necessarily having the feeling that a *goal* has been reached. . . . Experience shows . . . that there is a relatively large number of patients for whom the outward termination of work with the doctor is far from denoting the end of the analytical process. It is rather the case that the dialectical discussion with the unconscious still continues, and follows much the same course as it does with those who have not given up their work with the doctor. Occasionally one meets such patients again after several years and hears the often highly remarkable account of their subsequent development. It was experiences of this kind which first confirmed me in my belief that there is in the psyche a process that seeks its own goal independently of external factors.'[1]

Professor Jung speaks of this as 'seeking the solution to some ultimately insoluble problem,' but here, indeed, he naïvely begs the question. Whether it is insoluble or not is the point at issue. The Christian who sees in this purposive goal-seeking the working of the Holy Spirit in every man at the natural level will see no reason to draw this conclusion, which is certainly not forced upon us by the evidence. He will rather see in the fact that no final goal seems ever to be reached a confirmation of his belief that 'here we have no continuing city,' since man is made for God, and can finally rest in nothing less than the Beatific Vision.

It is, however, with the earlier stages of this process that we are

---

[1] C. G. Jung: *Psychology and Alchemy* (Kegan Paul 1953), pp. 4, 5.

concerned here; and what Jung has to say about these seems to agree tolerably well with what we find in the Scriptures. There is, for example, the belief widespread among Biblical and other ancient writers that dreams reveal this teleological process, and not merely in the sense that they indicate the operation of wishes which have been repressed by the individual, as Freud maintained. It is true that dreams were almost universally regarded in the ancient world as supernatural visitations, whereas the psychologist to-day thinks of them as purely natural phenomena. This point, however, is of secondary importance, especially as *some* dreams—to say the least—would be regarded by most Christians as more than merely natural phenomena. A good instance is provided in the Acts of the Apostles by the account of S. Peter's dream at Joppa (*Acts* 10. 9 ff.). This incident is one of great significance, and although we are still mainly concerned with the natural, as contrasted with the supernatural, working of the Holy Spirit, it will be best to deal with it now.

It will be remembered that at midday S. Peter went on to the roof of the house in which he was staying at Joppa in order to pray. He was hungry for his midday meal, and, while they were getting it ready, he dropped off to sleep—it is to be hoped not before he had finished his prayers. He then had the well-known dream in which he saw the sail let down from heaven containing all manner of animals and insects, and heard a voice telling him to eat them. He demurred: but the thing happened three times, so that, when he awoke, the dream set him thinking. It must have been vivid. Just at that moment the deputation of Gentiles from Cornelius arrived at his door. Streeter drew attention to the fact that the word translated 'sheet' (ὀθόνη) in our English versions means a mainsail, and this makes it highly probable that it was, in fact, a dream. The actual word used by S. Luke in the first account is ἔκστασις and this might refer to any experience which 'shakes' a person. In the following chapter, when S. Peter is describing what happened, he says that he saw in an *ekstasis* 'a vision' (ὅραμα) which might well be applied to a dream regarded as divinely inspired. We may with reason suppose, therefore, that we are here dealing with a dream and that just before S. Peter dropped off to sleep he had caught sight of a sailing boat or sailing boats which supplied the imagery of the dream, in what we now know to be quite a normal way.

'While Peter thought on the vision,' we are told, 'the Spirit said unto him, Behold, three men seek thee. But arise, and get thee down, and go with them, nothing doubting, for I have sent them' (*Acts* 10. 19, 20). This makes it quite clear that we are here dealing with more than an ordinary natural process. And this interpretation is clinched by what followed—viz. the descent of the Holy Spirit upon the little group of Gentiles. Nor must we overlook the way in which S. Peter himself interpreted the incident when he later gave an account of what happened to the Church at Jerusalem. He indicates how at the same moment as the Spirit came upon the group of Gentiles he 'remembered the word of the Lord, how that he said, John indeed baptized with water; but ye shall be baptized with the Holy Ghost' (*Acts* 11. 16). According to the Johannine account, it was precisely this work of recalling our Lord's teaching to the minds of the disciples which was to characterize the supernatural Christian dispensation of the Spirit. Wherever we may draw the line between the natural and the supernatural working of the Spirit, therefore, there can be no doubt that the giving of specifically Christian teaching must be regarded as falling within the latter category. What was happening in this incident, therefore, was that the Holy Spirit was bringing to bear on the mind of S. Peter the power of our Lord's teaching, which his Jewish prejudice was causing him to resist and to ignore. This teaching was given in a vivid symbolic form, as is always the case with unconscious thought. It was given also with great emphasis: the sheet, or sail, being let down three times, and apparently the whole episode being repeated three times. What was this if it was not a case of 'being warned of God in a dream' not to cling to his Jewish prejudices? S. Peter himself, at least, had no doubt that it was the work of the Holy Spirit, for we are informed that, while the Apostle was pondering upon the meaning of the dream, he became aware that the Holy Spirit was directly and unmistakably speaking to him and giving him guidance. Perhaps we may see here a subtle connection between the threefold action of the dream and the three men.

Returning to the consideration of the working of the Holy

Spirit at the natural level, the clearest evidence of this to-day is to be found in the consulting room of the psychiatrist. It is one of the ironies of history that we should owe the technique of modern psychotherapy to one who was a materialist. It is a commonplace to say that when a person is 'cured' by means of the psychiatrist's help, it is often extremely hard to say precisely how the satisfactory result has been reached; but it is significant that in this connection the saying of Ferenczi that 'it is the love of the physician which heals the patient' has become a classic utterance.

Let us try briefly to understand the situation. When a person enters the consulting room of the psychiatrist for treatment, it is because he has some problem or symptom of which he wishes to be rid. It may be homosexuality which is troubling him, or the threatened breakdown of his marriage, or some physical symptom, such as insomnia or a buzzing in his ears, or one of literally scores of possible symptoms. What he has to learn to accept in the course of the 'treatment' (which is, incidentally, not a satisfactory term to denote the patient-psychiatrist relationship) is that his real trouble is not the condition or symptom which has driven him to the psychiatrist. He has to learn that this is merely the mask or façade which conceals an unwillingness and an inability to accept his limitations and the limitations of others in such a way as to enable him to live harmoniously—still less creatively—with his fellow men.

The process by which he makes this discovery may be long and painful. He has to wrestle with the tendency to refuse to come to terms with the facts, i.e. 'psychological' facts. He has to learn that things are not always what they seem; that what he thought to be his moral integrity may be no more than a mask for his own pride and moral snobbery; that what he always supposed that he hated and shunned was, in fact, something alluring which has been enticing him unconsciously. In a word, he has to become fully conscious of all kinds of unrecognized tendencies in his own soul instead of turning to them a blind eye. All through, the psychiatrist is standing by, not to give him 'treatment' but to help him to self-knowledge, always scrupulously avoiding the bestowal of either praise or blame. This detached attitude of the psychiatrist will often provoke the patient almost to bursting point; and yet if the former allows himself to be drawn away from this detachment he will fail the patient.

The process which we have been describing usually takes place by means of an examination and assessment of the patient's dreams, and/or by 'free association.'[1] In this way are progressively revealed the hidden and frustrated tendencies, which have been responsible for the patient's breakdown. The psychiatrist does not direct or seek to control these tendencies. To do this would be fatal to the 'treatment.' He stands by in the same kind of way as the midwife stands by, in order to help to bring them to birth. What could more clearly show the working of the Holy Spirit?

God does not make men by mass production or deal with them so. As von Hügel used frequently to say, the spiritual director must never seek to dominate those committed to his care; for each individual soul has its own particular *attrait*. Even so, the psychiatrist, though he be a materialistic agnostic, is, in fact, whether he knows it or not, the instrument of the Holy Spirit. That is why, provided that he be a man of integrity who knows his job as a psychiatrist, a Christian may receive benefit at his hands. No Christian who has read much of psychiatric literature (and still more, who has ever done psychiatric work) with a relatively unbiased mind can fail to be impressed by the fact that the evidence from this field cries aloud for the recognition of the power and working of the Holy Spirit in every man—i.e. at what we have called the natural level.

This is true in two respects. The first is that the unconscious workings of the patient's mind are most obviously teleological and purposive, as we have seen; his only hope of healing resides in a frank understanding and acceptance of these workings. In the second place, the role of the psychiatrist, even if he be an avowed materialist *per impossibile*, is nothing if not a revelation of the way in which the Holy Spirit works. A quotation from a modern psychiatrist will make this clear. 'Even where the technical approach which the therapist favours requires a completely

---

[1] I.e. the patient tells out the ideas which come spontaneously into his mind until he is told to stop. Experience shows that some patients find it very difficult to allow thoughts passively to express themselves. They come from the unconscious.

detached and impersonal attitude, he nevertheless intends his patient to trust him—for instance, with manifestations of rage and fear, of aggression and sexuality, with which the analysand could not trust himself. The analyst is from the first committed to accept his patient as he is—to accept and not to reject him. If the patient finds that the worst he can do to the analyst does not break the relationship; that he is not despised on account of fears and desires which made him despise himself; that throughout this bitter process of self-revelation the analyst's attitude to him remains unaltered—it is hardly surprising if this is interpreted as love. The doctor has taken the weight of all the pent-up aggression, the guilt-ridden sexuality, the wretched inferiority, and has not turned against the patient for these misdeeds. The eternal principles of substitution, coinherence, and exchange which give life to all truly human relationships are at work here too.'[1]

2. THE SUPERNATURAL OPERATIONS OF THE HOLY SPIRIT

Our inquiry has clearly brought us to the edge of the field of the supernatural operations of the Holy Spirit. Jung tells us that his experience has taught him the truth which Christianity has consistently proclaimed, viz. that man is made for God. There is, as he puts it, a correspondence between the human soul and God. This correspondence he calls 'the archetype of the God-image.' It is not clear, however, what Jung means by the archetypes, which play such a prominent part in his teaching. In one place, he says that 'the archetype is an explanatory equivalent of the Platonic Form or Idea.'[2] This would mean that they are objective Realities; and yet elsewhere he repudiates any claim to be dealing with objective facts or truths, which he says are not the concern of the psychologist. He writes: 'The word type is, as we know, derived from τύπος 'blow' or 'imprint'; thus an archetype presupposes an imprinter. Psychology as the science of the soul has to confine itself to its subject and guard against overstepping its proper boundaries by metaphysical assertions.'[3]

Nor is it at all clear how Jung understands the soul or personality. Clearly it cannot be identified with the conscious mind;

[1] *Christian Essays in Psychiatry*, ed. Philip Mairet (S.C.M. Press 1956), p. 145.
[2] *Von den Wurzeln des Bewusstseins*, p. 5.
[3] *Psychology and Alchemy*, p. 14. (E.T.)

but on the other hand neither can it be said to be the conscious plus the unconscious, for (Jung says) in so far as anything is unconscious it is not definable. He argues: 'Since we cannot possibly know the limitations of something unknown to us, it follows that we are not in a position to set any limits to the self. It would be wildly arbitrary and therefore unscientific to restrict the self to the limits of the individual psyche, quite apart from the fundamental fact that we have not the least knowledge of these limits, seeing that they also lie in the unconscious. We may be able to indicate the limits of consciousness, but the unconscious is simply the unknown psyche and for that very reason illimitable because undefinable. Such being the case, we should not be in the least surprised if the empirical manifestations of unconscious contents bear all the marks of something illimitable, something not determined by space and time. The quality is numinous and therefore alarming, above all to a cautious mind that knows the value of precisely delimited concepts. One is glad not to be a philosopher or theologian and so not bound to meet such numina professionally.'[1]

In all this we see the limitations of a purely psychological approach to the problems with which Jung is dealing. It is clear that for their solution we have to pass to the field of theology and metaphysics. But though psychology cannot solve these problems, it may be able to point the way to their solution, and it would seem that this is what Jung's teaching does.

In the first place, it is clear that what Jung has said about the numinous quality of the unconscious harmonizes exactly with what Christians have always believed about the guidance of the Holy Spirit. They are in no doubt that He directs them, both individually and collectively, by subconscious inspirations and movings; and while it may be true that we cannot draw a clear line between the self and the not-self in the field of the unconscious, Christians are in no doubt that such a line could be drawn if we had the requisite knowledge.

In the second place, there are certain ambiguities in what Jung says not only about the archetypes but also about the relation of the conscious to the unconscious; but it will, I think, be found that these can be removed if what he has to say is interpreted by

[1] *Psychology and Alchemy*, p. 174.

the doctrine of the Holy Spirit. Thus, according to Jung, it is of great importance that a projected image should not be allowed to replace what he calls the 'unconscious content' of the mind. When this happens, he says that the latter ceases to exert the formative influence on consciousness which it normally possesses. Jung cites as an example of this the way in which the *imitatio Christi* motive in Christianity easily degenerates into a merely formal and external worship which does not touch the depths of the soul. 'The divine Mediator stands outside as an image, while man remains fragmentary and untouched in the deepest parts of him.' He says: 'It may easily happen, therefore, that a Christian who believes in all the sacred figures is still undeveloped and unchanged in his inmost soul because he has "all God outside" and does not experience Him in the soul. His deciding motives, his ruling interests and impulses do not spring from the sphere of Christianity, but from the unconscious and undeveloped psyche, which is as pagan and archaic as ever. Not the individual alone but the sum total of individual lives in a people proves the truth of this contention. The great events of the world as planned and executed by man do not breathe the spirit of Christianity but rather of unadorned paganism. These things originate in a psychic condition that has remained archaic and has not been even remotely touched by Christianity. The Church assumes, not altogether without reason, that the fact of *semel credidisse* (having once believed) leaves certain traces behind it, but of these traces nothing is to be seen in the march of events. Christian civilization has proved hollow to a terrifying degree: it is all veneer, but the inner man has remained untouched and therefore unchanged. His soul is out of key with his external beliefs; in his soul the Christian has not kept pace with external developments. Yes, everything is to be found outside—in image and in word, in Church and Bible—but never inside. Inside reign the archaic gods, supreme as of old: that is to say, the inner correspondence with the outer god-image is undeveloped for lack of psychological culture and therefore has got stuck in heathenism. Christian education has done all that is humanly possible, but it has not been enough. Too few people have experienced the divine image as the innermost possession of their own souls. Christ only meets them from without, never from within the soul; that is why dark paganism still reigns there.'[1]

All that Jung says here becomes far more intelligible if the movings of the unconscious at the deepest level are the movings of the Holy Spirit. Certainly Jung has shown ample reason to believe that Freud's doctrine of a closed unconscious is not in accord with the facts. It is the more unfortunate that Jung himself apparently fails to see the bearing of the Christian doctrine of the Holy Spirit on what he has written.

Jung's teaching, as it stands, is, in fact, self-contradictory. On the one hand, the unconscious is said to be archaic and static and unchanged; and yet, on the other hand, we are told that the unconscious should be allowed to exert its beneficial, formative influence on the conscious mind. It is difficult to see how this can happen if the unconscious is regarded as merely 'archaic' and static. But if, on the contrary, it is continually open to the gracious influence of the Holy Spirit, and—in the case of Christian believers—to the supernatural power of the Holy Spirit taking of 'the things of Christ' and making them known, we can see why it is that it can have that beneficial formative influence; also why it is harmful when that influence is replaced by adherence to a projected image. When this is the case, it is an unconscious in which not only the supernatural operations of the Holy Spirit but even His operations at the natural level have been frustrated by human sin. In other words, it is human sin which seeks to keep the unconscious at the level of the archaic. But it is hard for the psychologists to acknowledge this, for 'sin' is a theological word.

This reveals only too clearly the unsatisfactoriness of trying to understand all the problems of human personality solely at the psychological level. If there be a God and if man has interposed a barrier between himself and his Creator by wilful disobedience, seeking to order his own affairs in his own way, it is obvious that they must result in disharmony, putting his nature out of joint; and no attempt to understand the situation can succeed if it fails to take account of this.

However we may interpret them, the facts show clearly enough that man—every man—*is* in some degree emotionally frustrated.

[1] *Psychology and Alchemy*, pp. 11, 12.

From the first he finds co-operation with others difficult because of his fatal egocentric bias which makes him a prey to fears which cannot be ascribed solely to the failures of society.

Freud has come nearer than any other great psychologist to a recognition of this in drawing attention to the phenomenon known as Narcissism, whereby libido or psychic interest and energy is concentrated upon the ego instead of going out towards others. Unfortunately, however, Freud for no good reason assumed that Narcissism is the natural and primary condition of the ego instead of being a perversion. Freud does not argue for this but rather assumes it.[1] If, however, we decline to make that assumption, but, on the contrary, assume that the natural state of the ego is one in which the psychic energy flows outwards freely towards co-operation with society and that Narcissism is the perversion, we have here a statement in psychological terms of what theologians call original sin. We can then see that, in terms of the doctrine of the Holy Spirit, this means that His natural influence is frustrated by human selfishness, but that man, in his true nature, is not self-centred but altruistic.

The limitations of the purely psychological approach to the problems with which we have been thinking are clearly shown in another way, viz. by the place assigned by the psychiatrist to 'love' in the re-education of the psyche, which is the essence of psychiatric 'treatment.' Attention has already been drawn to the widespread acceptance by psychiatrists of the celebrated dictum of Ferenczi that it is the love of the physician that heals the patient. But this is no ordinary affection. It is technically known as 'the transference.'

The transference is the name given in psychiatry to the emotional relationship between the patient and the doctor which emerges with the gradual release of the repressed emotions which have given rise to the symptoms which have driven the patient to seek the help of the psychiatrist. Naturally enough, when liberated they attach themselves to the nearest person at hand, viz. the psychiatrist. Whatever particular emotions they are, in the last resort they are the result of a lack of the right kind of love in the past, especially the earliest years of the patient's life.

[1] He advocates the strange theory that the intra-uterine condition of the foetus is Narcissistic.

All the time, however, there have been other forces in his life which have been seeking to assist him to keep his balance; just as there have been similar forces which have operated in his physical organism leading to the maintenance and restoration of bodily health. Owing, however, not only to an inherited evil bias but also to the various ways in which his fellow human beings have failed him psychologically in the past, he has been unable to keep on an even psychological keel. Consequently, he needs the aid of the mental physician even as he needs the aid of the ordinary physician for bodily ailments. The former, however, is no more able than the latter to 'cure the patient.' All he can do is to co-operate with the healing forces of nature; and this is but another name for the Holy Spirit. Just as the ordinary physician treats symptoms, so does the psychiatrist. But instead of doing so by the use of drugs, he does it by understanding and the right kind of sympathy. It is precisely the giving of the right kind of sympathy which comprises the skill of the psychiatrist. It is a task which involves the greatest delicacy and skill. To give the patient the wrong kind of sympathy will only root him more deeply in his illness. What, therefore, in fact, the psychiatrist is doing in the course of 'treatment' is to give the Holy Spirit the chance which He did not get when the patient was a child.

It must be clearly understood that all mental illness arises from the loss, or at least the serious diminution, of the capacity to 'love,' in the Christian sense of that much misunderstood word. That is to say, the psychoneurotic patient is always in varying degrees enmeshed in his own egocentricity. The different 'schools' of psychiatry—Freudian, Adlerian, Jungian, and the rest—attempt to account for and to assess this bias in different ways; but, though not agreed as to its nature, they are at one in acknowledging its existence. And, in effect, the 'love' must be the same for all schools: for it consists in being pulled out of that egocentricity in one way or another.

The Christian theologian, therefore, is bound to prick up his ears when he hears this, and call to mind that in the tradition of Christian theology the Holy Spirit is regularly associated with 'love'—*agapē*, *philia*, *caritas*, or *amor*. He is bound to ask if Ferenczi's famous dictum does not need to be amended to—'It is the love of the Spirit which heals the patient.' Certainly the doctrine of the Holy Spirit throws not a little light on the patient-psychiatrist relationship.

First, it explains why the course of any analysis, or prolonged psychiatric treatment, cannot be mapped out in advance, even by the most experienced psychiatrist. To quote from a modern exponent of the art: 'A wind begins to blow—softly, and, at the start, almost imperceptibly; but (and this is the point) "where it listeth." The *direction* of the new current within the man's life is not fixed in advance.'[1] The patient has, in one way or another, become cut off from the instinctual roots of his being—in a word, from the beneficent leadings of the Holy Spirit, the Life-Giver. Healing comes when the Holy Spirit is allowed by the patient to have free course within him. The task of the analyst is to assist the patient in allowing this to happen—not *de haut en bas* (that leads to deadlock), but by coming alongside his patient and sharing, so far as may be, his experience with him. There is only one word which can do justice to this attitude and that is the word *agapē*; and it is precisely this which is the most distinctive 'fruit' of the Spirit, according to the New Testament. It is the work of the Paraclete. The word 'Paraclete'—literally, 'one called alongside to help'—here takes on a new meaning; for this is an exact description of the good psychiatrist, of whatever school.

Secondly, the doctrine of the Holy Spirit reveals how it is that the psychiatrist so frequently cannot explain exactly how the patient has reached a state of recovery. For it has not come about from what he, the psychiatrist, has done, but rather by virtue of the operation of the Spirit who has blown 'where he listed.' In this respect, after all, mental healing is similar to physical healing. *Mutatis mutandis* the words of the surgeon, who wrote outside his operating theatre, 'I dressed the wound, God healed it,' apply to psychological healing.

In the light of what has just been said, it can be seen that the commonly expressed fear that if a Christian consults a non-Christian psychiatrist he is endangering his faith is not really well founded.[2] For if the psychiatrist knows his job, and is a man of integrity (as most psychiatrists are), he is, in fact, as we have

---

[1] *Christian Essays in Psychiatry*, p. 141.
[2] Possibly an exception should be made if the psychiatrist is a 'hard-boiled' Freudian.

already seen, the instrument of the Holy Spirit, whether he recognizes it or not, even as an agnostic surgeon is.[1] If he were to try to impose his unbelief upon a patient, he would be a bad psychiatrist, even as a Christian psychiatrist would be if he did the same *mutatis mutandis* to an agnostic patient. If the patient is a Christian believer, naturally he will make his 'treatment' a matter of prayer, and thus will assist the working of the Holy Spirit, whether the psychiatrist be a believer or an unbeliever. It may well be the case, of course, that the patient's religion is partly based, perhaps largely based, upon neurotic foundations. These will have to be removed in the course of treatment, but however painful the process, in the end, if the Holy Spirit is given free course, all will be well. The patient will emerge from his fiery trial, not as though some strange thing had happened unto him, but able to see the gracious influence of the Holy Spirit, working through it all.

Thirdly, and most important of all, the doctrine of the Holy Spirit makes it clear why deprivation of love is at the root of all psychological mal-development. Thus a modern psychiatrist writes: 'The child who is given love can afford to love, to give what he has received, so that he grows up to be sociable, affectionate, and a good companion in marriage. *Given love*, the child identifies himself with those he loves, and so gets from them a stable ideal by which he can co-ordinate, direct, and harmonize his energies for the purposes of life. So he becomes healthy-minded, strong in will, and determined in character. If, however, the child is *deprived of love* or, what is the same thing from the child's point of view, *feels* himself deprived of love, he reacts abnormally to life.'[2]

We must be careful not to misunderstand this situation. S. John wrote truly: 'We love, because He first loved us.' There is in every child that is born into the world the capacity to give love—which capacity we can now see is the work of the Holy Spirit working at the natural level. Unfortunately, every child is also born into a sinful environment—'Born in [i.e. into] sin,' as the Prayer Book says in a much misunderstood phrase. That is to say, it is born into a society of persons who by sin have perverted their capacity to love; in other words, persons who are not un-

---

[1] This does not mean that psychiatric treatment is necessarily beneficial any more than a surgical operation is necessarily beneficial. In each case more harm than good may result. But this is not the fault of the Holy Spirit.

[2] J. A. Hadfield: *Psychology and Mental Health* (Allen & Unwin 1950), p. 124.

selfish but selfish. This means that the small child is not encouraged to express its capacity to love, but tends to be driven in upon itself. But this is not all. Every child appears also to inherit a fatal egocentric bias, which has no parallel in the lower animals. However we may seek to explain this tendency (not very happily named 'original sin' by theologians) its existence cannot be questioned by any impartial observer. This means that the work of the Holy Spirit at the natural level is deeply frustrated in us all.

Some theologians have followed Calvin and taught that the child's nature is utterly corrupt. This would mean that the Spirit is quenched in every man, but it is not in accordance with the facts. The Spirit still works in every man and is continually leading him to desire to love. Unfortunately, only too often those who have charge of the young child fail to recognize this. Instead they are apt to regard him exclusively from their own point of view; and thus the child feels rebuffed and deprived. The situation is well illustrated by the case of the pretty little boy with a mass of curls, shown off by his mother on the sea front every morning. The child said: 'I am bored to death by my beautiful curls; I wish that my mother would love *me*.'[1] The situation is somewhat paradoxical. We show our love to a child most really by allowing the child to be itself and to give what it has to give. Or, to put the matter differently, there is such a thing as pseudo-love which can only smother the love which the child might give. Thus we see that what is happening in the case of the neurotic is that the neglect of the gracious influence of the Holy Spirit by the parents and elders may lead to the deep frustration of His working in the child. It is, however, the work of 'grace'—the grace of Christ—to set free that love, as the individual learns to respond to the love of the Spirit, who is the Spirit of Christ. Thus, as S. Augustine said, does God crown His own gifts.

The Significance of Rebirth and Water-baptism

Before the end of the first century Christian baptism was associated with rebirth. This at least is clear from S. John 3. 5,

---

[1] Quoted by J. A. Hadfield, *op. cit.*, p. 127.

where the true text undoubtedly reads: 'Except a man be born of water and the Spirit, he cannot enter into the kingdom of God.' It is, however, difficult to suppose that our Lord should have said this at the beginning of His ministry (as the Fourth Gospel suggests), for at that time 'baptism' could refer only to John's baptism, which was not regarded as being baptism of the Spirit. Christian baptism was not yet instituted. But this does not alter the fact that very shortly after Pentecost, Christian baptism *was* regarded as involving rebirth. There are various references to this in the Pauline epistles, where the writer thinks that the submerging of the baptized person in the water symbolizes a burial with Christ and the rising up from the water, a resurrection with Christ, this last being nothing less than a rebirth (*Rom.* 6. 4; *Col.* 2. 12; *Titus* 3. 5). And this doctrine of baptismal regeneration gained universal acceptance in the Church.

Whether or not this belief was due to the explicit teaching of our Lord given to His disciples before His Ascension or not, it is impossible to say with certainty. But if there is any truth in our contentions about the way in which the Holy Spirit teaches and guides men in the unconscious depths of the mind, there is no doubt at all that this was the teaching of the Holy Spirit to the Church. For in unconscious thought water is a regular symbol for rebirth, as every psychiatrist knows. Let us follow out this symbolism.

In the first instance, water in both dreams and folklore symbolizes the unconscious mind. So Jung writes: 'Water is the most frequent symbol for the Unconscious.'[1] He quotes in this connection a letter in which the writer wrote to inquire why he constantly dreamed about water: 'Almost every time I dream it is about water: either I am having a bath, or the water-closet is overflowing, or a pipe is bursting, or my home has drifted down to the water edge, or I see an acquaintance about to sink in the water, or I am trying to get out of the water, or I am having a bath and the tub is about to overflow, etc.'

It is because of this symbolism that the widespread tradition arose that the earth floats—not in space, as we think of it, but in the waters of 'the great deep' (*Gen.* 7. 11). The same idea underlies the references to the waters under the earth (*Exod.* 20. 4;

[1] C. G. Jung: *Von den Wurzeln des Bewusstseins*, p. 24.

Ps. 24. 2). The meaning of this is not obscure to the psychologist. It is an allusion to the mystery of the creation—a secret hid in the depths of the unconscious. *Omnia exeunt in mysterium.* And it is significant that this mystery is directly associated with the Spirit of God in Genesis 1. 1. The early Christian fathers took this as a reference to the Holy Spirit; and we may do the same, provided that we recognize that this meaning (involving as it does a Trinitarian theology) could not have been present to the mind of the Old Testament writer. It is, however, legitimate for us to see here a reference to Him who is 'the Giver of life.'

Water, however, in dreams symbolizes not only the unconscious but also rebirth. This is intelligible enough, for the foetus before birth lies in the uterine waters. Moreover, it is more than likely that this association is the root of the idea that water symbolizes the unconscious; for in the womb the babe lies unconscious in the waters. However this may be, this conception throws much light on the doctrine of baptismal regeneration, as clearly taught in S. John 3. 5. For water, in fact, as Jung points out, equals unconscious spirit. This, as he shows, is a commonplace in the thought of the alchemists.[1] Consequently, the association of water-Spirit baptism with rebirth by the early Church is easily understood.

This brings us to a third meaning associated with water-baptism, viz. the remission of sins. It is part of the universal Christian tradition that there is 'one baptism for the remission of sins.' Here the connection of thought is obvious enough; for that water brings cleansing needs not to be argued.

There is one more symbolical meaning for water, and that is death. This idea is enshrined in Bunyan's immortal tale: 'Now I further saw that betwixt them and the gate was a river, but there was no bridge to go over; the river was very deep. At the sight, therefore, of this river, the pilgrims were much stounded; but the men that went with them said, "You must go through, or you cannot come at the gate." . . . They then addressed themselves to the water, and entering, Christian began to sink, and crying out to his good friend Hopeful, he said, "I sink in deep waters, the billows go over my head; all his waves go over me." . . . And with that a great darkness and horror fell upon

[1] Ibid., pp. 259 ff.

Christian, so that he could not see before him; also here he in great measure lost his senses.' It may seem surprising that water should symbolize both birth and death; for the two ideas appear to be contradictory. The contradiction is resolved, however, when it is remembered that when water symbolizes death in dreams it also symbolizes the entrance to a new life, as it does in the *Pilgrim's Progress*. Indeed, the association between water and the unconscious *ipso facto* carries with it the thought of death, for when a person is unconscious he resembles one who is dead. Consequently, this idea found most natural expression in the symbolism of baptism by immersion. As we have seen, it would appear to be from this symbolic action that the whole idea of rebirth arose. And it is easy to see why the early Church should have associated its rite of initiation with the passage of the Hebrews through the Red Sea, which was tantamount to a burial under the waters and a safe emerging from them.

If there is any truth in the foregoing contentions, we should expect to find this same idea of rebirth in Jewish proselyte baptism which also involved total immersion. And this is what we do find in the Talmud. 'A newly converted proselyte is like a newborn child' (*Yebamoth* 48b).[1] But we do not find in Jewish literature, so far as I am aware, that this change was actually *effected* by baptism, which was understood merely to effect cleansing (cf. *Ezek.* 36. 25). It may well be that it was the influence of what later came to be called 'confirmation' upon the preceding rite of water-baptism, i.e. the conferring of the gift of the indwelling Spirit, which led to the distinctively Christian doctrine of rebirth by the Holy Spirit, as implied in the conversation between our Lord and Nicodemus.

Whether or not our Lord explicitly taught the doctrine of baptismal regeneration by the Holy Spirit, therefore, it was at any rate implicit in the whole conception of death/resurrection which Christ underwent and which He taught His disciples that they must undergo. We must become as little children. We must deny ourselves and lose our souls in order to find them. So He taught. If, therefore, Christian baptism, with its death/

[1] Admittedly this is much later in date than the New Testament and admittedly there is no clear reference to proselyte baptism in the earlier Mishnah; but it is psychologically impossible to suppose that the Jews should have borrowed the idea from the hated Christians.

resurrection symbolism, and all the unconscious associations which, as we have seen, went with it, was interpreted as effecting the rebirth of the baptized, this can be regarded as neither surprising nor illegitimate. We should not fail to observe, however, that this symbolism is entirely distinct from that of sealing and anointing, the source of which must be sought elsewhere. Thus our findings about the relation of water-baptism and confirmation and their respective effects are confirmed.

Identification

The question of rebirth brings us to the consideration of the 'mechanism' which Freud called identification. This corresponds to imitation in the lower animals, but it is far more powerful. This is primarily an unconscious process and leads the child—the very small child—to adopt within itself the moods, ideas, and standards of those upon whom it is dependent; this means in practice its parents. The infant not only imitates them, but identifies itself with them. It will often say: 'I am mummy doing the cooking' or 'I am daddy digging the garden.' This identification is possible because the very small child has not yet learned to distinguish between the world of imagination and the 'real' world—between the world of fancy and the world of fact.

Thus arises within the child's mind what Freud called the super-ego. Freud held that this super-ego constitutes what we call conscience. In this he was mistaken; for if this were the case, conscience would be based simply upon fear of punishment, since the super-ego according to Freud represents nothing more than the fear of social disapproval, manifested by the earliest representatives of society (in the infant's experience), i.e. the parents. But conscience is not based upon the fear of punishment; for it involves the highly significant little word 'ought.' This embodies something quite distinct from the fear of social disapproval. That is why it is recognized that it is right to obey conscience at the cost of opposition to the whole world: and that is why this has often happened in the history of mankind. 'We must obey God rather than men.' In other words, conscience is the reflection in the mind of man of the law of the Creator; and apart altogether from the thought of punishment it has power and authority. This is the power and authority which is manifested by love and not by fear of punishment. But having said this, it *is* true that the contents of conscience are derived from the super-ego. Conscience itself is the *form* of obligation. Its content in any given case is derived through personal experience. That is why conscience has to be educated.

Thus it comes to pass that the mechanism of identification may lead to most unhappy results if the persons with whom the child identifies himself are not the right kind of parents. If, for example, the child's father is tyrannical in nature, the child's super-ego will be a tyrant; and for the rest of its life (it may be) he will carry round this tyrant super-ego with it. Thus the words of the Old Testament about visiting the sins of the fathers upon the children find a new and terrible meaning. To such a conscience the child is bound to produce a morbid reaction. If he is of strong fibre, he may turn into a rebel and be for the rest of his life 'agin the government'; or, worse still, he may become the victim of what is called an obsessional neurosis.

From what has been said it should be clear that somebody greater than any ordinary human being is required to bring unity and harmony to the self through the super-ego. In a word, the individual requires a saviour. He is in need of salvation. And it is just here that a right doctrine of the Holy Spirit can throw much light on the situation. We have seen that He works teleologically deep down in the mind of the ordinary person. Freud was greatly mistaken in holding that the human being is fundamentally impersonal—or, to use his expression, an 'id' or 'it,' fundamentally non-moral, and a closed system. The evidence indicates, on the contrary, that the individual, himself essentially personal, is subject to personal, teleological influences in his unconscious mind, which we may equate with the influences of the Holy Spirit, the Life-giver. Unfortunately, this influence has been hindered and frustrated by the sin, i.e. the wilful disobedience to conscience,[1] of countless generations of human beings. Consequently, the newborn child begins life, not only among sinful human beings all around him, but also carrying deep in his unconscious the imprint of past sinful generations which tends to frustrate the gracious influence of the Holy Spirit within him. His nature is not utterly corrupt, however, as Calvin

[1] For we must obey even an erring conscience.

taught. Fortunately, God has not left Himself without witness in any human soul. But the witness is confused by the echo of human sin down the ages.

Thus man needs a saviour, i.e. somebody outside him who will give him a fresh start. This, as Christians believe, he received through the Incarnation of the Son of God, who after His earthly life, passion, and Resurrection, powerfully renewed the Holy Spirit, who was working all the time within man, by providing the latter with a perfect object of identification—the Perfect Man. In other words, added to the natural working of the Holy Spirit there is a supernatural working through Christ, who may be said to dwell in the heart (i.e. the mind) of the believer.

This is the teaching of S. Paul. He says, 'I live; yet not I, but Christ liveth in me' (*Phil.* 1. 21)—language which has given rise to what has been called Pauline 'Christ mysticism,' perhaps not a very happy title. But by whatever name we call it, it is clearly nothing else than a case of identification—identification not with father or mother, but with Christ. This, as we have seen, is always more than a consciously willed process. It is primarily unconscious, the work of the Holy Spirit, and of what theologians call 'grace' which is generally recognized now to be largely unconscious.

In the Johannine writings this same teaching is even more fully expressed. The believer dwells in Christ even as the branch abides in the vine (*S. John* 15. 4). Because Christ lives he shall live also (*S. John* 14. 19). The Holy Spirit will come to the believer as 'another Paraclete' taking the place of the visible Saviour (*S. John* 14. 14). But this 'identification' is most fully worked out in the great discourse on the Bread of Life: 'He that eateth My flesh and drinketh My blood abideth in Me, and I in him. As the living Father sent Me, and I live because of the Father; so he that eateth Me, he also shall live because of Me.' And then, significantly, it continues later on: 'It is the Spirit that quickeneth; the flesh profiteth nothing'—surely 'Spirit' here must be written not with a small 's' as in our English versions, but with a capital (*S. John* 6. 56, 57, 63). Thus our Lord is represented as taking charge of the super-ego. 'We have the mind of Christ,' writes S. Paul (1 *Cor.* 2. 16). This means much more than that we have access to Christ's teaching. It means, in fact, identification with Christ.

This process of identification with our Lord, however, is by no means free from dangers. There are two which are common. The first is that instead of Christ taking over the super-ego, this may be done by a Christ-substitute. This is likely to be the person's father or mother dressed in our Lord's robes. When this happens, the super-ego will be a menace to the individual, because it will be an unworthy object of identification. Perhaps it will be too harsh and rigid, and will in consequence produce the evil results of ultra-authoritarianism. On the other hand, it may be too easygoing. In this case, God will be conceived as what C. S. Lewis has called 'our grandfather in heaven.' *Corruptio optimi pessima.* There are few things in the world worse than a debased and unworthy religion, and it is by no means an uncommon phenomenon.

The second danger which besets the process of identification with Christ consists in the subtle danger of identifying ourselves with perfection. Thus the neurotic (i.e. psychologically maladjusted person) may adopt the Christ-identification in phantasy as a substitute for a genuine taking of Christ into his mind. The psychotic (i.e. insane person) may be fully persuaded that he is himself the Messiah returned again to earth. The surest safeguard against both these dangers is a clear recognition of the person and work of the Holy Spirit in the Church. For it is His work to bring about the growth of the Body. That is the key consideration, the recognition of the need for growth and development. The apostle who said 'I live; yet not I, but Christ liveth in me' also said later on in the same epistle: 'Brethren, I count not myself to have apprehended' (*Phil.* 3. 13). All this is finely set forth in the Epistle to the Ephesians: 'Till we all attain unto the unity of the faith, and of the knowledge of the Son of God, unto a fullgrown man, unto the measure of the stature of the fullness of Christ: that we ... may grow up in all things into Him, which is the head, even Christ. ... That ye be renewed in the spirit of your mind. ... And grieve not the Holy Spirit of God, in whom ye were sealed unto the day of redemption.'

However we may choose to interpret the allusion to 'sealing' by the Holy Spirit, we do not stretch the meaning of this passage if we see in it a clear recognition of the fact that the Christian, while being identified with Christ (i.e. in the Body of Christ), needs to grow in likeness to Him, and that this happens under the influence and power of the Holy Spirit. But this demands of him a humble, teachable attitude, one which is constantly on the watch for the gracious admonitions and leadings of the indwelling Spirit of Christ, who will teach us in all kinds of ways (and not least in our dreams interpreted symbolically) the path of holiness and likeness to our Redeemer. We might even dare to bring this out by transposing the phrases in S. Paul's famous declaration: 'It is not I that live and yet it is I,' the weak and wavering disciple, in the fellowship of the Church.

The Power of the Spirit

There is a tendency in popular thinking to suppose that the energy of human nature is limited in quantity in the same kind of way as the amount of water stored in a tank is limited by the storage capacity of the tank. But the evidence contradicts this. It makes it clear that every human being is apparently in touch with almost unlimited resources. We are all familiar with the fact that, in an emergency, we become possessed of powers which we should have supposed were quite beyond us. McDougall cites the case of a boy who being chased by a wild animal leaped over a fence which he could never afterwards clear even when he had grown to manhood and had gone into hard athletic training.

At such times we seem to be able to draw upon hidden sources of strength. It used to be customary for psychologists to speak of these innate sources of strength as 'instincts' and to say that, when any of the fundamental human instincts are stimulated these powers are called forth. Thus it is (for example) that under the influence of the parental 'instinct' the animal is able to fight furiously and even successfully against one which is physically bigger and stronger. In like manner the human mother seems to be possessed of almost superhuman strength in caring for a large family of small children or in nursing a sick child. Again, when the instinct of self-preservation is stimulated and the emotion of fear aroused, greatly increased powers seem to be available to the individual animal or human being, as in the case of the boy in the instance just mentioned.

In more recent psychological thinking, however, the practice of speaking of these innate drives or tendencies as human instincts has fallen into disfavour, on the ground that the word 'instinct' is better confined to denote the more specialized activities of the sub-human species than the innate tendencies of man. There is no need here to embark on a discussion of this vexed question of terminology. It is sufficient for our purpose to recognize the undeniable fact that man inherits certain innate tendencies to action and unlearned reactions apart altogether from what experience teaches him. Beneath the level of fully conscious behaviour, in other words, there lie deep springs of action; and once these are tapped man has access to immense resources of physical energy.

It is fair to claim that these so-called springs of action are simply another name for the power of the Holy Spirit, the Life-giver. When they are touched in the ordinary course of experience they may be regarded as a manifestation of the power of the Holy Spirit working at the natural level. A good instance of this is afforded by what the old physicians used to call the *vis medicatrix naturae*, by which alone medicine and surgery alike can be of any avail at all. When, however, this power is called forth by what is believed to be a supernatural stimulus, we have an instance of the operation of the Holy Spirit at the supernatural level.

Sometimes, indeed, it may be difficult to decide in which category an act falls: as, for example, when we read of the abnormal power which was available to Samson: 'Behold, a young lion roared against him. And the spirit of the Lord came mightily upon him, and he rent him as he would have rent a kid' (*Judges* 14. 5, 6: in R.V. there is no capital 's' for spirit). This doubt, however, does not affect the argument that incidents of this kind seem to show that man is in touch at the subconscious level with enormous hidden resources of power and that it is more satisfactory to regard them as in some sense external to him—as is done by the Biblical writer—than to think of them as simply part and parcel of his own personality.

We must, however, observe that these hidden resources

provide something more than physical power or strength. They also make available that mental power which is commonly known as inspiration. Here, at least, it is usually taken for granted that man is in touch with resources which are external to himself. To speak of a self-inspired person would involve a contradiction in terms.

Inspiration has often been understood in a somewhat mechanical fashion, as if the inspired person were almost an impersonal tool in the hands of God. Such is the standpoint of what is commonly called verbal inspiration, a belief which existed among the Jews and which has too much influenced Christian thought. But in point of fact the most significant feature of this idea of inspiration is that the latter reaches man via the subconscious levels of the mind—a conception which has been endorsed by scientific psychology. Philo's teaching affords a good example of this. He illustrates what he has to say by reference to the passage in Genesis 15 about Abraham's sacrifice of the heifer, the she-goat, the ram, the turtle-dove, and the pigeon. We read: 'And when the sun was going down, a deep sleep fell upon Abram; and lo, an horror of great darkness fell upon him.' Philo interprets the going down of the sun as the sinking of the human reason and the rising up in its place of the divine reason. 'So the setting of the reason and the darkness that gathers round it generates an ecstasy and heaven-caused madness.' It is easy to see that what Philo is trying to say is that inspiration does not come through the volition of the conscious mind, but through the operation of forces from below (cf. the metaphor of rising and setting), i.e. from what we should call the unconscious and that this inspiration is at its highest when the prophet speaks in ecstasy, consciousness being in abeyance.

In the New Testament, however, this teaching is corrected by S. Paul in his well-known dictum, 'the spirits of the prophets are subject to the prophets' (1 Cor. 14. 32), and in what he has to say about speaking with tongues. But there can be no doubt that the phenomenon of ecstasy did much to convince men of the reality of the divine afflatus. Herein lies its real value, and not in the claim that the human consciousness, as such, has no part to play in inspiration. S. Paul, in the passage from which we have just quoted, is most emphatic in his insistence upon the fact that ultimately the deliverances of subconscious inspiration must be conformable to sound reason. He says: 'Howbeit in the church I had rather speak five words with my understanding, that I might instruct others also, than ten thousand words in a tongue' (1 Cor. 14. 19).

It is, indeed, when we come to consider what we may call works of inspiration in the light of the critical reason that inspiration looks most impressive. We seem to see here the operation of a greater mind guiding the thoughts and actions of those whom we deem to be inspired. These thoughts and actions may in no sense have occurred as a result of the suspension of conscious reasoning or thought; it is rather the case that they seem to manifest what the collect calls 'a right judgement in all things.' Our experience teaches us clearly that we frequently have to pass judgement or to decide upon courses of action with a good deal of uncertainty. But if we seek to rely upon the guidance of God, while using our own powers of judgement to the best of our ability and taking the best advice available to us, it not seldom happens that on looking back we are able to see that we have been led to take what is clearly the right course. This may happen in relation to both greater or lesser matters.

Sanday cites some impressive examples of this in his Bampton Lectures. He points out how certain events in Biblical history which from the point of view of a contemporary must have seemed of very little importance indeed—mere accidents as we might suppose—have proved in the sequel to have been of outstanding and even decisive importance. He cites the decision of the Hebrew prophets to commit their discourses to writing, which at that time was undoubtedly far less effective than living speech. Yet it was the first step which led to the establishment of Holy Scripture. Sanday quotes as another example of the same kind of thing S. Paul's calling 'one of his companions to his side to dictate to him what perhaps at first was meant to be a few lines of encouragement to one of the Churches which he had lately founded or recently visited in person. The letters by degrees got longer and include teaching as well as encouragement, until they grow into elaborate treatises like the Epistle to the Romans. When the Christian remembers that the letters so written form the greater part of his *corpus* of authoritative theology, he cannot help seeing a marked disproportion between the circumstances of its origin and the magnitude of the result. Here, too, he may see the directing mind at work with objects within its ken which no one saw of those more immediately concerned, neither writer nor scribes nor readers, nor (we may add) for some time to come those who were entrusted with the custody of the letters when written.'[1]

Examples like these help us to see the question of the operation of the Holy Spirit in what is called inspiration in rather a different light. We recognize that the essence of inspiration is not the over-riding of the critical reason but the keeping open of the lines of communication between the human *psyche* and the Holy Spirit. We learn from the evidence of psychology that these lines of communication lie in the unconscious, but, of course, no science can pronounce as to the moral or metaphysical value of anything which reaches us in this way. To the psychologist, *qua* psycho-logist, the ravings of a maniac patient and the utterances of a saint alike may come through the same mechanism—if the phrase may be allowed. But to separate the precious from the vile is the work, not of science, but of philosophy and religion. It may indeed be true that there are certain types of individual in whom these lines of communication are broader than is the case with the average persons. This is suggested by the well-known saying that genius and madness are closely allied. But this does not alter the fact that the Holy Spirit may, according to His own purposes, make special use of persons with this kind of make-up. Indeed, what else should we expect Him to do?

We must, therefore, claim that modern science lends no support to the standpoint of the followers of Karl Barth and the neo-Calvinists who seek to deny reason in order to magnify the reality of inspiration.

It is, indeed, a strange fact that Calvin nowhere in his *Institutes* comes to grips with the question of what constitutes inspiration. Indeed, he seldom uses the word 'inspiration' in connection with Holy Scripture. He claims, indeed, that it is inspired, but the only criterion by which he asserts that this can be established is the *testimonium Spiritus* in the heart of the elect. To such as have this, Calvin argues, the supreme authority of Scripture is self-

[1] W. Sanday: *Inspiration*, pp. 403, 404.

evident. 'Enlightened by Him [the Holy Spirit] we no longer believe, either on our own judgement or that of others, that the Scriptures are from God; but, in a way superior to human judgement, feel perfectly assured—as much so as if we beheld the divine image impressed on it—that it came to us, by the instrumentality of men from the very mouth of God. . . . Because we feel a divine energy living and breathing in it—an energy by which we are drawn and animated to obey it, willingly indeed and knowingly, but more vividly and effectually than could be done by human will or knowledge.'[1]

This antithesis between faith and reason which is implicit in Calvin and only too explicit in some of his modern disciples is one for which no support can be derived from psychological science. Indeed, it seems to arise out of a very real confusion of thought whereby the fact that inspiration reaches us by the route of the unconscious is taken to imply that it is in no wise subject to the mature judgement of conscious reason. Once this conclusion is drawn, the door is opened to all the cranks and fanatics and a chaos of competing sects—and this is what has happened under the influence of unbridled protestantism. Yet we find in the New Testament itself very plain warnings against anything of the kind. Thus we find S. Paul writing to the Corinthians warning them against this: 'What is it then, brethren? When ye come together, each one hath a psalm, hath a teaching, hath a revelation, hath a tongue, hath an interpretation' (1 Cor. 14. 26). Chaos lies that way, but Calvin and his followers appear to be incapable of recognizing the fact.

The subconscious or unconscious origin of 'inspired' thought, however, can be understood in quite a different manner, as we must now endeavour to show. The essential and primary fact which is fully established by psychological research is that the contents of the conscious mind enter it from two directions. On the one hand, they enter it through fully conscious sensation and perception. On the other, they enter it from below the threshold of consciousness. The human organism is not a purely passive receptacle into which the contents of conscious experience are poured or—to use the different and more familiar figure—a *tabula rasa* on which conscious experience writes. It is rather the

[1] Calvin: *Institutes* I, chapter 7.

meeting-place of a two-way traffic: some comes from the conscious sphere and some from the unconscious. And it is from the latter that come all 'our bright ideas.' Baron von Hügel used to say that he had no more conception how he got his bright ideas than how he got a bar of chocolate after inserting a coin into a machine. In each case they just came.

Experience makes it quite clear that we cannot control these thoughts (and desires) which come from the unconscious.

> We cannot kindle when we would
> The fire that in the heart resides.

But there seems to be no sufficient reason to deny the statement in the Prayer Book that it is God 'from whom all holy desires, all good counsels' proceed. It may be that these desires and counsels come when the conscious mind is in abeyance—as in ecstasy, or in ordinary sleep, when they are given in the form of what we call dreams. But it may equally happen that they come when we are fully awake. In either case, however, they must stand before the bar of the judgement of conscious reason.

The point that I am trying to make is this. It is true that inspiration comes *via* the unconscious and that this is the normal channel of the Holy Spirit's illumination and power. But it is sheer bad logic to argue that because this is the case on the one hand, we have to accept *every* thought and desire which comes spontaneously into the mind as coming from Him; or on the other, that because an inspiration reaches us when our consciousness is in abeyance it is any more (or less) likely to be a divine inspiration. In either case, we have the duty to weigh the deliverances which come to us through the unconscious.

Such is clearly New Testament teaching. There we are taught to believe that we are in touch not only with the Holy Spirit but also with evil spirits. Thus S. John wrote: 'Beloved, believe not every spirit, but prove the spirits, whether they are of God: because many false prophets are gone out into the world.' He then proceeds to provide a test: 'Hereby know ye the Spirit of God: every spirit which confesseth that Jesus Christ is come in the flesh is of God: and every spirit which confesseth not Jesus is not of God' (1 S. *John* 4. 1–3).

Unfortunately, this criterion does not take us very far, for the writer is apparently concerned only with what we should call 'spiritualistic phenomena' when it is possible to question directly the alleged source of inspiration. Plainly we need something quite different when we are concerned with those thoughts and leadings which come to us in the ordinary day-to-day experience of life. It is here that the mind of the Church as expressed in the general tradition of the Church is of paramount importance. For it provides a safeguard against the eccentricities of sheer individualism. This at the Reformation led to the position satirically expressed in the lines describing the contemporary attitude to the Bible:

> Hic liber est in quo quaerit sua dogmata quisque;
> Invenit et pariter dogmata quisque sua.

> This is the book in which every one seeks his own opinions:
> And in like manner every one finds his own opinions.

In the last three or four hundred years we have suffered with a vengeance from the effects of this state of mind, which has broken the unity of Christendom into fragments. We are beginning to see that there is no sufficient justification for this exaltation of private judgement. Certainly no support can be found for it in the findings of psychological science. The fact is that this Bibliolatry is nothing more than the worship of the individual in disguise. What is, in fact, enthroned is not the Bible but *my* interpretation of the Bible. But what ground is there in psychology or theology for this idolatry of private judgement? The answer must be: none at all.

The truth is that this extreme individualism which has led to the riot of Protestant sectarianism is a reaction against the extreme authoritarianism of Papalism. In the Middle Ages, the ordinary man or woman was not encouraged to read the Scriptures; indeed, until the invention of printing there were no Scriptures readily at hand for him to read. And if there had been, for the most part he would have been too illiterate to do so. The tragedy was that when the time came when the man in the street could read for himself, he did not always find what he had been taught by the priest endorsed by the Scriptures. Consequently, the Protestant individualistic reaction set in. And this, fortified by the deplorable interference of 'Princes' in the proper affairs of the Church, provided little opportunity for the true *koinonia* of the Spirit—which alone can hold the balance between extreme authoritarianism and extreme individualism—to manifest itself.

There is, however, another aspect of the question of inspiration which we have to settle. The individual not only needs a wise guide and authority to enable him to know what he ought to *believe*; he also needs a guide to help him to know what he ought to *do*—in a word, how to regulate his conduct in the day-to-day affairs of life. At the Reformation, the guidance which he had been content to accept on the authority of the Church was challenged by the new doctrine of the autocracy of the individual conscience. This led to a chaos in moral practice hardly less than the chaos of rising sectarianism. This may be illustrated in various ways. One of the best is to think of the ban on 'usury' which obtained in the Middle Ages and the doctrine of 'the just price.' The Reformers were in no way anxious to abolish those controls; but they opened sluice gates which allowed them in a short time to be submerged by the flood tide of developing commerce and the increasing complexity of business life. And ever since then there has been nothing which could be described as an agreed Christian moral standard among those who have jettisoned the traditional moral guidance of the Church.

Here, again, the tragedy has been that the fragmentation of Christendom, arising by way of reaction from the over-authoritarianism of Papalism, has prevented the Holy Spirit from making clear to the whole Christian people what His mind and will on those practical issues are: or, at any rate, has made it increasingly difficult for the devout Christian to obtain the moral guidance which he needs in the day-to-day affairs of his life.

The Supernatural Community and the Fellowship of the Spirit

We saw in Part II of this book that the coming of the Holy Spirit at Pentecost resulted in the creation of the *koinonia* or fellowship. We read: 'And they continued steadfastly in the Apostles' teaching and fellowship [literally, in the fellowship], in the breaking of bread and the prayers' (*Acts* 2. 42). This fellowship is called 'the Church' (or *ekklesia*) in Acts 5. 11 (in 2. 47 the best text does not read 'the Church'), and this term soon established itself as the official name for the *koinonia*. This was to be expected, for it was the term used to describe the Jewish Church ('the church in the wilderness' of Stephen's speech (*Acts* 7. 38)) from which the Christian Church sprang. In some ways this application of the old term to the new fellowship was unfortunate; for it made it only too easy to forget that the Church of Christ is a new creation, fundamentally different in kind from the Jewish Church. That this was our Lord's teaching is clear from S. Mark 2. 21, 22, where He speaks of the mistake of trying to sew a piece of unshrunken cloth on to an old garment, or to put new wine into old wineskins.[1]

The newness of the Christian Church as contrasted with the Jewish Church rests upon the fact that the latter was based upon natural kinship. In this it resembled all primitive communities. Yahweh was the God of the Hebrews, and He never ceased to be regarded by the Jews as a national deity, right up to the time of Christ. And it is the same to this day. The movement known as Zionism bears witness to this. Judaism has always been religio-political, i.e. a Church-State. So we have re-established (with most unhappy political results) the modern state of Israel.

The Christian *ekklesia* or *koinonia*, on the other hand, was in no sense based on natural kinship or nationality. From the first moment of its creation it transcended all national limits. That is the essential meaning of the account of the descent of the Holy Spirit, described in Acts 2. In the words of an epigram,[2] which deserves to become famous, it is based not upon race but upon grace. The Council of Jerusalem, described in Acts 15, clearly saw this, and refused to regard it as merely a new Jewish sect. It was the great achievement of S. Paul to drive this nail home. He wrote to the Galatians: 'There can be neither Jew nor Gentile, there can be neither bond nor free.' Even the inequality of the sexes (hitherto taken for granted) is overcome, for he goes on: 'There can be no male or female: for ye are all one man in Christ Jesus' (3. 28). Again in Colossians 3. 11 he writes: 'There cannot be Gentile and Jew, circumcision and uncircumcision; barbarian, Scythian, bondman, freeman: but Christ is all, and in all.'

All this is clearly shown by the use of the words 'brother' and

---

[1] Even if this saying is 'a community product' the point holds.
[2] Coined by Stanley Jones in *The Christ of the Indian Road*.

'brotherly love' (*philadelphia*) in the New Testament. The former is the term used as the equivalent of 'a Christian' in modern usage. We never meet the latter expression in the Bible; it is always 'a brother.' Consequently, the virtue of 'brotherly love' was characteristic of the Church. In his earliest epistle, therefore, we find S. Paul writing: 'Concerning brotherly love you have no need that any one should write unto you; for you yourselves are taught of God to love one another' (1 *Thess.* 4. 9). This is the essential fruit of the *koinonia*, and came to be known as *agapē*, a virtually new term to denote a new quality of life, which by the time that one of the latest books in the New Testament was written had become so distinctive as to supersede the earlier term (2 *S. Pet.* 1. 7).

We have now to see how this universal (or catholic) community provides the only completely satisfactory environment for the growth and development of human nature, and to consider what light is thrown upon it by modern psychological and philosophical studies. We must first observe that human nature consists of a complex of opposing tendencies which have been named in different ways. They can be described as tendencies to aggression and to submission, or to self-assertion (or self-realization) and to self-sacrifice, or to independence and to sociability. Whatever terms are used, however, these opposing tendencies are obvious enough, and they are the cause of the difficulty which human beings experience when they try to live together. There is more than a grain of truth in Schopenhauer's simile of the freezing porcupines, which crowd together in order to keep themselves from freezing to death, but which separate as soon as they feel one another's quills sticking into them. Thus they move backwards and forwards uneasily, trying to find the mean distance which makes life most tolerable.

According to the New Testament, the Christian *koinonia* provides the solution of this practical problem. The self-asserting and the self-denying tendencies in men find their harmony in those who by personal devotion to Christ are united to one another, for they live to a centre outside themselves which draws them all together as if by a magnet. Another way of putting this is to say that the Christian community or Church is the guardian of freedom; for freedom can be fully experienced only in so far as these two tendencies are balanced. We can put this in yet another way by saying that freedom is the capacity to do as we please. Clearly, therefore, universal freedom must mean that everybody is free to do as he pleases. But this cannot happen until each individual is pleased to do that which is compatible with the good pleasure of every other individual. This obviously necessitates the existence of a common mind which will harmonize their varying claims and interests. And this is exactly what S. Paul claims for the members of the Church when he says: 'We have the mind of Christ' (1 *Cor.* 2. 16)—a mind made known to us by the Holy Spirit.

This question of the common or group mind is one which has been strangely neglected by psychologists. Indeed, its investigation has scarcely, if at all, been advanced since McDougall wrote his book, *The Group Mind*, thirty years ago. Not all his contentions have stood the test of time, but there can be no doubt that he was right in carefully distinguishing between the mentality of the 'crowd' or temporary aggregation of persons, and the stabilized 'group' as he called it. He indicated five factors, which in his opinion are constitutive of the latter, and we cannot do better than consider these with reference to the Christian *koinonia*.

1. The first factor is continuity. If a group is to maintain itself with any degree of permanence there must be some means of establishing its continuity. This is absolutely essential. In the case of the state one of the most effective methods of doing this is kingship. A long series of crowned sovereigns is obviously a powerful instrument for maintaining the continuity of the group. In the case of the Christian Church this continuity was maintained for the first fifteen centuries by the Apostolic Ministry and succession. Even if those who maintain that in some places this succession was maintained at first by presbyter-bishops rather than monarchical bishops are right, this does not essentially affect the position. There seems to have been a regular succession of ordainers as of ordained, and there is no early evidence at all for the new theory of the ministry invented by Calvin and Luther at the Reformation, whereby the ministry was appointed and *ordained* democratically, ordination not being restricted to any one class of ministers. The result of this breach of continuity has been the creation of almost innumerable sects and the fragmentation

of the outward and visible unity of the *koinonia*. At the present day it is becoming recognized increasingly that the restoration of visible unity is dependent upon the re-establishment of this broken continuity. Hence the various reunion schemes all take this for granted, and are all 'episcopal' in nature.

It is most important here to distinguish carefully between Papalism and the maintenance of the threefold Apostolic Ministry. Protestant writers persist in making a comparison between the two in connection with the doctrine of the Holy Spirit. Papalism by making the Pope the Vicar of Christ does crowd out from His rightful place the Holy Spirit, who, in fact, is the only Vicar of Christ. 'I will pray the Father, and He will give you another Paraclete, who shall abide with you for ever, even the Spirit of truth' (*S. John* 14. 16). And in the Papal system it is fair to say that 'the gospel is identified exclusively with what is spoken *by* the Church, and there is no provision whereby the gospel may be spoken *to* the Church.' Professor Hendry, the author of this quotation, goes on to say: 'The heart of the Protestant position is found in its conception of what may be called the abiding polarity between Christ and the Church. . . . Take any authoritative statement of the Roman theory, such as that given by Leo XIII in the encyclical *Satis cognitum*, and reduce its pontifical magniloquence to the simple style of the New Testament: it makes Christ appear to have said to His disciples: "When I go away, you will take My place." This, of course, is very different from what He did say. He promised that His place would be taken by the Spirit (*allos Parakletos*), toward whom the Twelve would stand in the same relation of polarity as they had stood to Christ during His bodily presence with them.'[1] That is well and truly said; but it is a sheer *non sequitur* to say that the acknowledgement of the necessity of the Threefold Ministry to preserve the continuity of the Church is 'to place it on the side of Christ over against the Church' and to assign to it 'the exclusive function of re-presenting the gospel to the Church.'[2] The Holy Spirit remains the Lord of the Church; but even He cannot preserve its organic unity if the backbone of the Church—its ordered historical ministry—is broken. Are not the innumerable divisions of

[1] G. S. Hendry: *op. cit.*, pp. 63 and 65. [2] Ibid., p. 61.

fissiparous Protestantism enough to convince any fair-minded student of this?

2. The next factor is what McDougall called 'a sentiment for the group.' He was using this word 'sentiment' in a somewhat technical way to indicate a settled and permanent emotional regard for an object. How important this is can be seen by the value attached to national flags, which serve to focus this senti-ment of nationality and, in so doing, to increase and strengthen it. The same purpose is fulfilled by national anthems. In the early days of the Church it is clear that this sentiment for the group—the 'brotherhood,' as it was called—was very strong. And this state of affairs was still further strengthened by the Persecutions. It was not in irony that those outside the Church exclaimed: 'See how these Christians love one another.' As we should say, there was in the Church a most powerful *esprit de corps*. And this phrase is here most significant. In this context it refers not merely to the subjective feeling which animated the members of the Church in relation to one another and the brotherhood as a whole, but to the objective presence of the Holy Spirit, who was the power uniting them closely together. Unfortunately, how-ever, when the Persecutions finally ceased, this sentiment was weakened by two changes which occurred. The first was the building of 'churches' in the form of bricks and mortar. This led in course of time to the transferring of the word 'church' from human beings to buildings, and it became easy for people to forget that the Church is, and must always consist of, human beings. Thus the idea of 'going to church' subtly undermined in people's minds the idea of 'being the church.' This disastrous consequence was made easier by the rise of the practice of infant baptism and the flooding into the church of crowds of purely nominal 'brothers.' In fact, the word 'brother' in like manner became debased, especially in its plural form, 'brethren,' until it had become an almost meaningless ecclesiastical term, as it commonly is to-day.

Thus the sentiment for the Church was greatly weakened. Moreover, owing to the fact that human beings are always liable to be influenced far more by the concrete than by the abstract, the sentiment which at one time was directed towards the Church in the true sense of the term became deflected towards particular buildings to which individuals severally became attached. In a disastrous sense they too often could not see the wood for the trees; and this state of affairs is still only too common.

3. The third factor is rivalry. A group sentiment is increased and strengthened by rivalry with another group, or other groups. A familiar instance is provided by the friendly rivalry between the universities of Oxford and Cambridge. We are also only too familiar with the operation of this factor in the national sphere. Here, again, in the case of the Christian Church, there has been a change for the worse. In New Testament times, the rivalry was between the Church and the world, understood as being 'society organized apart from God.' This is very clear in the late Johannine writings in the New Testament. Consequently, one of the most deadly of all sins, in the eyes of early Christians, was the sin of apostasy—of desertion. In the eyes of the author of the Epistle to the Hebrews it was clear that this could never find forgiveness (*Heb.* 6. 4–6). How far have we moved from this standpoint in modern times in this country, when multitudes appear to hold that you can be a good Christian without having anything to do with your fellow Christians *as such*. This is often expressed in the well-known saying that you can be a good Christian without going to church. The rivalry between the Church and the world has gone for the simple reason that the line of demarcation between the two has also disappeared.

It is true that the factor of rivalry does still operate in the Church, but it operates in entirely the wrong way. The primitive rivalry between the Church and the world has degenerated into rivalry between different Christian 'denominations,' as they are called: a horrid word for a horrid thing! The brethren are easily betrayed into greater concern for being a good 'Catholic' or a good 'Protestant' than for being good Christians, let alone good members of the universal brotherhood of Christ. Indeed, the fatal divisions of Christendom have almost obscured the existence of this brotherhood from the eyes of multitudes of Christians.

4. The fourth factor is the possession by the group of a body of tradition. In the case of a nation this is embodied in its age-long laws and customs. The same applies to the Christian Church. In a comparatively short time the Christian baptismal creed came into existence, and this provided a vital nucleus of

tradition which held the Church together. Indeed, from the very earliest days there existed a core of tradition which even an early convert like S. Paul received, as he tells us, when he first became a Christian. Writing to the Corinthians he says: 'For I delivered unto you [he employs the word regularly used for the handing on of tradition] that which I also received [he uses the word regularly employed for the receiving of tradition], how that Christ died for our sins according to the Scriptures; and that He was buried; and that He was raised the third day according to the Scriptures' (1 *Cor.* 15. 3, 4). The Scriptures here mentioned are, of course, the Old Testament Scriptures; but to these were gradually added the Scriptures of the New Testament—the Apostolic Scriptures. And in the fourth century there was added to the early baptismal creed—known to us as the Apostles' Creed—the Creed of Nicaea, subsequently enlarged to take the form of our 'Nicene Creed.' Thus in the Apostolic Creeds and the Apostolic Scriptures the Church has from early days possessed a very solid body of tradition.

The influence of this has been considerably weakened, however, by the invention of printing, which made it possible for the Scriptures to obtain a certain independence of the Church, each individual being in a position, if he chose, to interpret it according to his own lights. This separation of the Apostolic Scriptures from the Church has led to what is nothing less than a divorce of the one from the other, the Scriptures being even set up in opposition to the Church. This most unfortunate cleavage has reinforced the tendency to separation created by the jettisoning of the Apostolic Ministry already mentioned, and has made for great confusion and the creation of many sects.

5. Finally, McDougall mentions differentiation of function through the organizing of the group. In the nation this takes place through the development of systems of government, both central and local. In this country, for example, what we know as democratic government is an essential element in maintaining the stability of the group. Similarly, the Church developed; but in this case it was recognized from the first that the development and differentiation of various functions within the Church was under the guidance and direction of the Holy Spirit. So S. Paul says: 'Now there are varieties of gifts, but the same Spirit; and

there are varieties of service, but the same Lord; and there are
varieties of working, but it is the same God who inspires them
all in everyone. To each is given the manifestation of the Spirit
for the common good' (1 Cor. 12. 4–7, American R.S.V.).

Unfortunately, this natural development—or, rather, supernatural development—under the guidance of the Holy Spirit has
had to battle against forces which would crush the liberty of
prophesying. The most powerful of these has been the growth
of Papal power, which has, in fact, produced exactly the opposite
effect of what was intended. It has, indeed, resulted in the
closely-knit authoritarian Roman Catholic Church, but at the
heavy price of the creation of a deep cleavage between Roman
and non-Roman Christianity. We shall see further into the
meaning of this when we come to consider the meaning and
place of liberty in the group.

Enough has been said to show how the *koinonia* of the Spirit
has fulfilled the essential requirements for the stability of the
group as indicated by McDougall's analysis. We have also seen
how failure to comply with these requirements has led to the
divisions of Christendom, and to grievous lapses from the
Christian standard and ideal. Nevertheless, despite all these there
is a very deep underlying unity which binds together the *Una
Sancta*, as it is called in the notable Oecumenical Movement,
and this is due to the fact that in the case of the Church the group
mind is not a mere figure of speech but what S. Paul calls 'the
mind of Christ' (1 Cor. 2. 16) or 'the mind of the Spirit' (*Rom.*
8. 27). It is a real mind which is working out the divine will and
purpose. Indeed, if the word purpose is to have any intelligible
meaning it presupposes the existence of a mind. For purpose can
exist only in a mind, and, as we have seen, in purely human
communities there is rightly speaking no group mind. What is
commonly understood as 'purpose' in such communities is no
more than the resultant of the interplay and conflict between the
individual purposes in the minds of the members of the group.
'The psychological factors involved in large-scale group action,'
wrote M. Ginsberg, 'are extremely inchoate and obscure "an
impalpable congeries of hopes and fears," which certainly has not
the character of voluntary decision. As has been well said, what

is general in common action is not will, and what is will is not general.'[1]

We need not do more than mention the claim which has been put forward that there may be a purpose which is unconscious, and, indeed, that this is the only kind of purpose which can be claimed as existing in the universe as a whole. The fatal objection to this line of argument is that to talk of 'unconscious purpose' is a contradiction in terms. As Dr. W. R. Matthews has said in this connection: 'Obviously a philosopher who should tell us that the world realizes ends "by a kind of instinct" or "by the force of generation" may be making good poetry, but he is not talking philosophy, unless he can show us that "instinct" or "the power of generation" are concepts which are so luminously clear that they need no further explanation. So far as I know, no one has done this.'[2]

If, however, we accept the Christian doctrine of the Holy Spirit we have a solution of this difficulty. Ginsberg is widely astray when he says, 'A large movement like Christianity was, no doubt, never as a whole present to any one mind,'[3] for he ignores what S. Paul calls 'the mind of the Spirit' (*Rom.* 8. 26). This is the mind which has guided the Church throughout the course of its history, and still guides it, despite the stubbornness of men's wills and their disobedience to God's calls.

We can, however, go further than this. The Holy Spirit not only has guided the supernatural community from the first, as is so artlessly stated in the Acts of the Apostles, where there are many references to His guidance. He also works at the natural level, as our Lord clearly saw, overruling and guiding even the minds of non-Christian men and women. There is, in the words of the collect, a 'never-failing Providence which ordereth all things both in heaven and earth.'

Such, then, according to the New Testament, is the *koinonia* of the Spirit. It is a religious community sharing through the Holy Spirit the supernatural life of Christ. Here we may follow Professor MacMurray in making a careful distinction between two types of association. One is the type of association which is constituted by the sharing of a common purpose. The other

---

[1] M. Ginsberg: *Sociology* (Home University Library), pp. 122, 123.
[2] W. R. Matthews: *The Purpose of God* (Nisbet 1935), p. 91.   [3] *Op. cit.*, p. 127.

type of association exists by reason of the fact that it shares a common life. He calls these, respectively, a society and a community. He points out that, of course, these two principles of association are not mutually exclusive; a society may also be a community. But, he writes: 'This is not necessarily so; and even where both principles are effective in the same group, they may be effective in very different degrees. But the principles themselves are radically distinct. . . . Thus, though the members are persons, and the group is an association of persons, the members (of a society) are not associated *as persons*, but only in virtue of the specific functions they perform in relation to the purpose which constitutes the group. . . . The State is, thus, the central institution of society, that is to say of the functional association of a human group. It is organic; not personal'.[1] On the other hand, the Church is a community in the highest sense of the term; for it exists by reason of sharing a common life. This is the supernatural life of the Spirit, which is in the New Testament contrasted sharply with the life which is not of the Spirit.

Now the acid test to apply here is the test of freedom. Freedom, we must remember, is of two kinds, viz. freedom *from* external compulsion, and freedom *to* do what is right. The State, at its best, is the guardian of the former. But it cannot ensure the latter. This is the function of the Church, which is led by the Spirit. 'Where the Spirit of the Lord is, there is liberty.'

In the first instance, this holds good at the natural level. It is natural for human beings to associate together and to live as friends. It is fear which divides men and estranges them from one another. And superfluity of fear is the result of man's rebellion against God. By setting himself in opposition to his heavenly Father man thereby bedevils his relationship to his fellow men, who are his brothers. The good State reduces and mitigates this fear by promoting and defending justice; but it is unable to abolish it. Only the Church, by uniting men to their Father in heaven and to one another, without any distinction of race or nation or class, can promote positive freedom, i.e. what we have called 'freedom to' and contrasted with 'freedom from.'

What happened at Pentecost was the outpouring of the Holy

[1] J. MacMurray: *Conditions of Freedom* (Faber 1950), pp. 54 and 55.

Spirit who renewed the will to community (which had been weakened by racial antagonisms) through the creation of *agapē*, which, as S. John says, 'casts out fear' (1 S. John 4. 18). This quality or gift of *agapē* is at root the will to fellowship based upon our Lord's teaching. What He taught in this connection is twofold. First, we all share in a common humanity, which must be allowed to override all divisions. This is the essential teaching of the Parable of the Good Samaritan, where we see the opposite process pilloried, when religion itself is allowed to override the dictates of a common humanity. Secondly, our Lord taught that by devotion to humanity we are showing devotion to Him, the implication clearly being that He sums up in His own person the whole of humanity. This tremendous claim is the basis of the teaching of the Parable of the Last Judgement (*S. Matt.* 25. 31 ff.). The Christian, by his love for his Lord, will automatically share in what, in a famous phrase, has been called 'the enthusiasm for humanity.' The fact that Christians unfortunately do not always do this does not alter the fact that some of them, at least, do, and that the Christian Church is the strongest force in the world for pulling down racial, national, and social barriers between men.

That is why Christianity is necessarily the path to freedom. To be completely free is to be completely oneself, and this can happen, paradoxically enough, only when one is taken out of oneself. This latter can occur only in community. That is why the creation of the Christian community, which transcends all barriers, is also the creation of the basic condition of freedom.

Why, then, it will be asked, has this New Testament *koinonia* or community not prevailed more powerfully? The answer is that men are afraid of freedom. To quote MacMurray again: 'We flatter ourselves too much when we imagine that we love freedom and strive wholeheartedly towards freedom. On the contrary, there are few things which we fear so much. No doubt we find the *idea* of freedom attractive; but the reality is another matter. For to act freely is to take a decision and accept the consequences. . . . Here, then, is the paradox of freedom. We are free to choose between freedom and security.'[1] If we choose security, he goes on to point out, what is happening is that we are using our free choice to frustrate ourselves. 'If we persist in

[1] *Op. cit.*, p. 19.

this choice we destroy ourselves. If we aim at security we aim at the impossible, and succeed only in multiplying the occasions of fear, and magnifying our need for security. There is no security for us except in choosing freedom. For our insecurity *is* our fear, and to choose freedom is to triumph over fear.'

MacMurray has here unmasked the source of the tendencies which have always made the realization of the *koinonia* of the Spirit so terribly difficult. To the unredeemed man, as he has shown so clearly, security is preferable to freedom; but really and truly to desire freedom is a mark of the redeemed man. Hence the strength of the disastrous but persistent tendency to debase the Christian community to the level of a society which exists to guarantee security. Only too often has the false equation been made: salvation = security. Yet it is significant that the only occasion in which the word 'salvation' occurs in the English Authorized Version of the Bible is in the incident of Zacchaeus, when, after making what must have seemed, by all the standards of worldly prudence, a most risky declaration, our Lord exclaims: 'To-day is salvation come to this house' (*S. Luke* 19. 9).

It is not difficult to trace the influence of this disastrous equation of salvation and security through the Middle Ages, when the idea of the Church-State (or super-State) took form, and the Papacy developed as the great guarantor of salvation. And at the Reformation essentially the same error underlay the conception of national Churches which resulted. In this country the so-called 'Free Churches' sought to break away from this. But the last error has been worse than the first, viz. the fragmentation of Christendom, or schism run riot.

The only hopeful course is to recover the conception of *community*—the community of the Holy Spirit—and this can come to pass only by a true appreciation of the five factors, which are essential to the stability of the group. Unless the Church succeeds in doing this, she cannot hope to play her rightful part in the creating of international unity.

Something may be said at this point about the place of the leader in a group or community. It is generally recognized that in ordinary human groups and communities a leader is essential; and modern social psychology has made a serious attempt to analyse the conception of leadership. Various experiments have been carried out to this end. On the whole, psychologists take the view that the commonly accepted idea that a person is 'a born leader' is false; at least, if it is understood to mean that such a person would be a leader in any circumstances. The reason for this is that leadership is too closely bound up with varying circumstances. Thus Professor Sprott says: 'In America, for example, the political régime is such that the shrewd, self-seeking, vigorous political boss has a place, and therefore a niche is provided for people with appropriate qualities, and thus a reward is offered for the possession of these. Under the English system there is no place for such a character.'[1] Again, he says: 'A political régime may be almost said to choose its leaders.' There is more than a grain of truth in this, though it may be most fully seen in the case of crowd leadership. Thus in Paris, in the 1848 revolution, a man who was taken by the police exclaimed: 'Let me go. I must follow the crowd over there. I am their leader.' He spoke more wisely than he knew.

The truth seems to be that in all human groups leaders are, in part at least, followers. This is patently true in some cases where we see 'leaders' vainly trying to control their followers; some trade union leader, for instance, trying to settle an unofficial strike. This dependence of leaders on followers, however, is not necessarily in principle wrong for the simple reason that the only way to exclude this element in the situation is some form of dictatorship, where the individuals are deprived of all but a semblance of freedom by being forcibly prevented from speaking their minds.

Thus we see that the position of a merely human leader is paradoxical. In a real sense he has to be a follower, unless the freedom of the individual is to be sacrificed. On the other hand, if he is only a follower in the sense that he is no more than the mouthpiece of popular opinions, he is failing 'to give a lead.' There seems to be no escape from this dilemma at the human level. The leader is in constant danger of exerting too much pressure or too little.

But what happens when the leader is not merely a human being but also God Himself? Clearly God cannot in any sense be a mere follower. On the other hand, if even He dominates

[1] W. J. H. Sprott: *Social Psychology* (Methuen 1952), p. 79.

and plays the dictator human freedom is destroyed. Here we have the paradox of the Christian idea of grace. On the one hand, all is of God; on the other, human freedom must be preserved if men and women are to remain persons and not to become automata.

This is not the place to discuss at length the Christian doctrine of grace; but some observations on the bearing of the doctrine of the *koinonia* of the Spirit on it may not be irrelevant. We have seen that the life of the individual Christian is bound up with the life of the Christian community and that this community alone can guarantee his true freedom. For only here are the barriers of race and nation and economic and social status transcended. In other words, if the Church were *in fact* the perfect community which it is *in ideal* the environment of each individual Christian would be such that he could do what he pleased because everybody else was acting in such a way as to make this possible. And this could come about because in S. Paul's phrase each member of the community was not 'looking to his own things' only but also 'to the things of others' (*Phil.* 2. 4).

Although this ideal is not fully realized in the Church we constantly see examples of its realization on a small scale; and this comes about because the individual Christian is living in an environment where the *koinonia* of the Spirit is a fact. And when the ideal is thus partially realized we can at least begin to discern what things would be like if it were universally realized. Apart from this environment constituted by the *koinonia* of the Spirit, the individual is shut up in a vicious circle. He cannot do as he pleases, because what he wants to do conflicts with the wishes of others; and the wishes of others conflict with his wishes for precisely the same reason, viz. that they desire what is incompatible with what he desires. Plainly, what is required is some common ground where they can meet and adjust their mutual relationships. This is provided by the objective power and presence of the Holy Spirit, and if the individual enters upon that ground of his own free will, he finds that he has escaped from the vicious circle in which he was previously enclosed. He finds himself in a community where (ideally at least) it is 'the done thing' to look to the interests of the other members of the community and not only to his own.

Thus we can begin to see how the grace of the Holy Spirit can influence and determine the behaviour of the individual members of the Christian community without infringing their liberty. The creation of such an environment is possible only by the grace or power of God, and that is why grace must be 'prevenient.' But we can begin to see how this is not incompatible with the continuance of man's free choice. The paradoxes of the Christian doctrine of grace, in other words, have been largely created by our inveterate habit of regarding grace as the result of a solitary encounter between God and the individual; instead of being, as it were, triangular—viz. the relations between God, the Christian community, and the individual, and *in that order*. If, as happened in too much Reformation theology, the community is placed third in order of time, as being merely the result of the coming together of converted individuals,[1] the problem becomes a stark antithesis between the grace of God on the one hand and the liberty of the individual on the other—an antithesis which cannot be resolved.

What has just been said can be put differently by quoting again another saying of S. Paul's: 'Where the Spirit of the Lord is,' or perhaps we should render 'where the Spirit is Lord'—i.e. in the *koinonia* of the Spirit—'there is liberty.' But if we try to convert this proposition and say: 'Where there is liberty, there is the Spirit of the Lord,' we may be misled; for liberty is an ambiguous word, as we have seen. It may stand simply for the freedom of human choice apart from compulsion: what we have called 'freedom from.' But full freedom must include also 'freedom to.' And it is only this last kind of freedom which is capable of revealing the presence of the Holy Spirit. Mere freedom from external compulsion does not of itself guarantee this. But the supernatural freedom which the Holy Spirit bestows upon our Lord's disciples is freedom to live their full lives—to full self-realization, if we like to put it that way. 'If the Son shall make you free, you shall be free indeed.' And it is in the *koinonia*, or fellowship of the Spirit, that He does this.

[1] It is significant that theologians of the Protestant tradition are breaking away from this view. See, e.g., Bultmann, *op. cit.*, I. 93f.

APPENDIX

THE DOCTRINE OF THE HOLY SPIRIT IN RADICAL PROTESTANTISM

GEORGE FOX has been chosen as the representative of what is sometimes called Radical Protestantism because we see in him the full logical development of the doctrine that the light of the Holy Spirit is shed first and foremost in the mind and heart of the individual. 'The inner light' shines directly from Christ into the heart of each and every man. There are, however, others who may be placed in the category of Radical Protestantism who would not accept the extreme individualism of Fox's teaching. Unfortunately, there is no outstanding theologian among them, and, indeed, no single individual whose influence has been comparable with that of Fox, with the solitary exception of John Wesley. But such writers as Richard Baxter, Richard Sibbes and John Owen come to mind in this connection.

There are three respects in which what we may call Radical Protestants of the right differ from Fox. The first is the way in which they relate the Holy Spirit to Holy Scripture. Fox maintained that he had the Holy Spirit as much as any New Testament writer, and that the authority of Scripture did not stand above the authority of the inner light in every believer. The right wing Radicals, on the other hand, taught that the Bible is unique in its authority. So, for example, Baxter says: 'The Holy Spirit, by immediate inspiration, revealed unto the apostles the doctrine of Christ and caused them infallibly to indite the Scriptures. But this is not the way of ordinary illumination now.'[1]

Secondly, there was a difference of opinion regarding the place of the Sacraments in the Christian life, or rather, the place of the Ordinances, as they were usually called. Fox held that these were superseded by the Dispensation of the Spirit in which we now live, and so he swept them all away. The more moderate Radicals, however, on the basis of the authority of Holy Scripture, retained Baptism and the Lord's Supper; but they gave them a new meaning, so that they tended to become peripheral in the Christian life. Indeed, the doctrine of the inner light in any form tends to make the use of the sacraments of secondary importance.

Thirdly, there was a difference of opinion concerning the work of the Holy Spirit in the unbeliever and in the heathen. As we have seen, Fox clearly recognized the existence of this, though he failed entirely

[1] R. Baxter: *Works*, II, 104.

211

to distinguish between the natural and the supernatural operations of
the Spirit. He believed that the Spirit of Christ was at work in all
men without distinction. But the moderates held that it was only
believers who had 'the witness of the Spirit,' and that it was only they
who were led by the Spirit of Christ. As to unbelievers and non-
believers they were not agreed. Some, like Baxter, hold to the belief
that the Holy Spirit operates in all men at the natural level, but that
the unregenerate do not possess the Spirit of Christ. Others adopt
the view that only the elect have the light of the Spirit.

There is, however, one fundamental question which Radical
Protestantism has to face in whatever form it exists, and that is, How
is the individual to distinguish between the inspiration of the Spirit
and self-deception? Fox, who was no theologian, never really faces
this issue; but the more theologically minded radicals saw that it was
a question which could not be evaded. It will be convenient to consider
Wesley's account of this matter; for it brings to a head the essential
theological and moral difficulties which beset the Radical Protestant
doctrine of the Holy Spirit. The classic utterance is Wesley's sermon
on 'The Witness of the Spirit.' This, he teaches, is immediate in the
mind of each believer. 'The Spirit beareth witness with our spirits
that we are the sons of God' (*Rom*. viii. 16). This witness 'is an inward impression on the soul, whereby the Spirit of God directly
witnesses to my spirit, that I am a child of God; that Jesus Christ
hath loved me: that all my sins are blotted out, and I, even I,
am reconciled to God.'[1] Wesley recognizes the possibility of self-
deception here; that the nominal Christian may and often does have
a confident but illusory belief that he is a child of God; but he claims
that a little honest self-examination will soon convince such a one that
he is self-deluded. Wesley claims, as Calvin did, that, in fact, the
internal witness of the Spirit, is self-evident. In reply to the question,
How may one who has the witness within himself distinguish it from
presumption? Wesley writes: 'How, I pray, do you distinguish day
from night? How do you distinguish light from darkness? Or the
light of a star, or glimmering taper, from the light of the noon-day
sun? . . . In like manner, there is an inherent, essential difference
between spiritual light and spiritual darkness.'[2] But the question is
posed, How shall I know that my spiritual senses are, so to speak, in
working order? Wesley replies: 'By their fruits ye shall know them,'
and he proceeds to quote S. Paul's list: 'Love, joy, peace, bowels of
mercies, humbleness of mind, meekness, gentleness, long-suffering.
And the outward fruits are, the doing good to all men; the doing no

[1] John Wesley: *Collected Works*, I, p. 202.   [2] Ibid., pp. 211, 212.

evil to any; and the walking in the light; a zealous, uniform obedience to all the commandments of God.'[1]

Well and good. Such persons are known as saints, and it may be agreed that they bear obvious witness to the presence and power of the Holy Spirit. Unfortunately, however, they are as rare as they are conspicuous whenever they occur; and—here is the rub—they are as rare in the sphere of Radical Protestantism, as they are rare in other Christian traditions. The fact of the matter is that Perfectionism will not do. The Christian Church is a school for saints, and not a society of saints—using that word in the modern sense. The facts compel us to acknowledge the existence of those who, as our Lord teaches, bring forth thirtyfold and those who bring forth sixtyfold as well as the very few who bring forth a hundredfold. Indeed, Wesley does to some extent recognize this, for he rejects the crude Perfectionism of Zinzendorf. He admits that in the believer the flesh may still lust against the Spirit. Nevertheless a Perfectionist he remains. He cannot get away from the words of 1 S. John 3. 9: 'Whosoever is born of God doth not commit sin' and 'We know that he which is born of God sinneth not' (1 S. John 5. 18). He writes: 'In conformity, therefore, both to the doctrine of S. John, and to the whole tenor of the New Testament, we fix this conclusion, "A Christian is so far perfect as not to commit sin." '[2] It is only fair to say that Wesley's Perfectionism has not been accepted by all his followers; but if it is rejected, the internal witness of the Spirit clearly becomes a most uncertain guide.

It might have been expected that Wesley, as a Churchman, would have sought to buttress this weak spot in his defences by bringing in the mind and authority of the Church. The mind of the individual Christian can find guidance in the general mind and *consensus* of the Church. But Wesley does not do this; nor does he seem to appreciate fully the place of the Church in the life of the individual believer. Thus in his *Reasons against a Separation from the Church of England* his arguments are all appeals to expediency. There is no suggestion that schism is a sin or that the Church of Christ is essentially a single visible society. His belief in the Church, in fact, seems not to be organically attached to his belief in the witness of the Spirit. The latter he derived from his famous conversion experience on 24th May, 1738; the former he inherited and was brought up in; hence he accepted without question the Scriptures and the two Dominical Sacraments. But the two elements were not fully integrated in his mind.

Another way of stating this criticism is to say that Radical Protestantism has never really appreciated the New Testament doctrine

[1] Ibid., pp. 213, 214.   [2] *Op. cit.*, III, pp. 202, 203.

of the *koinonia* of the Spirit in the Body of Christ—a *koinonia* which is both a corporate and an individual experience. Radicals when they refer to the fellowship of the Holy Spirit think of it as a mutual recognition of the working of the Spirit in the hearts of individual believers. This, in Baxter's phrase, is 'connaturality of Spirit in the saints.' But this is quite different from an experience which is *per se* corporate and which can occur only in the corporate worship and life of the Church. So far as I am aware, Wesley shows no appreciation of this point, which, as I think, is fundamental to a right understanding of the New Testament doctrine of the Holy Spirit. Indeed, as one studies the history of the Puritans and their successors one is impressed by the contrast between the orderly life of the Spirit-guided Church of the New Testament—though disturbed in places, especially in disorderly Corinth—and the life of sectarian Christianity.

There is one point in particular where their understanding of the N.T. doctrine of the Spirit went astray, and that is in their interpretation of the N.T. Church as a democracy. Thus William Erbury wrote: 'The Independent or baptized Churches (both is one) are a pure Democracy.'[1] As Dr. G. F. Nuttall has said, 'It was the church meeting which gave birth in England to political democracy, not *vice versa*.'[2] But a careful study of the New Testament makes it quite clear that the early Church was not democratically governed, as we understand the matter. There is no trace of the modern idea that the vote of the majority of believers is a mark of the mind of the Spirit. As we have already seen, unanimity is one thing, but a majority vote is another. The Quakers have been nearer the truth in this matter than other Radical Protestants in their habit of avoiding the practice of counting votes at their business meetings and seeking rather to ascertain the sense of the meeting as a whole. This *consensus fidelium*, on the widest scale, indeed, has all along been fundamental in the life of the Church and has had a decisive influence upon its history. But this has little to do with democracy understood as 'government of the people, for the people, by the people' through the voice of the majority.

This one-sidedness, though, to my thinking, regrettable, is fully intelligible. It was a reaction against the over-authoritarianism of the Papacy; and there can be no doubt that it has liberated a great missionary force in the world. Christ has been proclaimed in the power of the Spirit, and for this we must thank God. But we are coming to see that schism in the visible Church of Christ is not in accordance with the mind of the Holy Spirit; and millions of Christians are beginning to pray fervently for the healing of the wounds in the Body of Christ.

[1] W. Erbury: *Testimony*, p. 63.
[2] G. F. Nuttall: *The Holy Spirit in Puritan Faith and Experience* (Blackwell 1946), p. 120.

Shine in our hearts, O Holy Spirit, with the pure light of the knowledge of Thy truth, and open the eyes of our minds to Christ's teaching, that in all things we may think and act according to Thy good pleasure, and that, meditating on those things which are holy, we may live continually in Thy light.   Amen.

INDEX OF BIBLICAL REFERENCES

OLD TESTAMENT

NEW TESTAMENT

INDEX OF NAMES

223